A. J. Ayer

The Central Questions
of Philosophy

Penguin Books

PENGUIN BOOKS

Published by the Penguin Group
27 Wrights Lane, London w8 5tz, England
Viking Penguin Inc., 40 West 23rd Street, New York, New York 10010, USA
Penguin Books Australia Ltd, Ringwood, Victoria, Australia
Penguin Books Canada Ltd, 2801 John Street, Markham, Ontario, Canada l3r 1b4
Penguin Books (NZ) Ltd, 182–190 Wairau Road, Auckland 10, New Zealand

Penguin Books Ltd, Registered Offices: Harmondsworth, Middlesex, England

First published by Weidenfeld & Nicolson 1973
Published in Pelican Books 1976
10 9 8

Copyright © A. J. Ayer, 1973
All rights reserved

Made and printed in Great Britain by
Richard Clay Ltd, Bungay, Suffolk
Set in Monotype Plantin

To

Guida Crowley

Contents

Preface

This book reproduces the series of Gifford lectures which I delivered at the University of St Andrews in 1972–3. It comes only marginally within the provisions of Lord Gifford's bequest, which set up a trust, in 1885, to establish Lectureships in Glasgow, Edinburgh, Aberdeen and St Andrews for the purposes of 'Promoting, Advancing, Teaching and Diffusing the study of "Natural Theology", in the widest sense of that term'. It was however, stipulated that the lecturers 'may be of no religion, or they may be so-called sceptics or agnostics or free-thinkers, provided only that the "patrons" will use diligence to see that they be able reverent men, true thinkers, sincere lovers of and earnest inquirers after truth'. In this instance, the patrons at St Andrews, to whom I am much indebted not only for the invitation but also for their friendly hospitality, permitted me to devote only one out of ten lectures to the topic of theology. The lecture is sceptical, in that it is mainly concerned with showing that we have no good reason to believe that there is a God, but it is at least an earnest inquiry after truth.

The bulk of the book, as its title indicates, is more strictly philosophical. It begins with an attempt to explain what philosophy is and after a few historical comments goes on to give examples which illustrate the special character of metaphysical arguments. Various theories of meaning are examined and an account is given of the range of problems which philosophical analysis may be taken to cover and the different methods which have been used to deal with them. Proceeding to the theory of knowledge, I show how it is possible to start with sensory qualities and construct on this basis a realistic theory of the physical world. Among the topics which are subsequently discussed are those of the relation of body and mind, the analysis of personal identity, the grounds for attributing consciousness to others, the problem of inductive reasoning, the character of scientific laws, the analysis of conditional statements, the theory of probability, the nature of causality, the concept of logical necessity, the status of abstract entities, such as classes, propositions and universals, the nature of moral judgements and the freedom of the will. My approach to the theory of knowledge follows a line which I first laid down in my book *The Problem of Knowledge* and in the two chapters which centre round the problem of inductive reasoning, I have reproduced ideas which are already to be found in my book *Probability and Evidence*. I have to thank the publishers Macmillan and Penguin Books, in the first case, and Macmillan and Columbia University Press, in the second, for allowing me this repetition.

In writing this book, I have attempted not only to interest those who are already familiar with the questions with which it deals, but also to provide an introduction to the subject for the general reader. These aims are not easy to reconcile, but I have done my best.

A. J. Ayer

New College
Oxford

6 February 1973

I The Claims of Metaphysics

A Philosophy and Science

What is philosophy? Even for a professional philosopher this
question is very difficult to answer, and the fact that it is so difficult
is itself indicative. It brings home to philosophers how peculiar
their subject is. For one thing, it aims at yielding knowledge; or,
if this be thought to go too far, at least it comprises propositions
which their authors wish us to accept as true. Yet it seems to have no
special subject matter. What can a philosopher be said to study, in
the way that a chemist studies the composition of bodies or a
botanist the variety of plants?

A possible answer is that being a subject with many branches
philosophy has not one but many objects of study. So, it may be
said, metaphysics investigates the structure of reality, ethics the
rules of human conduct, logic the canons of valid reasoning: the
theory of knowledge discovers what it is in our power to know. This
answer is not incorrect, but it could be misleading. Ethics is indeed
concerned with human conduct, but it is not descriptive of human
conduct, in the way that psychology and sociology are. It can be
prescriptive, but its interest is rather in what lies behind the
prescriptions; not so much in formulating rules of conduct as in
considering what basis there can be for them. If the theory of
knowledge discovers what it is in our power to know, it is not in the
sense in which an encyclopaedia may be said to give a conspectus of
our knowledge. It aims rather at establishing criteria for knowledge;
criteria which may possibly set limits to what can be known. We
shall see later on that the theory of knowledge is primarily an
exercise in scepticism; the advancement and the attempted
rebuttal of arguments which are intended to prove that we do not
know what we think we know. Logic, indeed, is a special case. As a
formal science it ranks with mathematics, from which it is hardly
now distinguishable. But as it becomes assimilated to mathematics,

so it becomes detached from philosophy. Philosophical questions can be raised about logic, as they can about mathematics. They are not, however, questions within a logical system, but questions about the status of logical propositions, the character of logical concepts, the legitimacy of certain types of proof.

The thread which is emerging is that philosophy has to do with criteria. It is concerned with the standards which govern our use of concepts, our assessments of conduct, our methods of reasoning, our evaluations of evidence. One thing which it may do is to bring to light the criteria which we actually employ; another to adjudicate if they are found to conflict; another, perhaps, to criticize them and find better substitutes for them. But here we are beginning to go too fast. For how, it may be asked, is any of this distinctive of philosophy? Surely every discipline has its own criteria. A mathematician does not need to be told what is a valid proof, or a physicist what is a convincing theory, or what weight to allow to an experiment. Lawyers are skilled at estimating evidence. It is the historian's business to assess the value of his sources. What has the philosopher to contribute? And with what authority?

The easiest way to answer this question will be to show philosophy at work in one of its branches, and for this purpose I shall start with metaphysics. In its original use, the term 'metaphysics' meant no more than 'after-physics'. Aristotle wrote a book on physics and 'metaphysics' was the title given by commentators to the books which came after it in their catalogue of his works. There was, however, also the suggestion that metaphysics, operating in the same area as physics, was intended to deal with questions which physics left unanswered. But what could these questions be? I imagined someone's saying earlier that metaphysics investigated the structure of reality. But is not this just what the natural sciences do, except that what they do would not ordinarily be described in such a portentous fashion? In what way can metaphysics go beyond them?

A superficial answer is that each of the special sciences deals only with a fragment of the world. Metaphysics goes beyond them in being concerned with reality as a whole. This is true in the negative sense that the range of metaphysics, whatever it may be, is not circumscribed in the same way as that of a special science. But if the suggestion is that the metaphysician does the same work as a scientist, only on a larger scale, it is not only inaccurate as a description of what has commonly passed for metaphysics, but also unattractive as a course for any philosopher to adopt. For how would he set about depicting the whole of reality except through the depiction of its parts ? The best that he could hope to achieve would be to compile an encyclopaedia which would set out all the theories and hypotheses which were currently accepted in the various branches of science. This would be a very difficult task for one man to accomplish, and by the time that he had completed it, some parts of the work would almost certainly be out of date. For this reason it would be better undertaken as a co-operative enterprise. If it were well done, it could serve a useful purpose. Even so, there must surely be more to metaphysics than the compilation of scientific works of reference.

It may be objected that I am being unfair. What is expected of our metaphysician is not just that he should assemble all the scientific theories of his time but that he should then integrate them into a world-picture. He is to realize the Hegelian ideal of unifying our various scraps of knowledge into a higher synthesis. But the trouble with this is that it is not at all clear what such a world-picture could amount to. One could perhaps envisage something of the following sort. Someone might succeed in ful-filling Einstein's aim of unifying physics by constructing a general theory which would incorporate both quantum physics and the theory of relativity. It might then be shown that the other sciences were all reducible to physics. To some extent, indeed, this has already been achieved. There is good reason to believe that the laws of chemistry can be derived from those of physics, and that biological laws are derivable from chemical laws. If it could then be shown that the laws of psychology and sociology were derivable from biological laws, the programme would be complete. If it could be completed, one might regard the fundamental physical theory, in terms of which everything else was explained, as supplying a general picture of the world. Since this theory would have to be extremely abstract, it could yield only a very schematic picture, but this is unavoidable. For concrete detail we should need to return to the encyclopaedia.

But now we must ask how it is to be determined whether such a programme can be carried out. There might, indeed, be objections of principle to the reduction of the mental to the physical, or the organic to the inorganic, and it might be a philosophical undertaking to determine whether this was so. But from that point onwards the problems would be scientific. If it were established that no valid objection of principle stood in its way, the work of devising a theory which would account for mental states and processes in terms of the operations of the nervous system would fall to the physiologist. It would be for the biochemist to find the bridge between organic and inorganic entities. The metaphysician whose theories are not similarly testable by observation would have nothing to contribute.

A more ambitious conception of metaphysics is one that places it in competition with the natural sciences. The suggestion is that the sciences deal only with appearances: the metaphysician penetrates to the underlying reality. This idea has been more prevalent in Eastern than in Western philosophy, but it remains attractive to those who wish to think of philosophy as outranking science and to those who associate the natural sciences with a materialism that offends them. The difficulty about it is primarily that of making it intelligible. We are, indeed, accustomed to the fact that appearances can be deceptive, but when this fact is analyzed, it is found to consist, not in a conflict of appearances with something of another order, but rather in their conflict with one another. We interpret some observations in a way that further observations do not corroborate. So far, therefore, from supporting the conclusion that reality is veiled from us, the discovery that things are not always what they seem appears to be incompatible with it. What possible experience could authorize our making a distinction between appearances as a whole and a quite different reality?

B Evaluation of Mystical Experience

The answer which some would give to this is 'mystical experience' The mystic develops a special faculty which enables him to see what he reports to us, no doubt inadequately, by saying such things as that reality is spiritual, or that time and space are not ultimately real, or that everything is one. But what are we to make of this? The question is not whether mystical experiences are worth having. The verdict of those who have actually had them is very decidedly that they are. The question is whether they yield knowledge; and if so, what it is that they establish. If what they are said to establish does not make sense or, on any literal interpretation, is obviously false, then at the very least the case for their being cognitive has not been made out. You can say, if you please, that the information which they yield is incommunicable to those who are not equipped to receive it, but this also puts an end to the argument. So long as there is no intelligible proposition before us, there is nothing to discuss.

But is it as simple as that? There is a story by H. G. Wells, called 'The Country of the Blind', in which a man finds his way to an isolated village of which all the inhabitants are not only blind but ignorant of the possibility of sight. Remembering the adage that in the country of the blind the one-eyed man is king, the hero of the story expects to dominate them, but instead finds himself treated as a simpleton because he does not possess their sensitivity of hearing and touch. When he tries to convince them of the power of his faculty of sight, they think that he is romancing. Could it not be that the mystic, relatively to the rest of us, is in the position of the man alone able to see in the country of the blind?

The analogy is persuasive, but there is a point where it fails. The claims of the seeing man could to a certain extent have been tested by the blind. He could have described the positions and shapes and sizes of objects at a distance, and his audience could then have discovered by touch that his descriptions were true. He could not, indeed, have explained to them what colours looked like, but given enough resources he might have taught them to arrange colours in the same compartments as he did; for instance, by the use of a machine, read tactually or auditorily, which registered differences of wave length. In the actual story, the seeing man was not skilful at devising such tests; and he was handicapped both by the incredulity of his audience and by their having so thoroughly explored their limited environment that there was little new information with which he could have tried to impress them. Nevertheless, it is easy to imagine changes occurring which he would have been the first to detect. On the other hand, it is not easy to see what changes could occur in our world that the mystic would be in a better position to detect. It is not clear what would have to happen for his statements to be generally testable. Indeed, this is not even an appropriate demand to make of him, if his claim is not that he has a more extensive knowledge of what we take to be the world, but rather a vision of some ulterior reality.

But is it not logically possible that the data of sight and touch should be so dissociated that we could attach no useful sense to speaking of the same objects as being both visible and tangible, and if that were so, would not the analogy hold? The seeing man would have access to an autonomous world of the nature of which he could give the blind no inkling. All that he could intelligibly report would be that it did exist. Very probably they would disbelieve him, or even say that he was talking nonsense. But then they would be wrong.

I think that the premiss of this argument can be accepted. For instance, I find it conceivable that our sight should operate in such a way that all visible objects were beyond our reach; or it might be that they all had the properties that are attributed to ghosts; or, more prosaically, that they were all like after-images. One can imagine even our inhabiting a predominantly tactual, non-visual world in our waking hours, and a visual world in our dreams; if they were equally coherent, this would put a strain upon our concept of reality. There is, however, no need to embark upon such fantasies. The same result can be obtained more simply by supposing that we come upon creatures who differ from us in having an extra sense the deliverances of which are internally systematic but not such as to enable us to correlate them with anything that we are capable of perceiving. Having come to believe that these creatures really did have such experiences, should we have any good reason to doubt that they were cognitive?

The answer to this question would depend upon the way in which these experiences were described to us. *Ex hypothesi*, we could be told nothing significant about their content, but we could be informed whether those who had them agreed in the accounts which they gave of them and the interpretations which they put upon them. We could enquire whether they classified them as merely subjective states, or as revealing what to us were unknown properties of objects which we were otherwise able to identify, or as being experiences of objects, not otherwise perceivable, which were spatio-temporally located. In either of the last two cases, we might very well allow the claim that these were cognitive experiences. The question is not significantly different from that raised by the reports of apparitions which are recorded in the annals of the Society for Psychical Research. In many instances, there is little or no doubt that the experiences occurred, though for some reason they were much more frequent in the nineteenth century than they have since become. Most people, however, would put them down as hallucinations, partly because this is the hypothesis that best accords with our general picture of the world, partly because the apparitions were not reported as being regularly visible even to those who claimed the power of seeing them. Were there to be evidence that they were constantly detectable, at roughly the same places, by those who possessed these special powers, we might reasonably come to believe in their reality.

But now it becomes clear that what is at issue here is whether or not we have underestimated the variety of things that are to be found in the world. The possession of an extra sense, or of a special power of vision, might conceivably disclose the existence of objects, or properties of objects, which would otherwise have escaped our notice. It would not, however, follow that our previous conception of the world had been anything worse than incomplete. It would not follow that we had been mistaken in attributing reality to the items that we had previously identified, or even that they were in any degree less real than the items that we were now in a position to incorporate. Consequently these more or less fanciful analogies are of no service to the mystic who wishes to down-grade the material world by comparison, let us say, with the spiritual world which he supposes that his experiences reveal to him. And, indeed, it is surely obvious that no experience, however intense, can possibly establish such propositions as that reality is spiritual, or that time and space are unreal, or that things which appear to be different are in some manner identical. To obtain any such results one would have to formulate an adequate criterion of reality, and one would have to show by argument that the things which were commonly taken to be real did not satisfy it.

C Appearance and Reality: Some Metaphysical Positions

To do them justice, this is how the metaphysicians who have sought to persuade us that the world is really very different from what it appears to be have commonly proceeded. Thus, in Plato's theory of Ideas, which he may indeed later have discarded, the world made apparent to us by our senses is contrasted with an intellectually apprehensible world of Ideas or Forms.[1] In the sensible world, things come into being and pass away, they have different properties at different times, they simultaneously have properties like

[1] See especially his *Phaedo* and *Republic*, Books V to VII.

that of being big or small, which vary with the things to which we relate them. By contrast the forms, which may be identified with the common properties to which later philosophers have given the name of universals, exist eternally and do not change. Thus, the quality of goodness abides, on this theory, independently of its incidence in the sensible world; so does the quality of redness, no matter how things change their colour; so does the form of a table, no matter what tables actually exist. The forms determine the character of perceptible things and these things partake of reality just to the extent that they participate in the forms. The superiority of the forms consisted, for Plato, in their immutability and also, it would seem, in their being objects of the intellect rather than the senses. Whether this entitled him to make them the touchstone of reality is, of course, another question.

Though their conceptions of the world were very different both from one another and from that of Plato, the idea that knowledge of the way things really are is to be obtained through the exercise of pure reason and not through sense-perception is one that was shared by the seventeenth-century Rationalist philosophers, Descartes, Spinoza and Leibniz. Of the three, Descartes is, in modern terms, the least metaphysical, since the picture of the world to which his reasoning led him could just as well have been the product of the study of contemporary physics. His peculiarity lay in supposing that he could reach these scientific conclusions by purely logical deduction from self-evident premisses. Spinoza, on the other hand, though influenced by Descartes, constructed a system which could hardly be represented as a scientific theory. By reflecting on the concept of substance, he professed to be able to deduce that there could be only one substance, to which he gave the name of 'God or Nature', the popular idea of a God who was the transcendent cause of nature being held by him to be self-contradictory; that the attributes of thought and extension, which Descartes, in his dualism, had taken to be respectively characteristic of mind and matter, were perfectly corresponding attributes of this single substance; and that everything within nature was rigorously determined. Leibniz also reflected on the concept of substance, but in his case his reflections led him to the conclusion that there must be not one substance but infinitely many.[1] On the logical ground that in every true proposition of the subject-predicate form the

[1] See his *Monadology*.

predicate had to be contained in the subject, he held that each of these substances, to which he gave the name of monads, was internally self-sufficient, in the sense that all its properties were determined by its nature. It followed that monads could not interact, but by a pre-established harmony, each of them mirrored the same universe from its own point of view. This was the work of God, the creator of the system: for Leibniz, so far from agreeing with Spinoza that the proposition that any such creator existed was self-contradictory, believed himself able to demonstrate that it was necessarily true.

Descartes and Leibniz, like Plato, were mathematicians, and Spinoza shared with them the belief that a metaphysical system should exhibit the deductive reasoning and the logical necessity that are characteristic of mathematics; his principal work, inadequately entitled *Ethics*, was composed, as he put it, in a geometrical manner: its metaphysical propositions were set out in the form of definitions, axioms and theorems. In a very different way, concern for mathematics also plays a dominant part a century later in the philosophy of Kant. Kant's *Critique of Pure Reason* is not cast in the form of a geometrical treatise, neither did he believe that metaphysical propositions were comparable to those of mathematics. On the contrary, one of his most important contentions was that the rationalists had been entirely mistaken in supposing that they could discover the nature of things merely by the exercise of reason: he sought to demonstrate that reason was bound to lose itself in contradictions if it ventured beyond the limits of possible experience. At the same time he started with the assumption that the propositions of mathematics, as well as certain other propositions, like the law of universal causation, were both *a priori* and synthetic; by which he meant that they were and could be known to be necessarily true, without the support of experience and without being demonstrable merely by the law of non-contradiction; and his principal aim was to show how this was possible. His answer was that we know such propositions to be true because their truth is necessary for the world to become an object of our experience. Thus, he thought that mathematics was guaranteed by the intuitions which we had of space and time; and he held that the world, as we knew it, was bound to satisfy these intuitions because we imposed them upon it as a prior condition of our having any perception of it. For the same reason he held that the world was bound to satisfy the very general concepts to which he gave the name of categories: they were imposed by us upon it as a prior condition of its being accessible to our understanding. Thus, for Kant, the world that we know is partly our own creation. We can infer that there is a raw material upon which we go to work. But what things are in themselves, independently of our processing of them, is something that we can never know.

The distinction between things as they appear to us and things as they really are does not play an interesting part in Kant's system, just because he leaves himself with nothing to say about the nature of things as they really are. For this reason, perhaps, his followers tended to discard the notion of things in themselves, and to conceive of reality as itself partaking of thought. Thus, Hegel represented the history of the world as a spiritual progress; the necessary ascent of what he obscurely called the Absolute Idea. Unlike Karl Marx, who retained the belief in a necessary historical development, but substituted material forces for Hegel's spirit, Hegel's English disciples, who dominated the local scene at the end of the nineteenth century, retained the belief that reality is spiritual, but discarded the idea of temporal progress. Thus, both Bradley and McTaggart, the two most distinguished of these neo-Hegelians, maintained that neither space nor time nor matter could be ultimately real, since our conception of them involved insuperable contradictions. McTaggart took the remarkable view that what we misperceive as physical objects in spatio-temporal relations are really immaterial selves eternally contemplating one another with spiritual love.[1] For Bradley, reality consisted in the Absolute, an undifferentiated whole of experience, which could be positively described only in the vaguest and most general terms, since any limited description, which abstracted only a part of it, would be false to its nature.[2]

I do not propose to discuss these various metaphysical systems in detail, though I shall have something to say later on about the reality of abstract entities,[3] such as Plato believed in, and something also about the question, raised by Kant, whether it makes sense to talk of things in themselves, apart from their relation to our manner of conceiving them.[4] The point to which I now wish to revert is

[1] See his book *The Nature of Existence*.
[2] See especially his *Appearance and Reality*.
[3] See below pp. 203–10.
[4] See below pp. 12, 49, and 110–1.

that of the possibility of the more ambitious kinds of metaphysical enterprise. How could it be validly determined, by reason alone, that the world is so very different from what it appears to us to be?

To begin with, it is surely obvious that there is something amiss with the attempt to incorporate the world in a deductive system, in which everything follows logically from a set of self-evident first principles. For what could these premises be? If they are to have any claim to be self-evident, they must presumably be abstract principles, like the principles of mathematics or formal logic; at the least, they must set out relations between concepts; and how then can they either generate the information which we derive from experience or provide an acceptable alternative to it? This is not to deny that a scientific theory can be cast into the form of a deductive system: if the system is logically rigorous, we can be assured that if any objects satisfy its premises, they also satisfy its conclusions; but that there are objects which do satisfy the premises is something that cannot be known *a priori:* it has in the end to be discovered by observation. The more factual content a deductive system appears to have, the greater the likelihood that factual assumptions are concealed in the axioms or the definitions. For instance, Spinoza's argument depends very largely on a definition of substance as something that contains in itself the reason for its own existence, and on the axiom that if something does not contain in itself the reason for its own existence, the reason for its existence must lie in something else. But if it were possible that anything other than a purely abstract entity should contain in itself the reason for its own existence, it would be a question of fact, to be determined by empirical evidence, whether anything did so; and similarly, when it had been found that an object did not meet this requirement, it would be a question of fact whether the reason for its existence lay in something else, or whether, perhaps it had no discoverable reason for its existence at all.

In one way, this is not a good example, since the condition which Spinoza lays upon substances could not possibly be satisfied. For what he meant by a reason was a logical ground, and nothing that exists concretely can contain a logical ground for its existence, in the sense that the fact that it exists can be deduced merely from the description of its character. It has been argued that God is the one exception to this rule but I shall show later on that this is not so.[1]

[1] See below p. 213-5.

Whether one thing can ever supply a logical ground for the existence of another is a more complicated matter, since it depends upon
the way in which the things in question are described. For example,
it is not logically necessary that any man should be a debtor, but
if he is truly described as a debtor, the existence of a creditor is
logically entailed. What can, I think, be said is that if any two things
are spatio-temporally distinct, it must be possible to describe the
character of either one of them in a way that carries no reference to
the other. This is not to say that there is no cause why either of
them should exist. The point is rather the one first made by Hume
that causality, as holding between distinct events, is not a logical
relation.

The objection, then, to Spinoza's attempt to characterize the
world in advance of any experience of it is that he devises a framework into which it not only might not, but could not fit. We cannot
assume, however, that the same would apply to every enterprise
of this sort. We are not in a position to say that nothing can be
determined *a priori*. It is vain to attempt to dissociate the world as
it is in itself from the world as we conceive it. Alternative conceptual
systems may be possible, but we can only criticize one from the
standpoint of another. We cannot detach ourselves from all of
them and compare them with a world which we envisage from no
conceptual standpoint at all. Accordingly, the world's freedom to
surprise us may be limited in advance by the general features of the
machinery which we use for describing it. How far these extend
beyond the laws of logic is a matter for argument. It may even be
maintained that what we take to be the laws of logic are not sacrosanct, on the ground that there could be alternative systems of
logic, just as there are alternative systems of geometry. Even so, it
would at least seem to be necessary that any such system should
contain, or at any rate be governed by, some principle of consistency. We might have a system in which truth and falsehood were
not treated as exhaustive alternatives: we might even choose in
certain cases to speak of a proposition as being both true and false.
This might, for example, be one way of representing processes of
change: there are suggestions of it in what is called Hegelian logic.
But however many divisions were allowed for in our scale of truth,
and whatever names we chose to give them, it would still have to
be the case that if a proposition was assignable to one compartment,
it was not assignable to another. As in a game, the possible moves

can be as various as you please, but if you have made a move, then you have made that move and not a different one. If the moves were not so distinguished, the game could not be played. Thus, the reason why the world cannot contravene the laws of logic, whatever they may be, is that they determine what can happen by determining what can be described. As Wittgenstein put it in his *Tractatus*, 'It used to be said that God could create anything except what would be contrary to the laws of logic, – the reason being that we could not *say* what an "illogical" world would look like'.[1]

The conclusion which we have just reached is that the concepts which we apply to the world, since they have to conform to the laws of logic, must at least be self-consistent: they must not issue in contradictions. This seems a modest requirement, but it was contended by the neo-Hegelians that almost all our concepts fail to meet it. For, as we have seen, their ground for holding that space and time and matter were alike unreal was that our notions of them were self-contradictory. In Bradley's case, this charge was mainly sustained by his belief that there was something logically vicious about the idea of there being relations between different terms. If the relation entered into the being of the terms, it welded them into a whole from which they could not be independently abstracted; if it did not enter into their being it merely constituted an extra term with no intelligible connection with the terms which it was supposed to relate. Bradley did make some concession to science and to common sense, in as much as he allowed that the things which we seem to perceive as spatio-temporally related had the degree of reality which accrued to them as appearances. He insisted, however, that they were not ultimately real.

Unfortunately, it is not easy to see what this concession is worth. To begin with, it is not at all clear what can be meant by talking of degrees of reality. Surely whatever may be in question is either real or not: there is no room for anything in between. One may indeed say of a character in fiction that it has more or less verisimilitude, but however life-like it may be, it remains a character in fiction: there is no process by which it can slide into becoming a real person. Neither is it clear what can be meant by saying that something is real as an appearance. If what is to be understood is that the thing really does appear, then the inference to be drawn is that it is real

[1] L. Wittgenstein. *Tractatus Logico-Philosophicus* (tra. D. F. Pears and B. F. McGuinness) 3.031.

without qualification, though we may allow for the possibility that it is appearing under some disguise. If what is to be understood is that the thing only appears to be real, then the conclusion that it is not real follows. The only other possibility is that the word 'real' is here being used in some special sense, but then this needs to be explained.

The conclusion that what Bradley calls appearances are unreal without qualification would in any case seem to follow from his charge that the concepts under which they fall are self-contradictory. For if a concept is self-contradictory it necessarily has no application, and no appearances can fall under it. The most that is possible is that something should appear, in the sense of being thought, to fall under it, so long as the contradiction is not detected. What is not tenable is the view that things are misperceived as standing in spatial and temporal relations, for if the concepts of space and time were self-contradictory there would be nothing to constitute the misperception: it would have no intelligible content. The theory is that the apparent world is a disguised form of a deeper reality; but unless both A and B answer to coherent descriptions, the suggestion that A masquerades as B makes no sense.

If this is so, these metaphysicians do not succeed in saving the appearances. What we need rather to ask is how they could think themselves capable of destroying them. Is it not plainly absurd to say that space and time and matter are unreal? If this were taken literally, it would follow, as G. E. Moore pointed out,[1] that nothing ever happens before or after anything else, that, for example, a man's birth does not precede his death, that nothing ever moves, that a man's head is at no distance from his feet, indeed that he has neither head nor feet. It would follow too, as Moore also remarked, that if this view were true, no philosopher could ever have propounded it. For philosophers, if they exist, are human beings with material bodies, and their theories are propounded at particular places and times. In the same way, if Zeno had been right in asserting that the concept of motion was self-contradictory,[2] he could not have asserted it; for whether he spoke or wrote some part of his body would have had to move.

Refutations of this sort seem too easy. Metaphysicians who make these apparently outrageous claims should not be taken just to be

[1] In his 'A Defence of Common Sense' *Philosophical Papers*.
[2] See below pp. 17–21.

denying obvious facts. But how then are they to be taken? The best way to try to answer this question will be to examine specimens of their arguments.

D Time and Motion: Some Metaphysical Arguments

Let us begin then with the argument by which McTaggart sought to demonstrate the unreality of time.[1] McTaggart begins by remarking that we have two ways of ordering events in time. We speak of them as being past, present or future, and we also speak of them as being before or after or simultaneous with one another. He then argues that the first of these ways of speaking cannot be reduced to the second, since the second makes no provision for the passage of time. Whereas the same event is successively future, present and past, there is no change in its temporal relations to other events. The fact that one particular event precedes another is equally a fact at any time. So to do justice to our concept of time, we have to make use of the predicates of past, present and future. But then, McTaggart argues, we fall into contradiction. For these predicates are mutually incompatible, and yet they are all supposed to be true of every event.

The obvious answer to this is that there would be a contradiction if we supposed these predicates to be simultaneously true of the same event, but that this is not what we suppose at all; we apply them to the same event successively. McTaggart considers this answer, and his rejoinder to it is that it escapes the contradiction only at the cost of launching us on a vicious infinite regress. We say of a contemporary event that it is present, has been future, and will be past; and what this means, according to McTaggart is that the event is present at a present moment, future at a past moment, and past at a future moment. But then the same difficulty arises with respect to these moments. Each of them is assigned the incompatible predicates of being past, present and future. We can again try to escape the contradiction by saying of the moments in their turn that they are present at present moments, past at present and future moments, and future at past and present moments, but then the same difficulty arises with respect to this second series of moments, and so *ad infinitum*.

The argument still seems sophistic, but it does pose a problem. So far as I can see, there are only two ways of meeting it. The one

[1] See *The Nature of Existence*, Vol. II paras. 329–33.

which I favour is to deny the contention that the predicates of being past, present and future cannot be reduced to the predicates of temporal order. If we take this course, we shall have to maintain that what is meant by saying of an event that it is past, present or future is just that it is earlier than, simultaneous with, or later than some arbitrarily chosen event which is contemporaneous with the speaker's utterance. On this view, the passage of time simply consists in the fact, which is itself non-temporal, that events are ordered in a series by the earlier-than relation. The passage of an event from future to present to past merely represents a difference in the temporal point of view from which it is described. This analysis has the effect of assimilating time to space, and it is, indeed, for this reason that some philosophers object to it. They feel that the river of time has somehow been turned into a stagnant pond.

The other course is to maintain that being present is not a descriptive property of an event, assigning it to a moment which itself can be described as present, past or future, but the demonstrative property of occurring *now*. Once this is established, the past and future can safely be defined by their relation to the present. The regress is avoided by the fact that 'now' is tied to an actual context. We are not required to say when now is: our use of the word shows it. The disadvantage of this course, as opposed to the previous one, is that it introduces an irreducible element of subjectivity into our picture of the world. It entails that an observer outside the time series, if such a thing were possible, would not be able to give a complete account of temporal facts.[1] To do so, on this view, one has to put oneself into the picture, as an observer undergoing the passage of time.

We see, then, that while McTaggart did not prove time to be unreal, in the sense of showing all our temporal judgements to be false, his argument does throw light upon the concept of time. It confronts us with the alternative either of assimilating time to space, with the threat that we shall then be failing to do justice to the passage of time, or of giving an account of temporal facts which is incurably subjective. His argument is destructive to the extent that it denies us the privilege of having only the best of both these approaches. It shows us also that the analysis of temporal facts is not so straightforward as we might have hoped.

[1] cf Michael Dummett 'McTaggart on Time' *The Philosophical Review*, October 1960.

For my second example, I take Zeno's paradoxes. Zeno of Elea who lived in the fifth century B C was a disciple of Parmenides, the earliest philosopher who is known to have maintained that Reality is One. Parmenides described the world, which he took to be material and finite, as being 'like the mass of a well-rounded sphere', and he argued, on logical grounds, that there could be no differentiation within it. This entailed, among other things, that nothing really moved, and this was the conclusion which Zeno's paradoxes were intended to establish.

It is, as we have already seen, a conclusion which we can easily show to be absurd, but once again the question becomes less simple if we consider not just the conclusion itself but the steps by which it is reached. As reported by Aristotle, to whose book on *Physics*[1] we owe our knowledge of Zeno's work, Zeno advanced four closely connected arguments. The most famous of these is the paradox of Achilles and the tortoise, which on the face of it is designed to show not that motion is impossible but that we are mistaken in our acceptance of what appears to be the obvious fact that a faster runner can overtake a slower one. The argument is that in order to catch the tortoise, which has received a start, Achilles has first to reach the point from which the tortoise started; but by the time he gets there the tortoise will have advanced to a further point, and by the time Achilles gets to this further point, the tortoise will have gone a little further still, and so *ad infinitum*.

Essentially the same reasoning is deployed in the paradox known as the Dichotomy where Zeno argues that no distance can ever be traversed. For in order to traverse the full distance, it is necessary first to traverse half of it, and in order to traverse half of it, it is necessary first to traverse a quarter of it, and before that an eighth, and so again *ad infinitum*.

The third paradox is that of the arrow. Here Zeno argues in favour of the apparent contradiction that an arrow in flight must always be at rest. This argument depends upon correlating times to places. The assumption is that if an object occupies a variety of places during a period of time, there are shorter periods of time during which it occupies each one of them. But then at each of these moments of time it will be at the corresponding place. Consequently, it will always be at rest.

The paradox of the arrow is echoed by that of the Stadium, the

[1] Book 2, section 9.

most difficult to follow in Aristotle's account, which is supposed to show that 'half a given time may be equal to its double'.[1] We are asked to imagine a stadium containing three equal rows of objects, one of them stationary, and the other two moving at uniform speed in opposite directions. The moving rows pass the stationary row at the same time, so that there is a moment at which all three rows coincide. Let us illustrate this by a diagram:[2]

Position 1				*Position* 2		
A_1	A_2	A_3		A_1	A_2	A_3
$\leftarrow$	B_1	B_2	B_3	B_1	B_2	B_3
C_3	C_2	C_1	$\rightarrow$	C_3	C_2	C_1

Now let us consider the transition from the first to the second figure. For this change to be effected, B_1 and B_2 and C_1 and C_2, the leading members of the moving rows, have in each case to pass one member of the stationary row A. In the same time, however, both B_1 and B_2 will have passed two members of C, and both C_1 and C_2 will have passed two members of B. Let us think of each object as occupying a point at any given instant. Then, since their motion is uniform, we may assume that it takes the Bs and Cs an equal amount of time to pass any given object. But now we come upon the contradiction that they pass two objects in the same amount of time as they take to pass only one.

This last argument is the least impressive of the four, since it seems to depend upon the inconsistent procedure of treating the Bs and Cs as being in motion when they pass the members of the other rows but as static when they are themselves being passed. There is not even any appearance of contradiction in the fact that the relative rate of motion of the Bs and Cs, as measured by the rate of diminution of the distance between them, is twice as great as that of their motion with respect to the stationary As. Nevertheless, the argument does contain a serious puzzle. Let us assume that our figures represent the position of the rows at two successive instants. This assumption may be thought legitimate, since we can put the As as close together as we please and postulate that it takes just an instant to pass each A. Then at the first instant, C_1 is opposite

---

[1] i.e. the whole time. Aristotle. *Physics*, z.9.239 b 33.
[2] Taken from Bertrand Russell's exposition of the paradox in *Our Knowledge of the External World*, Ch. V.

B_1, and at the second instant, it is opposite B_3. When did it pass B_2? There is no room for any time in which this could have happened.

The solution of this puzzle is not at all commonplace. We have to deny the assumption that there are such things as successive instants. The moments of time form a continuous series, in the sense that between any two of them another intervenes. There are, consequently, an infinite number of moments in any period of time, however short, which is, indeed, only another way of saying that stretches of time are infinitely divisible. This is not the conclusion that Zeno drew, but it is a product of his argument.

The paradox of the arrow goes deeper, since it does not depend upon taking the units of time to be discrete. For whether the number of moments at which we can locate the arrow be finite or infinite, it remains true that at any given moment the arrow will be at some particular place. But how is this compatible with its being in flight? The answer is that its being in flight simply consists in the fact that over a continuous period of time it occupies a continuous series of places. If we are asked how it gets from one place to another, our answer must again be that its getting from one place to another simply consists in the fact that it occupies some intermediate place at any given intermediate time. This may appear to do away with the fluidity of motion, just as the first of our answers to McTaggart appeared to do away with the fluidity of time, but in this case at least the appearance is delusive. The fluidity of motion consists in its continuity, and the continuity of motion is secured by the continuity of space as well as time. There is, however, a sense in which Zeno was right. The arrow could be said always to be at rest if what is meant by this is that there is a one to one correlation between the places which it occupies and the times at which it occupies them. He was wrong only in assuming that its being at rest, in this special sense, was incompatible with its being in flight.

The other two paradoxes raise a different problem, though one that is also connected with difficulties concerning infinity. The problem in this case is how an infinite series can be either begun or completed, the argument of the Achilles paradox being, in effect, that the race can never end, and the argument of the dichotomy paradox that it can never begin.

Attempts have been made to dismiss the Achilles paradox on the ground that Zeno simply did not realize that the sum of an infinite series can be finite. To catch the tortoise, Achilles has indeed to make good the distance which originally separated them, as well as the further distance which the tortoise has advanced in the meantime, as well as the further distance which it has advanced while the first advance is being made up, and so *ad infinitum;* but since the sum of an infinite series can be finite, as, for example, the sum of the series $1/2 + 1/4 + 1/8$ etc. is equal to 1, his task presents no logical difficulty.

This answer seems to me insufficient. It may be used to prove that Achilles would in fact catch the tortoise, but this is not seriously in doubt. In the normal way, faster runners do overtake slower ones. The problem is how it is possible that they should, in the face of Zeno's argument, and this is not solved by a simple appeal to mathematics. How little it is solved becomes clear if we turn to the dichotomy paradox. It is no good our knowing that the sum of an infinite series can be finite if we are unable to explain how the series can ever come into existence.

Let us then try to attack the problem, rather than circumvent it. The crucial point, as I see it, is that the stages of a continuous series cannot be reached successively. If Achilles, or the runner in the dichotomy paradox, had to go through the infinite number of points in the courses one by one, they could, indeed, neither start nor finish. They could not start, because there is no point next to the starting-point which would be the first of their goals, and they could not finish, because there is no point next to the finishing point, from which they could immediately proceed to complete the course. The runners do, indeed, take a first and last step, each of which carries them a certain distance, but in taking the first step they *have* already covered an infinite number of smaller distances, and in taking the last step they *have* already covered the infinitely divisible stretch which separates the place to which the previous step had brought them from the finishing line. It is tempting to assume that in order to run a number of yards, it is necessary first to run a yard and before that to run half a yard and before that to run a quarter of a yard and so *ad infinitum,* but this assumption is false. What is true is that in the interval between the athlete's beginning to run and his putting any finite distance behind him he will have been at any given intermediate place at some intermediate time: what is not true is that this constitutes a progression. There are first and last steps that he takes but in the course of the run no first and last points that he occupies. If the attainment of each point on the course is represented as a task, then in taking any step, however short, the runner has accomplished an infinite number of tasks which it would be impossible for him to perform successively.

Again, this conclusion is far from commonplace. If anything, it goes against our untutored intuition. When we add it to what went before, we see that Zeno's paradoxes are not just ingenious sophistries. By taking them seriously we obtain unexpected insights into the behaviour of our concepts of space and time and motion. The same result, the clarification of a fundamental concept, was yielded by our examination of McTaggart's argument. It is, however, to be noted that in both cases these benefits were compensations for the failure to establish a metaphysical position. The question is whether this must always be so. We have seen that philosophical argument can illuminate our picture of the world. Can it also change it? Or must philosophy be restricted to the practice of analysis?

II Meaning and Common Sense

A The Verification Principle

The view that 'philosophy is not a body of doctrine but an activity', which 'aims at the logical clarification of thoughts'[1] was propounded by Wittgenstein in the 1920s and has since gained very wide currency. It was taken up enthusiastically by the Logical Positivists in the following decade and gradually developed into the linguistic movement of the 1950s when the clarification of thoughts was interpreted rather narrowly as an account of the way in which the expressions of a natural language are ordinarily used. There is, indeed, nothing new in the idea that the aims of philosophy include the clarification of thoughts. It goes back at least to Socrates who, if we can trust Plato's account of him, was primarily concerned to answer such questions as 'What is justice?' or 'What is knowledge?'. The controversial question is whether this is the only aim that philosophy can legitimately have. Why should it be so restricted? The reason is that all the other avenues of knowledge are thought to be already pre-empted. Having no right to trespass, philosophers are then directed to conceptual or linguistic analysis, as the only field which they can profitably explore.

Even this conclusion is not new, though it is only in recent times that it has gained widespread acceptance. It is, for example, already implicit in the famous passage with which Hume concludes his book *An Enquiry Concerning Human Understanding*. He has just divided all the legitimate forms of study into abstract science, the only objects of which are quantity and number, and enquiries regarding 'matters of fact and existence', which can be founded only on experience, and he then continues: 'When we run over libraries, persuaded of these principles, what havoc must we make? If we take in our hand any volume; of divinity or school metaphysics, for instance; let us ask, *Does it contain any abstract reasoning*

[1] L. Wittgenstein. *Tractatus Logico-Philosophicus* 4.112.

concerning quantity or number ? No. *Does it contain any experimental reasoning concerning matter of fact and existence* ? No. Commit it then to the flames: for it can contain nothing but sophistry and illusion.'[1]

But what of Hume's own work, which he did not think deserving of committal to the flames ? He was not so heroic as Wittgenstein who said of the propositions in the *Tractatus* that 'anyone who understands me eventually recognizes them as nonsensical, when he has used them – as steps – to climb beyond them'.[2] Not so heroic, and also not so disingenuous; for if the propositions of the *Tractatus* were nonsensical, we should not be expected to believe them. Hume does not apply his criteria to his own philosophy, but he most probably regarded it as coming within the domain of experimental reasoning. The distinction between philosophy and science was not explicitly drawn in the eighteenth century; indeed, the very word 'scientist' is a nineteenth-century coinage, designed to take the place of 'natural philosopher'. It is not, therefore, to be expected that Hume should have distinguished the subject-matter of his *Treatise of Human Nature* or his *Enquiry Concerning Human Understanding* from that of what we should nowadays call psychology. Nevertheless, it is only to a very limited extent, in these works, and then chiefly when he is writing about morality, that he advances any empirical generalizations which could be tested by experiment. His main business is with concepts, which he is indeed concerned not only to analyze but also to harness to the profit of his scepticism. We shall see later on how the practice of analysis is linked with the attempt to promote, or more often to counter the challenge which the sceptic poses.

At present we are concerned with Hume's attack on 'school metaphysics', from which the restriction of philosophy to analysis can be made to follow. The assumptions on which Hume was relying were taken up by the Logical Positivists and embodied in what came to be known as the principle of verifiability or, less accurately but more compendiously, the verification principle. As formulated by Moritz Schlick, the leader of the group of philosophers and mathematicians, calling themselves the Vienna Circle, who organized the logical positivist movement in the late nineteen twenties, the principle was that the meaning of a proposition

[1] David Hume. *An Enquiry Concerning Human Understanding*, Section XII.
[2] *Tractatus Logico-Philosophicus* 6.54.

consists in its method of verification. My own version of it, as expressed in my *Language, Truth and Logic*, was that 'a sentence is factually significant to any given person if, and only if, he knows how to verify the proposition which it purports to express – that is, if he knows what observations would lead him, under certain conditions, to accept it as being true or reject it as being false'.[1] Meaning was also accorded to sentences expressing propositions like those of logic or pure mathematics, which were true or false only in virtue of their form, but with this exception, everything of a would-be indicative character which failed to satisfy the verification principle was dismissed as literally nonsensical.

The two versions of the principle which I have quoted are not equivalent. As I stated it, the principle supplies a rule for determining only whether a sentence is meaningful. In Schlick's version it takes the further step of giving a procedure for determining what meaning a sentence has. It has often been assumed that the results are the same whichever form of the principle one adopts, but this need not be so. For instance, one may require that the propositions of a scientific theory be testable by observation, without holding that their content is reducible to that of the propositions in which these observations are recorded. If one adopts the principle of verifiability in any form one will, indeed, be inclined to equate what William James called 'the cash-value' of scientific theories with the range of observable states of affairs which they serve to correlate and predict; but this is not to say that the variety of situations in which it could be tested, or even the variety of ways of testing it, is fixed once for all in the formulation of a theory, still less that its content is limited to a description of the favourable tests which are actually carried out. To pursue James's analogy, there is more paper issued than is ever redeemed for gold.

An example which brings the distinction out more clearly is that of historical propositions. It is one thing to require of a historian that some possible observations should be relevant to the truth or falsehood of his assertions, but another to identify the meaning of propositions about the past with the present or future evidence which would be held to support them. This would entail, for example, that all that could now be meant by saying that Caesar crossed the Rubicon was that if we were to look in such and such

---

[1] *Language, Truth and Logic* (1st edition 1936) p. 35 (2nd edition).

history books we should discover that their authors affirmed it. This was, indeed, the position taken by C. S. Peirce and other American pragmatists, and by myself in *Language, Truth and Logic*, but it no longer seems to me tenable. Admittedly, if one came to doubt whether such or such an event did really occur, the only way in which one could hope to settle the question would be by the discovery of further evidence. In practice, speculations about the past, if they are not to be entirely idle, must relate to the traces which the past has left. Nevertheless, the logical point remains that those traces are fallible. However little reason one may have to distrust one's sources, their saying or indicating that such and such an event occurred does not logically entail that it did occur. And I think that this formal point needs to be respected, even when it has no practical application.

One might, indeed, try to construe the phrase 'its method of verification' in such a way as to produce a criterion which did not have this implausible consequence. Thus, one might leave it open who was to do the verifying; and then one might equate the meaning of an indicative sentence with that of the sentences which recorded the observations of those who were best placed to test the truth of the proposition which it expressed. In the case of sentences expressing historical propositions, these would be the persons who were or could have been present on the occasion. It might even be argued that one could, in principle, have been there oneself, but this is disputable. While it seems to make sense to say that one might have been slightly older or younger than one is, if only on the ground that one can be mistaken about one's age without falling into self-contradiction, it is doubtful whether the idea of one's living at a very different time is consistent with one's personal identity. In any case, it is not clear why the meaning of a sentence like 'Caesar crossed the Rubicon' should be thought to contain any reference to oneself, unless 'what it means to me' is construed not as 'what I understand by it' but as 'what difference my believing it would make to my expectations of future experiences', and then the reference must be to experiences one could actually have, rather than to the experiences which one might have if one were differently situated in space and time. On the other hand, if the talk of verification is to be taken impersonally, as referring simply to observable states of affairs, there is a shift to a rather different theory, which I shall presently consider, whereby the meaning of a sentence is equated with the truth-conditions of the proposition which it serves to express.

Even in its weaker form, in which it is designed only to demarcate literal sense from nonsense, the verification principle runs into difficulties. For one thing, it has never yet been adequately formulated. The suggestion that a sentence is factually significant to a given person if, and only if, he knows what observations would lead him to accept or reject the proposition which he takes it to express, is not satisfactory, because it does not take account of the fact that people may behave irrationally. Someone may be disposed to accept a proposition on the basis of observations which do not genuinely support it. For example, someone who prays for rain and sees it subsequently fall may treat his observation of the rainfall as a reason for accepting the proposition that God exists. A staunch verificationist might argue that what such a man really meant by saying that God existed was just that when he prayed he sometimes obtained what he wanted, but this would not be very plausible.

Accordingly, in the first edition of *Language, Truth and Logic*, I tried to give the principle a better formulation by delimiting a class of observation-statements which I called experiential propositions and then taking it to be 'the mark of a genuine factual proposition' that 'some experiential propositions can be deduced from it in conjunction with certain other premises without being deducible from those other premises alone'.[1] My reason for putting it in this way was to make provision for hypothetical propositions and for generalizations of law which could not be simply equated with any finite set of statements of particular fact. I said of this criterion that it seemed liberal enough, but this turned out to be an understatement, since the criterion in fact allowed meaning to any assertion whatsoever. This followed from the simple fact, which was first pointed out by Sir Isaiah Berlin,[2] that if 'O' is an observation statement, then whatever statement 'S' may be, 'O' follows from the conjunction of 'S' with 'If S then O' without following from 'If S then O'. alone. In the second edition of my book, I tried to meet this difficulty by recasting the principle as follows: I said that a statement was to be accounted directly verifiable 'if it is either itself an observation-statement, or is such that in conjunction with

[1] *op. cit.* p. 39.
[2] In an article entitled 'Verification and Experience'. *Proceedings of the Aristotelian Society*, Vol. XXVII.

one or more observation-statements it entails at least one observation-statement which is not deducible from those other premisses alone'. I said that a statement was to be accounted indirectly verifiable if it was the case 'first, that in conjunction with certain other premisses it entails one or more directly verifiable statements which are not deducible from these other premisses alone; and secondly, that these other premisses do not include any statement that is not either analytic, or directly verifiable, or capable of being independently established as indirectly verifiable':[1] and I then required of a literally meaningful statement, which was not analytic, in the sense of being formally true, that it should be either directly or indirectly verifiable in the way that I had just defined.

I hoped that this formula was elaborate enough at least to avoid the fate of its predecessor, but I was soon disappointed. For Professor Alonzo Church quickly pointed out[2] that even in its emended form, my criterion still allowed meaning to any statement whatsoever. The example by which he showed this was that of the complex formula 'Either (not–O_1 and O_2) or (O_3 and not–S)', where 'O_1' 'O_2' and 'O_3' are observation-statements which are logically independent of one another, and 'S' is any statement you please. Since this formula entails 'O_3' when conjoined with 'O_1', which *ex hypothesi* does not entail 'O_3' by itself, it satisfies my conditions for being directly verifiable. But then it will follow that 'S' is indirectly verifiable, since in conjunction with the formula it entails 'O_2' without its being the case that 'O_2' follows from the formula alone. Attempts have since been made to emend the criterion still further so as to escape Church's counter example, but none of them has so far been successful.

B The Criterion of Falsifiability

It is clear that Church's formula needs only to be slightly modified in order to pose the same threat to the principle of falsifiability, which was put forward by Sir Karl Popper,[3] not, indeed, as a criterion of meaning but as a method of demarcating scientific statements from those that he called metaphysical. Popper counted a statement as being falsifiable if it was logically incompatible with

[1] *Language, Truth and Logic*, p. 13.
[2] In a review of my book in the *Journal of Symbolic Logic*, 1949, pp. 52–3.
[3] In his book *Logik der Forschung*. English translation: *The Logic of Scientific Discovery*.

some class of what he called basic-statements, a basic statement being one which asserted the existence of some observable state of affairs at some particular place and time. Since not all scientific hypotheses are expressed in terms of what is straightforwardly observable, this criterion will be too stringent unless provision is made for indirect falsification, and it is not easy to see how this can be done except along the lines that I proposed for indirect verification. But then we have only to substitute 'not-O_3' for 'O_3' in Church's formula to obtain the unwelcome consequence that any statement whatsoever is falsifiable.

If it could be made logically watertight, the criterion of falsifiability would have the advantage over the verification principle that the notion of falsification is the more precise, at least in its application to scientific theories. The reason for this is that a single contrary instance is sufficient to refute a generalization, whereas, unless they exhaust its scope, which will not normally be the case if we are dealing with scientific laws, no finite number of favourable instances can conclusively establish it. Moreover, it is not always clear what is to count as a favourable instance. If we assume that a generalization is confirmed by anything that satisfies its antecedent and its consequent, and if we also make what seems the natural assumption that equivalent hypotheses are equally confirmed by the same evidence, then, as Professor Carl Hempel has shown,[1] we arrive at the unpalatable conclusion that everything which is compatible with a generalization confirms it. For the proposition that All A is B is equivalent to the proposition that everything that is not-B is not-A, and also to the proposition that everything is either not A or B, with the result that it is confirmed by everything except an A that is not B.[2] Neither, indeed, do the partisans of falsifiability escape this problem if they hold, as they do, that the procedure of science is to set up hypotheses and try to falsify them. For they then have to explain why the result of any observation which is logically compatible with the hypothesis, however seemingly irrelevant, does not equally accredit it.[3]

The criterion of falsifiability has its own disadvantages. Unless they are smuggled in by some such device as Church's formula, in

---

[1] C. G. Hempel. 'Studies in the Logic of Confirmation'. *Mind* LIV 213 and 214. For a discussion of this problem see my *Probability and Evidence*. I.3.

[2] I try to deal with this problem later on. See pp. 176–7.

[3] See below pp. 157–8.

which case all manner of nonsense comes in with them, open existential statements, which merely assert that something of such and such a sort exists, without saying where and when it exists, are not falsifiable. The proposition that there are abominable snowmen is probably false, but it cannot be strictly falsified, since we cannot search the whole of space at every moment of its existence. By the same token, the proposition that there are elephants, though established by observation, fails to satisfy the criterion and has to be accounted metaphysical, in Popper's peculiar sense of the term. The same applies to indefinite statements, like the proposition that some day the sea will encroach upon this land, since however long the sea fails to encroach, there is always the possibility that it will do so at some future time. On the other hand, the contradictories of these propositions *are* falsifiable. These anomalies are not so disturbing as they would be if the criterion of falsifiability were put forward as a criterion of meaning, but one might think that they made the class of empirical statements unduly narrow. A more serious objection is that the statements of probability which occur in science are not falsifiable, at least if they are interpreted, in the usual way, as predictions that the distribution of some property among the members of what may be an infinite class will reach and maintain a particular frequency. The reason for this is that however much the recorded statistics deviate from the predicted frequency, there is always the possibility that it will be reached at some later stage.[1] One can, indeed, make it a rule that the probability statement is to count as being falsified if the deviation goes beyond a certain limit, but this is to adopt a different principle. It is to forsake the neat logical criterion that was originally proposed.

C Meaning and Use

In the face of these difficulties, the tendency has been to give up the attempt to produce a general criterion of meaning, or even a formal rule of demarcation. This tendency is strengthened by the view, which is now very widely accepted, that the propositions of a scientific theory do not confront our experience singly but only as a body. This is illustrated by the fact that if the theory comes to grief, we may have some latitude in deciding which parts of it there is need to revise. The theory as a whole must be empirically testable, otherwise we could do nothing with it, but there may be no unique

[1] See below p. 168.

answer to the question which of its propositions are purely formal, and which have factual content: and there may be no clear way of distinguishing those that have empirical content from those that might be accounted metaphysical. What remains of the criterion of falsifiability is the demand that the theory as a whole be vulnerable to experience. If it is so interpreted that no possible experience could invalidate it, it is not a scientific theory, and may be accused of lacking any factual content.

The verification principle also survives in the equation, which many philosophers currently make, of the meaning of an indicative sentence with the truth-conditions of the proposition which it serves to express. The only objection to this view that I can see is that it is not very illuminating. It is not as though we could pick out the truth-conditions of a proposition independently of understanding the sentence which is used to express it. Admittedly, if one is uncertain about the meaning of what is being said, it can be useful to ask oneself in what circumstances one would accept it as being true, but this yields a sufficient answer only in those cases where the proposition in question straightforwardly refers to some observable state of affairs which one may be in a position to encounter. This will not apply to propositions about the past, nor to propositions about the experiences of other persons, unless one takes the implausible step of identifying their experiences with their overt behaviour, nor to scientific hypotheses containing theoretical terms which do not stand for anything that can be directly observed. It is true that one does not fully understand these hypotheses unless one knows what sort of experiments would be taken as substantiating them, or as substantiating the theories in which they figure; but, as we have seen, there are grounds for holding that the description of these experiments does not exhaust the meaning of the hypotheses or the theories which they serve to test.

The same comments apply to the slogan, made fashionable by Wittgenstein,[1] that the meaning of words consists in the way that they are used. The merit of this slogan was that it helped to disabuse philosophers of the idea that meanings are Platonic objects, already in being before we find the words to designate them. It also corrected the mistaken tendency to construe every word as if it were a name. For the misleading metaphor of words as pictures it substituted

[1] L. Wittgenstein. *Philosophical Investigations*, para 43, p. 20.

the metaphor of words as tools. One effect of this has been to call our attention to the variety of uses to which language is put; not only to state facts and formulate theories, but to make promises, promote actions, make requests, tell fictitious stories, tell jokes, utter obscenities, take oaths, play games and very much else besides. Nevertheless, the primary function of language is to state what is true or false, and here the identification of meaning with use is less accurate than its identification with truth-conditions. It is less accurate just because of those cases, of which I have given various examples, where the conditions in which we are justified in asserting a proposition are not the same as the conditions which make it true. For instance, we learn to employ the past tense by hearing it applied to events which we remember. But while the fact that one clearly remembers a recent event may be the best justification that one can have for believing that it happened, this is not what makes the belief true. What makes the belief true is just that the event did happen.

If the equation of meaning and use is taken literally, it comes close to the criterion which was put forward by the nineteenth-century American pragmatists. Their maxim, as C. S. Peirce formulated it, was that our whole conception of an object consists in our conception of its practical effects.[1] If the requirement is added that these practical effects be directly observable, we come back to something like the verification principle; indeed, though the logical positivists were mainly ignorant of pragmatism, many of their theses had been anticipated by Peirce and to a lesser extent by William James. The merit of this approach is again that it does away with occult properties. To say that an electrical current is passing through a wire is not to refer to something like an invisible wave, but to summarize a set of facts such as that, under suitable conditions, batteries will be charged, bells rung, engines driven and so forth. Electricity is what electricity does. To speak of gravitational attraction is not to imply the literal existence of mysterious entities called forces, but only to refer to such facts as that the ebb and flow of the sea is correlated with states of the moon or that unsupported bodies tend to fall. The corollary of this view is that concepts or theories which cover the same effects are equivalent in meaning, however much they may appear to differ in their content, and that concepts which are not related to any effects have no meaning in them.

[1] *Vide: The Collected Papers of Charles Sanders Peirce*, Vol. V, p. 402.

This position is attractive to the type of philosopher whom William James characterized as tough-minded,[1] but it encounters difficulties when one tries to work it out in detail. We have already seen that Peirce was led to take the implausible view that propositions about the past are equivalent to descriptions of the present or future evidence that might be forthcoming in their favour, and his account of scientific concepts is also not wholly convincing. The simple equation of forces with their effects overlooks the part that models play in scientific theories, and it also ignores the scientific practice of explaining functions in terms of structures. In the frequent case where the structural components are not directly observable, it may, indeed, be arguable that all that this comes to is the introduction of a wider range of effects with which the effects of the forces in question are linked, but, as I said before, it is doubtful whether even the widest range of effects which are ascribed to a scientific theory at any given time can properly be said to exhaust its meaning.

If the pragmatist position is not acceptable, it is mainly because of its failure to do justice to the texture of scientific theories, both to its openness, in that the range of the evidence which may bear upon a theory is not circumscribed, and to the fact that it is more closely woven than the texture of our observations. Thus, as Professor Hempel has pointed out,[2] the quantitative concepts which are employed in science cannot, in general, be defined in terms of what is actually observable. This applies even to such everyday concepts as those of length and weight. Thus, in any physical theory which includes Euclidean geometry there will be lengths which have irrational numbers, like the square root of 2, for their values, but no actual measurement can have an irrational number for its result. We might try to meet this objection by identifying an irrational number with the series of rational numbers of which it is the limit, but then we encounter the difficulty that this series is infinite, whereas any series of actual observations must be finite. A similar difficulty arises in the case of weight, where the possible values are, indeed, rational, but also infinite in number, since they form a compact series such that for any two of them there is another in between. The result is that there are theoretically more differences in weight than our observations can distinguish. We could perhaps conceive of these possibilities as being represented by an infinite number of conditional statements at the observational level, but apart from the difficulty of specifying the protases of many of these conditionals, the point of the pragmatic approach will then very largely be lost. The tough-minded insistence on cash-value begins to be softened when we cannot actually deliver the cash.

What we might do, as I shall suggest later on,[1] is to distinguish the meaning of a theory, or, to put it more accurately, the meaning of the sentences in which the theory is formulated, from its factual content. The factual content of the theory will be identified with the account which is derivable from it of what is actually observable. The sum total of such purely factual propositions, whether true or false, constitutes what the Cambridge philosopher F. P. Ramsey called a primary system.[2] This is contrasted with a secondary system, or set of systems, which is concerned with what Peirce called the arrangement of facts. The secondary system goes beyond the primary, in that it legislates for possible as well as actual cases and can also contain terms which are not directly related to anything observable. Since the distinction between fact and theory is only relative, we have some choice as to where to draw the line. We shall see that it is to some extent an arbitrary question what is to count as purely factual. Nevertheless, I shall argue that a reasonable decision can be taken. The meaning of the sentences which enter into the formulation of a scientific theory will then depend partly on the factual content of the theory and partly on the contribution, both to the structure and to the explanatory powers of the theory, that is made by the propositions which they express.

Returning to the question of the possibility of metaphysics, from which this discussion of meaning started, we are, I think, entitled to require of any metaphysical theory that it should function as a secondary system, at least to the extent of having some explanatory value. An objection which was often raised against the verification principle was that its own status was dubious. It did not seem to be necessary, in the sense that the denial of it was self-contradictory, and if it was put forward as an empirical hypothesis about the way

---

[1] See below pp. 109–10 and 142–7.
[2] *Vide* F. P. Ramsey. *The Foundations of Mathematics*, p. 212.

in which the word 'meaning' is actually used, the very fact that it denied meaning to statements which many people regarded as meaningful could be taken as evidence that it was false. The only answer that could be made to this objection was that the principle was advanced as a stipulative definition. It did not describe how the word 'meaning' was commonly used, but prescribed how it should be. But then why should anyone follow the prescription if its implications were not to his taste? We have, in fact, seen that the verification principle is defective on other grounds, but the same question arises with respect even to the much weaker proposal that I am substituting for it. Why should it be required of a metaphysical theory that it have some explanatory value? To this I can reply only by asking what interest could the theory have otherwise. If it does not aspire to truth, we need not worry. Let it be said that it is meaningful: the word 'meaning' is used very variously and there may be people to whom the theory is significant in some way or other. But if the theory does aspire to truth, there should be some way of deciding whether it attains it. Even if it has no factual content, in the sense which I am giving to the term, it should contribute something to the arrangement of facts. Otherwise we have no criterion by which to determine whether it is acceptable. Of course it may be said that my tying theories to observable facts begs the question, but what are the alternatives against which it is begged? Even a metaphysician like McTaggart, with his idiosyncratic conception of reality,[1] thought himself obliged to try to account for the appearances. If what we are charged with excluding is the existence of another realm, unconnected with anything that we ordinarily perceive, we return in effect to the question of mystical experience,[2] and the same considerations apply.

D The Claims of Common Sense

The distrust of metaphysics which has been a feature of much recent philosophy was partly brought about by the logical positivists, but it had an earlier source in the analytic movement which began to develop in Cambridge at the beginning of this century. The movement was originated by Bertrand Russell and G. E. Moore and was continued in his own fashion by Wittgenstein whose early work also stimulated the logical positivists. Though

[1] See above p. 10.
[2] See above pp. 4–7.

Russell has had a greater influence than Moore, not only in the world at large, but also through his purely philosophical writings, it was Moore who was chiefly responsible for the restriction of philosophy to analysis. He did not himself advance this view of philosophy, and indeed denied that he held it, but it was largely consistent with his practice and we shall see that it is an inference which one might easily draw from his views.

The salient feature of Moore's philosophical position was his defence of common sense. He did not go so far as to maintain that common sense was right in all its beliefs. For instance, it was once a common sense belief that the earth was flat, and Moore would not have denied the possibility that some beliefs which are now generally held might equally turn out to be erroneous. What he did maintain was the truth, and indeed the certainty, of a number of very general propositions which made up what he called the common sense view of the world.

The common sense view of the world, as Moore represents it, consists primarily in a belief in the existence of two different sorts of entities, material objects and acts of consciousness.[1] Moore does not define what he means, or what he takes common sense to mean by a material object, but he gives a list of examples which include human bodies, animals, plants, minerals, houses, railway engines, drops of water, the earth and the stars; and he also attributes to common sense the belief that all these objects are located both in space and time.

The belief that there are acts of consciousness is Moore's interpretation of a belief which the man in the street would more naturally express by saying that men, and possibly some other animals, have minds. Again, Moore does not try to define acts of consciousness, but he implies that they include such things as hearing, seeing, remembering, feeling, thinking and dreaming. He attributes to common sense the belief that these acts of consciousness are located in time and also, rather surprisingly, the belief that they are located in space, his view being that the attachment of acts of consciousness to human or animal bodies is thought to consist primarily in their being in the places where these bodies are. However, he also takes it to be a common sense belief that acts of consciousness are attached to bodies in the sense that they are causally dependent on them. Among material objects, this applies

[1] Vide G. E. Moore, Some Main Problems of Philosophy, Ch. I.

only to organisms and not to all of them. The great majority of material objects are not thought to have any acts of consciousness attached to them. Into whatever class they fall, they are regarded as things of which we can at times be conscious, but they are also thought to exist independently of our consciousness of them.

Material objects and acts of consciousness, together with space and time, which are said by Moore to be entities of some sort but not substantial things in the way that material objects and acts of consciousness are, constitute the only kinds of things, the existence of which, in Moore's opinion, is regarded as a certainty by common sense. He takes it to be a common sense belief that things of other sorts may exist, but not that they certainly do. At one time it was part of the common sense view of the world that God created it, but Moore thought that by the first quarter of this century enough ordinary people had become uncertain about the existence of God for it no longer to qualify as a common sense belief. I suspect that this conclusion was not so much the outcome of sociological research as of the fact that he wished to represent the common sense view of the world as being certainly true, and that he himself considered that there is no good reason to suppose that there is a God.[1] The same applies to the belief that human beings will continue to be conscious after the death of their bodies, which he might also have attributed to common sense if he had not himself thought that there is no good reason to hold it.

Another important feature of the common sense view of the world, in Moore's version of it, is the belief that we not only genuinely know that material objects and acts of consciousness exist, but also know a great many facts about particular examples of them. Among the facts of this sort which he claimed to know for certain were the facts that he had a body which had existed for some time, that during this time it had continually been in contact with or not far from the surface of the earth, that the earth itself had existed for many years past, that there were many other material objects including other human beings, from which his body had been at various distances at different times, and that many other material objects had come into existence and in many cases ceased to exist before he was born. He claimed also to know that he had had many experiences of various different kinds,

[1] *Vide* G. E. Moore, 'A Defence of Common Sense' in *Philosophical Papers*, p 52.

including the experiences of perceiving his own body and objects in its environment, that he had observed many facts about these objects, that he had remembered many facts of this kind which he was not currently observing, that he had held many beliefs, that he had often had dreams and often imagined things which he had not taken to be real, and that many other human beings had had similar experiences. Neither did he suppose himself to be unique in any of these respects. He thought it certain that many other human beings knew with respect to themselves and their environments facts corresponding to all those that he had listed.[1]

Since Moore offers no argument in favour of the proposition that there are acts of consciousness, he presumably took it to be self-evident. If he had thought it necessary he might have advanced the argument which leads to Descartes's first principle 'Cogito ergo sum' – 'I think, therefore I exist'.[2] If one doubts whether there are acts of consciousness, it follows that there are, since doubting is itself such an act. It is, however, to be noted that this argument itself rests on an assumption of an act of consciousness, namely the occurrence of the doubt.

The arguments which Moore advances in support of the common sense view concerning material objects are directed against the philosophers who reject it, whether because they believe that material objects are not real or, what is more frequently the case, because they believe that while there well may be material objects, the fact of their existence is not something that we can know for certain. His method of discrediting philosophers who deny the existence of material objects is to point out the absurdity of what this denial entails, including, as we have seen, the proposition that they themselves do not exist. Surprisingly, he thinks that he has an even stronger argument against philosophers who take what appears to be the more moderate view that we cannot know that material objects exist, since he maintains that this position is self-contradictory. The ground for this is that in saying that *we* cannot know that material objects exist, these philosophers imply that they know that there are other persons besides themselves, and persons have bodies, which are material objects. But if it is assumed from the start that persons have bodies, then the philosopher's knowledge of his own existence will be sufficient to prove that there is at least

[1] *Ibid.* pp. 32–5.
[2] See his *Discourse on Method*, part IV.

one material object. And if, like Descartes, one believes that it is logically possible for minds to exist independently of bodies, then the assumption that there are other persons need not carry the admission of the existence of material objects; for one might believe that those persons existed only as minds. Moreover, the philosopher who says that *we* cannot know that such and such, is, indeed, indicating that he believes there to be other persons, but can still consistently deny that this belief amounts to knowledge. He can make his point by saying that he cannot know whatever is in question, and that if there are persons besides himself, they cannot know it either. Consequently, this argument of Moore's is not decisive.

On the positive side, he has no argument to offer beyond the simple assertion that he really does know what he claims to know. Thus, in a lecture entitled 'Proof of an External World',[1] having quoted Kant's saying that it remained a scandal to philosophy that the existence of things outside us must be accepted merely on faith, without any satisfactory proof, he proposed to put an end to this scandal by the simple process of holding up his two hands and saying with the appropriate gestures 'Here is one hand' and 'Here is another'. His proof consisted in the fact that he knew these statements to be true, and that it followed logically from them that there were at least two things existing outside of us, in the sense that they were spatially located and also capable of existing unperceived. Moore then went on to prove that material objects had existed in the past, simply by reminding his audience that he had held up his hands a short time before. In neither case did he claim to be able to prove the premisses of his proof, but he insisted that his inability to prove them did not prevent him from knowing that they were true.

When Moore said that he had no proof of his premisses, he meant that he could not demonstrate them: he could not list a set of propositions from which it followed that they were true. This is not to say, however, that he had no evidence for them. He did have evidence, the evidence supplied in the one case by sense-perception and in the other by memory: and in saying that he knew that the propositions in question were true he was implying that in the circumstances this evidence was sufficient. But if these were the assumptions that he was making, they sustain an argument which

[1] *Vide* G. E. Moore, *Philosophical Papers*, Ch. VII.

has far-reaching consequences. As applied to the defence of common sense, the argument is that sentences like 'This is a hand' are used in such a way that our having such sensory experiences as Moore and his audience were having when he lectured does establish the truth of the propositions which they express. It is, indeed, possible that one is mistaken, as Moore himself was on one occasion when he pointed to a dummy skylight and claimed to know that it was a window to the sky, but such mistakes can be discovered and corrected. There are recognized ways of testing whether one is undergoing a perceptual illusion, and if these tests give no indication that this is happening, if one's perceptual judgement is corroborated by the further course of one's experiences, and by the testimony of other people, no serious doubt remains. Similarly, the use of sentences like 'I held up my hands a short while ago' is such that if one has what has all the appearance of being a clear recollection of the event in question, and others testify that they remember it too, and there is nothing in the circumstances to make us suspect that our memories are playing us false, then we are entitled to be confident that the event did occur. In short, there are recognized criteria for deciding such questions, and if these criteria are satisfied, the point is settled. To doubt or deny that there is a table in front of me when I can see it and touch it, in what are apparently normal conditions, is to be ignorant or feign to be ignorant of what 'perceiving a table' means.

I shall consider in a moment whether this argument is valid. The point that I now wish to make is that if it is valid there is no reason why it should apply only to the propositions which are acceptable to common sense. It is equally true of the propositions which figure in the formal or empirical sciences that there are recognized criteria for deciding whether they are true or false. To understand mathematics is, among other things, to know what constitutes a mathematical proof. To understand a chemical or biological theory requires knowing what experimental evidence would confirm or discredit it. In these cases also, if the appropriate criteria are found to be satisfied, there is no occasion for doubt: at the most, when we are concerned with empirical theories, we may be uncertain whether they will continue to hold good in the light of future experience, but this is a question to be decided by further experiment, so far as it can be decided at all. There is anyhow no opening for philosophy to gain a foothold. But if philosophy is not in a position to pass judgment on the truth or falsehood of the propositions which belong to any of these domains and if there is no other world for it to explore than that which is already covered by the cognitive arts and sciences, it is forced to turn to analysis, on the ground, as I said earlier, that this is the only avenue of knowledge that is not already bespoken.

Let us now take a closer look at this argument. The first point to note is that it over-simplifies the position both of the empirical and the formal sciences. There is, in fact, no universal agreement among mathematicians as to what constitutes a valid proof. There is, of course, a very large measure of agreement, but it does not go all the way. For example, some mathematicians will accept a *reductio ad absurdum* argument as proof of the existence of a number which satisfies such and such a function, others will attribute existence only to those numbers which they can positively construct. Neither is there universal agreement among physicists or biologists as to the status of their theories. Most physicists believe that in the field of quantum mechanics one has to be content with statistical laws, but there have been those, including Einstein, who hoped that a way might still be found of devising a deterministic theory which would do equal justice to the evidence. Most biologists now reject the Lamarckian theory that acquired characteristics can be inherited, but some of them doubt whether all the experimental evidence can be satisfactorily explained by the official neo-Mendelian theory of chance mutations. Now, in all these cases, the matter in dispute can be accounted philosophical. In the mathematical controversy, the issue partly turns on a question of logic; whether it is permissible to reject the law of excluded middle, according to which a proposition must be either true or false. In my other examples, it is very largely a question of the standards which a scientific theory should be expected to meet. Thus, Einstein's main reason for seeking an alternative to the prevailing quantum theory was that it did not consort with his picture of the world; he was not satisfied with an explanation in which things were ultimately left to chance. Admittedly, if this is a philosophical issue, it is one that a philosopher could not hope to resolve without a considerable knowledge of physics, but this does not remove it from his province. The divorce of philosophy from the natural sciences which took place, as we have seen, in the nineteenth century, was a product partly of the romantic movement which looked to philosophy for deliverance from scientific materialism, and partly of the great increase in scientific knowledge which led to very much greater specialization in the sciences. By now, there is, indeed, so much to be learned that a philosopher could not hope to have more than a superficial acquaintance with many branches of science: but that is no reason why he should turn his back on all of them.

A more radical defect in the argument which we have derived from Moore is that the distinction between knowing the truth of a proposition and knowing its analysis is not so sharp as the argument requires. In his defence of common sense, Moore makes the assumption that one could conclusively establish the truth of a proposition like 'Here is a hand' without at all knowing how it should be analyzed. But if one does not know how the proposition is to be analyzed, how does one know what proposition it is that one has discovered to be true? The usual answer to this objection is that we must distinguish between knowing the analysis of a proposition and knowing its meaning. A sentence like 'Here is a hand' has, in the context in which Moore used it, an ordinary sense which any competent English speaker would immediately understand. It is sufficient to take it in this sense in order to determine whether the proposition which it expresses is true. The question how to analyze this proposition comes later. But if analysis consists, as we shall see it does in this sort of instance, in the redescription of the circumstances which justify us in accepting the proposition which is being analyzed, then we cannot exclude the possibility of its showing that the way in which we have to construe our sentences, if we are to be justified in accepting the propositions which they express, is not the way in which they are ordinarily understood. Thus it is, as we shall see later on,[1] a philosophical question whether anything is capable of existing unperceived. The arguments which purport to show that nothing can so exist may not be valid, but they need to be considered: and until this point is settled we cannot be sure that the sense in which a sentence like 'Here is a hand' expresses a true proposition is the sense in which it is ordinarily understood; for certainly, as it is ordinarily understood, it does refer to something that can exist unperceived.

The great majority of philosophers nowadays do, indeed, believe in the capacity of material objects to exist unperceived, but not all of them conceive of these material objects in a way that accords

[1] See below pp. 99–106 and 221–2.

with common sense. Thus it has been argued, on scientific grounds, that things as they are in themselves do not have the properties that they appear to us to have when we perceive them. On this view, the true proposition which a sentence like 'Here is a hand' may be taken to express is that one's sensations of colour, shape and so forth are caused by a set of particles which are themselves colourless. In so far as common sense attributes colour to the material object with which it identifies the hand that we perceive, it is simply in error. Again, this view may be mistaken, but again the argument has to be met. We shall see later on[1] that it poses quite a difficult problem. Until such points are settled, the most that can be conceded to Moore is that when he said that his hands existed, he was saying something that he had the right to consider true, and this amounts to very little until we can determine what this something was. Indeed, if the sceptics are right, and their arguments too have a claim to be considered, it may have been no more than that Moore was having certain sensations, perhaps even no more than that certain sensations were occurring.

The procedure which Moore followed was that of trying to show that a concept undoubtedly had application by pointing to instances in which it was exemplified. For this reason, the argument which we have been examining has come to be known as the argument from paradigm cases. If such and such a state of affairs serves as a paradigm for the use of some expression, then the fact that the expression is used successfully is sufficient to prove that this state of affairs exists. In this way the sceptic is automatically ruled out of order. The argument fails not only, as we have just seen, because the fact that an expression is used successfully leaves room for considerable disagreement as to what it can legitimately be taken to refer to, but also because expressions in common use can be associated with theories which turn out to be unacceptable. Thus, there was a time when expressions referring to witchcraft were used successfully, in that there were recognized criteria for deciding whether some person was a witch, and these criteria were all too frequently found to be satisfied. Yet we do not regard this as a proof that witches existed. It is not easy to produce current examples, because concepts tend to be jettisoned when they become discredited, but I suspect that the concept of free-will, about which I shall have something

---

[1] See below pp. 82–8 and 110–11.

to say later,[1] may be one. Undoubtedly, the concept has application to the extent that we are often able to distinguish between cases where a person does something, as we say, of his own free-will and cases where he does something involuntarily or under constraint. We shall, however, see that it is at least very doubtful whether this distinction is sufficient to justify our holding him responsible in the one case and not in the other. If, as seems likely, our ordinary notion of responsibility involves the conception of the will as something self-propelling, it may very well not withstand critical scrutiny.

Common usage is not fixed. It changes under the influence of science, though the change is not always immediately apparent. We still speak of the motion of the sun, of its rising in the east and setting in the west, but the meaning of these words, at least to educated people, is not what it was before the acceptance of Copernican theory. Sometimes the change is philosophical. The theory of witchcraft was not empirically refuted; there were no crucial experiments by which the existence of witches was disproved. It was just that, with the development of the natural sciences, this anthropomorphic way of explaining untoward events ceased to be credible. It did not consort with the overall picture of the world which science favours.

This example shows that our ways of interpreting experience can change profoundly. We cannot safely assume that our existing apparatus of concepts will not eventually be thought in need of radical reform. There is, however, a restriction, if not to the lengths to which such reforms can go, at least with respect to the point from which they can start. If someone wishes to convince us that he has a better way of describing the world, he has to make it intelligible to us, and this means that he has to relate it to concepts that we already have. Not only that, but the need for a different system will not be recognized unless we can be persuaded that our actual system does not work so well, and for this it requires to be critically examined, with the resources of science but also of philosophy. This is not to say that philosophy is restricted to the practice of conceptual analysis, but it is only there that it can profitably begin.

[1] See below pp. 227–33.

III Philosophical Analysis

A Formal Analyses

Having argued that the practice of analysis should be at least the starting point for philosophy, I need to say a good deal more about what this practice is. In fact, it covers quite a number of activities, which differ from one another either in their methods or their aims or both. I distinguish several of them, without claiming that this is the only way in which they could reasonably be classified. In many respects, they shade into one another and it is a fairly arbitrary matter where one draws the lines between them.

The first type is that which led F.P.Ramsey, writing in 1929, to say that 'In philosophy we take the propositions we make in science and everyday life, and try to exhibit them in a logical system with primitive terms and definitions etc. Essentially, philosophy is a system of definitions, or only too often a description of how definitions might be given.'[1] The fact is, however, that very little has yet been done in the way of exhibiting even particular branches of science as logical systems. One reason for this is that the necessary combination of scientific knowledge and logical skill is rare, another that not many scientific theories have reached the stage where they can be usefully axiomatized. Neither is it always clear that the resulting gain in clarity will repay the labour.

What has more often been attempted is the formal definition of particular concepts which play an important role in science or in everyday discourse. Sometimes a term which is not used univocally in ordinary speech is resolved into terms with different senses, and an attempt is made by formal methods to define each of them precisely. This has happened in the case of the concept of probability. It may be that the ordinary use of such a term is too loose for these definitions to capture it exactly in all its variations, but the aim is not so much to give an accurate account of ordinary usage as

[1] F. P. Ramsey. *The Foundations of Mathematics*, p. 263.

to clarify and, if necessary, sharpen concepts in a way that will increase their utility to science. A good example of this is Einstein's definition of simultaneity, of which one could say that it brought to light implications in our use of the term which had previously escaped our notice; but it would probably be more correct to say that Einstein in his Theory of Relativity showed the ordinary concept of simultaneity to be defective and refined it. The same could be held to be true of Hume's definition of causality, though we shall see later[1] that the interest lies, not in Hume's actual definition, which is hardly acceptable in the form in which he presents it, but in the arguments which lead him to it. Another example of this first type of analysis, with which I shall be dealing later on, is that of the definition of truth.[2]

The philosophy of science, to which the refinement of concepts like that of probability is intended to contribute, develops an interest in the structure not only of scientific theories but also of scientific arguments. Moreover, the study of scientific arguments may be not only descriptive but also critical. Questions are raised about the reasons for preferring one theory to another, when they seem to be equally in accord with the factual evidence, and about the considerations that should guide us in deciding whether to abandon, or how to modify, a theory which some experiment has not borne out. There is also the problem of laying down the conditions under which an observation-statement confirms a hypothesis, and perhaps also making provision for different degrees of confirmation. This is connected with the more general problem of induction, in which the validity of any form of non-deductive inference is put in question. The attack on these problems may, indeed, include, or result in, the provision of formal definitions; for instance, attempts have been made to develop a formal theory of confirmation. If I put these studies into a separate category, it is because they are not limited to the clarification of scientific procedures, but are concerned also with the question how they can be justified.

B Logical Grammar

Next, there are the investigations which may be grouped under the heading of logical grammar, their purpose being to explain

[1] See below pp. 179–83.
[2] See below pp. 209–10.

distinctions which lay claim to belong to the architecture of our language. Here again, philosophers are concerned for the most part not just to clarify these distinctions but also to account for them; to consider how far they are forced upon us either by the nature of our experience or by the requirements of successful communication. For example, a distinction is ordinarily made between singular terms, like proper names, which are used to refer to particular objects, and general terms, which are mainly used to ascribe properties to the objects which the singular terms have served to pick out. There are, however, those who argue that since objects can always be identified by their properties, we do not need singular as well as general terms, any more than we need demonstrative as well as descriptive signs.[1] Since demonstrative signs include tenses, those who think that we can do without them are committed to the view, which we have seen to be debatable,[2] that the work which is done by tenses can equally well be done by specifying temporal relations. They are committed also to holding that we can say all that we want to say without having to use any words of which the meaning is dependent on the context of their utterance.

If words are signs, they are first of all sounds or inscriptions, and we need a theory which will explain how signs are constituted out of this material. Philosophers talk of indicative sentences as expressing propositions, but what are propositions? Do we have to conceive of them as abstract entities, existing independently of the sentences which express them?[3] Reserving this question, we may note that propositions are distinguished from one another in various ways; they may, for example, be simple or compound. Among compound propositions, some are truth-functional, in the sense that their truth-value, that is to say, their truth or falsehood, is wholly determined by the truth-value of their components; clearly the truth-value of the conjunction 'p and q' or the disjunction 'p or q' depends only on the truth-values of 'p' and 'q'. On the other hand, many hypothetical propositions appear not to be truth-functional. For instance, the validity of the proposition 'If I had struck this match, it would have lit' seems not to be affected by the falsity of its antecedent clause. But then the question how such propositions are validated presents a difficult problem.[4]

Again, an expression containing a nominative sign is said to be extensional when the replacement of this sign by another which refers to the same object yields a proposition which has the same truth-value as the one originally expressed. For example, 'Napoleon died at St Helena' and 'The victor of Austerlitz died at St Helena' both express true propositions. The same condition may be satisfied by predicative signs which apply to the same objects and by sentences which correspond in the truth or falsehood of what they express. Thus, in the sentence 'This is an equilateral triangle', the word 'equilateral' can be replaced by 'equiangular' without any change in truth-value: the formula 'It is true that p' will yield a true proposition when 'p' is replaced by any sentence which expresses a truth, and it will yield a false proposition when 'p' is replaced by any sentence which expresses a falsehood. There are, however, expressions which do not satisfy this condition, and are consequently said to be intensional. An important class of them is constituted by expressions which mention knowing or believing or other propositional attitudes. Thus, in the sentences 'I know that Napoleon died at St Helena' or 'I know that this is an equilateral triangle', the substitutions that were made in the previous examples could effect a change in truth-value, since it may be that while I know that Napoleon died at St Helena and that the triangle I am referring to is equilateral, I do not know that Napoleon was the victor of Austerlitz or that equilateral triangles are also equiangular. Similarly, in the propositional form 'I believe that p' the substitution for 'p' of a sentence expressing a true, or a false, proposition does not always yield a proposition which is correspondingly true or false, since I do not believe all true propositions and it is likely that not all the propositions which I believe are true. Intensional expressions are viewed unkindly by some logicians, because they complicate the processes of inference, and attempts have been made to show that we can do without them. This would be achieved if we were able to paraphrase the sentences in which they occur in such a way that substantially the same information was conveyed by sentences which do satisfy the condition of extensionality. It is, however, still an open question whether this can be achieved.

Another important class of intensional expressions consists of those that introduce modality, in the sense that they serve to characterize propositions not just as true or false, but as possible, necessary, or impossible. The reason why they are intensional is that some but not all true propositions are held to be necessary, and some but not all false propositions to be impossible: thus, in the sentence 'It is necessarily true that brothers are male', the replacement of the sentence 'brothers are male' by another which expresses a true but not a necessary proposition will not preserve truth-value. This can apply also to the replacement of signs of other types. A well-known example of Professor Quine's is the sentence 'Necessarily 9 is greater than 4', where the substitution of 'the number of the planets' for '9', though extensionally correct, turns what is thought to be a true proposition into a false one.[1] I say 'what is thought to be a true proposition', because logicians like Quine, who wish to get rid of intensional expressions, have cast doubt on the notion of necessity, maintaining that it has not been made sufficiently clear to be utilizable. This doubt extends to the distinction between analytic and synthetic propositions, with which the distinction between the necessary and the contingent is sometimes held to coincide. Again the argument is that the notion of meaning is not sufficiently clear for us to be justified in accepting the characterization of analytic propositions as those which are true solely in virtue of the meaning of the signs which express them.[2] However this may be, we are still left with the problem of accounting at least for the appearances of necessity.

There are philosophers who accept both the distinction between necessary and contingent and that between analytic and synthetic propositions, but do not treat them as coincident. Some, following Kant, believe that the propositions of pure mathematics, though necessary, cannot be shown to be analytic in any accepted sense of this term,[3] and some believe also that scientific laws exhibit what they call natural necessity. It is in this way that they distinguish generalizations of law from generalizations of fact. This would remove an awkward problem, if the concept of natural necessity were acceptable but I shall argue later that it is not, and that we must therefore find some other way of characterizing generalizations of law.[4] Since one of the distinctive marks of such generalizations is that they entail unfulfilled conditionals, this problem dovetails with the problem, which we have already noticed, of accounting for the validity of propositions which are not truth-functional.

[1] See W. V. Quine. *Word and Object*, pp. 195–200.
[2] For a further account of this distinction see below pp. 198–203.
[3] See below p. 199.
[4] See below pp. 147–50.

I shall be attempting to deal with most of these questions later on. All that I wish to say at this stage, before passing to my fourth class of analytical enquiries, is that in assigning to this group of questions the heading of logical grammar, I do not mean to say that they are merely verbal in a sense that might be taken to imply that they were trivial. Apart from their intrinsic interest, their examination throws light not only on the workings of our language but also on the character of the world which it serves to describe. There is in any case no sharp distinction between investigating the structure of our language and investigating the structure of the world, since the very notion of there being a world of such and such a character only makes sense within the framework of some system of concepts which language embodies. This is not to say that the world does not exist independently of our talking about it, or that any one system of concepts is as good as any other. We can and do bring different systems to the judgement of experience, and our observations lead us to believe that the world has existed, and probably will continue to exist, without containing any human beings to be conscious of it. Even so, our experience is articulated in language, and the world which we envisage as existing at times when we do not is still a world which is structured by our method of describing it. As I said before, we cannot detach ourselves from every point of view. If we abandon one we have to occupy another. The idea that we could prise the world off our concepts is incoherent; for with what conception of the world should we then be left?

C Analyses of Ordinary Usage

So far, we have been concerned only with the use of language to attempt to state facts or formulate theories to explain them. This is, indeed, the use that is chiefly of interest to philosophers, at any rate outside the sphere of moral philosophy, but it is not the only one that has been thought to deserve analysis. Though attempts have been made to develop a logic of imperatives, this analysis has mostly been informal. Examples are given of different types of speech-act, and attention is drawn to the different functions that they fulfil. The term 'speech-act' was coined by J. L. Austin in the nineteen-fifties and the concern with what it stands for is characteristic of the so-called school of ordinary language philosophy which Austin led. The natural language which these philosophers studied was English, and what they termed ordinary usage was the usage of educated English-speakers like themselves. This gave some of their work a rather limited interest, but some of it had a more general application. Thus, one of Austin's achievements was to discriminate a class of what he called performative statements. These are statements which do not so much report activities as help to bring them about. For instance, the judge who says to a convicted criminal 'You will go to prison for six months' is not thereby making a prediction; he is carrying out a ritual performance of which the man's going to prison is the probable effect. To say 'I promise' under the appropriate conditions is not just to report that one is making a promise but actually to make it. Some would say in this case that the sentence does not report anything at all, on the ground that my utterance would normally be characterized as sincere or insincere rather than as true or false, but I do not see why the sentence should not be held to fulfil a double function; both that of making a promise and that of asserting that it is being made. That a sentence need not be exclusively performative is shown by the example of 'I know that such and such', where the use of the word 'know' vouches for the truth of what follows in a way that merely saying 'I believe' would not. But in making this commitment I am also reporting what I take to be a fact about myself. The proposition 'I know that p' is not simply parasitical upon 'p', since they may have different truth-values. This occurs in the case where 'p' is true but I am not entitled to say that I know it.

The fashion for ordinary language philosophy, during the comparatively short period that it existed in any strength, generated more heat on either side than now seems to have been warranted. In its defence, it can be argued that there is no way of investigating concepts except as they are embodied in some language: if one is going to investigate a language, it is desirable to understand it thoroughly; and the language which one understands best is likely to be one's own. On the other hand, not all linguistic distinctions are of philosophical interest, and if the practitioners of this type of analysis had a weakness it was that they paid too much attention to niceties of English usage which had no discernible bearing on anything that any philosopher had ever regarded as a problem. Being influenced also by Moore, though less liberal in their conception of analysis, they tended to take the assumptions of common sense too much on trust, with the result that they largely missed the point of problems like the problem of perception where these assumptions are put in question. Even if one is not concerned to justify the common sense view of the world but only to analyse perceptual situations, in a way that takes account of the scientific evidence, an examination of the ordinary use of words like 'see' and 'hear' will not turn out to have very much to contribute.[1]

A good example both of the virtues and the limitations of the method is to be found in a paper of Austin's called 'A Plea for Excuses'.[2] The paper is concerned with some of the different grounds on which one may claim not to be responsible, or not to be fully responsible, for actions for which one might otherwise be held to blame. The subtle differences that there may be between doing things unintentionally, or inadvertently, or involuntarily, or by mistake, are adroitly exposed, and illustrated by felicitous examples. We are led to see that the standard dichotomy of voluntary and involuntary actions does not do justice to the intricacy of good English usage, nor, therefore, to the complexity of the facts. Since the use of an expression is characterized not only by the instances to which it is applied successfully, but also by those in which its application fails, and since the attribution of responsibility appears to presuppose that we are capable of acting freely, some light is thereby thrown upon the problem of free-will. Nevertheless, one feels that the core of this problem has not been touched. Philosophers have been perplexed by the question of free-will because it has seemed to them, rightly or wrongly, that there is a logical conflict between the common assumption that men do sometimes act freely and the plausible hypothesis that all their actions are causally determined: and the conflict is one that Austin's fine distinctions do nothing to resolve. Where they could be of service would be in helping to remould our concept of responsibility, if we came to the decision that it needed to be reconciled with the hypothesis of determinism.[3]

D Looking at the Facts

There is some affinity between the outlook of the Austinian school and that which is exhibited in the later works of Wittgenstein. It was Wittgenstein, as we have noted, who gave currency to the view that 'for a large class of cases ... the meaning of a word is its use in

---

[1] See below pp. 68–73.
[2] J. L. Austin. *Philosophical Papers*.
[3] See below pp. 232–3.

the language',[1] and in his *Philosophical Investigations* and else-
where, he devotes some space to the description of what he calls
language-games, these being examples which are designed to
illustrate the variety of purposes which language serves. We find
also in the later Wittgenstein an implicit respect for common sense,
as evinced by his saying that 'Every sentence in our language is
"in order as it is"',[2] and theoretically at least, though not so much
in practice, he goes even further than the analysts of ordinary
usage in limiting the scope of philosophical analysis. 'Philosophy,'·
he says, 'may in no way interfere with the actual use of language: it
can in the end only describe it. For it cannot give any foundation
either. It leaves everything as it is.'[3] This goes with the thesis that
it is not the business of philosophy to theorize even about language,
though the burden of this thesis is rather that one should not allow
one's vision of the facts to be distorted by preconceived theories
than that no theory can subsequently be applied to them. Wittgenstein's own examples would not make the impact that they do if
they were not designed to have a more general application.

Where Wittgenstein chiefly differs from the analysts of ordinary
usage is that he has little or no interest in usage as such. His descriptions of it are framed with a view to resolving philosophical
problems, which he sees above all as sources of perplexity. As he
puts it, 'A philosophical problem has the form: "I don't know my
way about."'[4] The philosopher does not know his way about
because he is lost in a maze of his own making. It is the purpose of
philosophical analysis to get him to see how he has gone astray:
when the confusion has been dispelled he will be able to realize
that his problem was illusory. This is achieved in some cases by
pointing out his mistakes but often by presenting him with examples
which will suggest to him how things really are: like a mental
patient, the metaphysician is made to participate in his own cure.
This view is characteristically summarized in a well-known passage
of the *Investigations*, where having again said that 'we may not
advance any kind of theory', Wittgenstein continues: 'There must
not be anything hypothetical in our considerations. We must do
away with all *explanation* and description alone must take its place.

[1] L. Wittgenstein. *Philosophical Investigations*, para 43, p. 20.
[2] *Ibid*. para. 98, p. 45.
[3] *Ibid*. para. 124, p. 49.
[4] *Ibid*. para. 123, p. 49.

And this description gets its light, that is to say, its purpose from the philosophical problems. These are, of course, not empirical problems; they are solved, rather, by looking into the workings of our language, and that in such a way as to make us recognize those workings *in despite of* an urge to misunderstand them. The problems are solved, not by giving new information, but by arranging what we have always known. Philosophy is a battle against the bewitchment of our intelligence by means of language.'[1]

Our intelligence becomes bewitched, not when we actually use our language to talk about the world, in the straightforward way we mostly do, but when we start reflecting on the way we use it. We make mistakes such as that of supposing that all words function like names, or that the things to which the same word applies must all possess one common quality, whereas there may be no more than what Wittgenstein calls a 'family resemblance' between them, as, for example, in the case of games; or that words like 'understanding' 'believing' 'anticipating' and the like must refer to inner processes. Wittgenstein does not deny the existence of inner processes, nor does he seem to wish to identify them with physical events, but one of his principal theses is that an inner process stands in need of outward criteria. Thus, in order to discover that someone understands what I am saying, I do not have to perform the impossible feat of inspecting his state of mind; it is sufficient that he responds to my words in some appropriate way. Even in my own case, when I consider what actually happens when I understand something that I hear or read, I do not commonly detect the presence of any distinctive mental episode. I may on occasions have a feeling which helps to constitute what is called a flash of understanding, but its occurrence is neither necessary nor sufficient to make it true that I understand whatever is in question. Not sufficient, because its presence does not guarantee my not misunderstanding, and not necessary, because in the normal way I understand things perfectly well without having any such feeling. We tend to assume that some mental occurrence of this sort must be present, in order to constitute the difference between, say, seeing words, in an unfamiliar language, simply as marks on paper and seeing words to which we attach meaning. What we do not realize, until we look candidly at the facts, is that the difference may

[1] *Ibid.* para. 109, p. 47.

consist in nothing more than a disposition to respond to the words in different ways.

Even in the cases where we do seem to be referring to inner processes, as when we speak about our own sensations, it would be a mistake, in Wittgenstein's opinion, to conceive of such processes as being logically independent of their characteristic outward expressions. His reason for this is that we learn to use the words which we interpret as standing for private experiences in situations where the experiences are publicly manifested, and that the meaning of these words is determined by the way in which we learn to use them. Accordingly, the philosophical problem of finding a means to bridge what seems to be the logical gap between a man's observable behaviour and the experiences of which only he is conscious is supposed to be resolved by our coming to see that the gap does not exist. But now it seems to me that the method has changed. We are no longer being invited just to look at the facts, but rather to adopt a theory of meaning, which is at least not evidently true. From the fact that I was taught to use the word 'pain' in situations in which I or some other person was showing signs of pain, it does not obviously follow that, having once learned to identify the sensation, I cannot subsequently distinguish it from its manifestations and refer to it independently: and in fact it seems to me that this is what I actually do. I shall resume this argument later on when we come to examine the question whether, and if so, how we are justified in attributing experiences to others.[1] The point which I now wish to make is that this is the sort of problem which, for me at any rate, the reading of Wittgenstein does not resolve.

The method of considering what typically has to happen for such and such a concept to be satisfied is characteristic of much that passes under the heading of informal analysis. The analysis is informal both in the sense that it dispenses with logical symbolism and that it commonly does not result in definitions. It is rather a matter of redescribing the facts so that they give a clearer insight into the working of the concepts which they exemplify. Thus, a philosopher who is concerned with the relation between knowledge and belief may be tempted to assume that knowing is a special state of mind, which is intrinsically different from a state of mere belief, or that knowing is distinguished from believing by being directed upon a different sort of object. Both these views appear to have been

[1] See below pp. 132-5.

held by Plato. But now if we look at what actually happens when someone is correctly said to know, or only to believe, that something is the case, we see that there need not be any difference in his state of mind. He may be as fully convinced of what he only believes as of what he knows; what prevents his belief from being knowledge may be just the unlucky circumstance that what he believes is false. Only what is true can be known, in the propositional sense of knowledge which is here in question, but this is a fact of grammar, not of psychology. It is not that knowing is an infallible state of mind, but just that we use the word 'know' in such a way that to say that something is known to be the case implies saying that it is true. This does not, however, entail that knowledge and belief are bound to differ in their objects, since it quite often happens that one and the same proposition is known to be true by some persons and only believed by others, who are in a less good position to estimate its truth. The reason for this is that one of the ways in which knowledge is differentiated from belief is that one cannot properly be said to know that a proposition is true unless one has good authority for accepting it, whereas the mere fact of acceptance may be enough to constitute belief. Admittedly, a rational man will not commit himself even to believing any proposition, unless he thinks that he has some adequate ground for taking it to be true, but the grounds which are thought to justify belief are in general not so strong as those which are required to authorize a claim to knowledge. Exactly how and where the line is to be drawn is a question which has proved remarkably difficult to answer, one reason for this being that in common speech the distinction is not sharp. We are usually able to decide the point in particular cases, though even here there may be differences of opinion, but it is open to doubt whether the particular decisions can be fitted tidily under any general rule. This might be thought a ground for emending our usage, were it not that the question of differentiating between knowledge and belief is of minor philosophical interest, in comparison with the more general question how our acceptance of different sorts of propositions is to be justified. What is important is to elicit the criteria of rational belief, rather than to determine the point at which it deserves a different name.

Very often the purpose of this sort of informal analysis is to show that some factor the presence of which has been thought to be essential for the application of a given concept is either dispensable or non-existent. This has already been seen in the case of Wittgenstein and it also comes out strongly in the work of his near contemporary, Gilbert Ryle. Thus, in his book *The Concept of Mind*, the main object of which is to discredit the dualistic conception of mind and body, vividly characterized by Ryle as the myth of the ghost in the machine, he attempts, among other things, to show that volitions are mythical, and one way in which he does this is by drawing attention to the fact that the mental processes which words like 'willing' might be thought to name simply do not occur. This is not to deny that men deliberate about their actions, or that having come to a decision they act upon it. The point is that they do just act upon it. What is denied is that the decisions are translated into action by the interposition of any such things as mental pistons. In the same way, Wittgenstein attacks the far too prevalent theory that objects are recognized by being compared with mental images. He does not deny that mental images occur, or even that they sometimes play a part in the process of recognition. If I go to a shop to match a fabric, and have failed to bring a specimen with me, I may try to conjure up a mental image of the pattern as an aid to selecting its equivalent. But the fact is that the cases in which mental images intervene are just those in which the work of identification, or recognition, does not proceed smoothly. When it does proceed smoothly, the identification is immediate and as it were automatic. The proof that mental images are dispensable is again that in most cases they simply do not occur.

In both these examples the appeal to the facts is reinforced by an argument of a type which is frequently to be found in philosophy: the argument being that if we were to assume that the entities, or alleged entities, in question played the part assigned to them, we should thereby be led into a vicious infinite regress. In the case of mental images, the crucial point is that if the image is to serve to identify an object, it must itself be identified. For instance, if I employed an image to identify the pen with which I am writing, I should have to know that the image was an image of a pen, otherwise it would not meet the purpose. But if nothing could be identified except by comparison with an image, then I should have to compare the image with another one in order to discover that it was an image of a pen, and so *ad infinitum*. To avoid the regress, we have to admit that some things can be identified directly, and then we have no reason to confine ourselves to images. If an image can be identified directly, so can the object which the image represents. Similarly, Ryle argues that if the actions for which we are held responsible were those that issued from volitions, then since we are held responsible for our alleged volitions, these would themselves have to issue from prior volitions, and so again *ad infinitum*.[1] In this case, however, the argument seems less convincing, since those who believe in volitions might reply that the fault here lies not in their concept of volition but rather in the concept of responsibility. Ryle uses a similar argument to more effect when he seeks to prove not indeed that inner processes of thought do not occur, but at least that they do not have to occur as accompaniments of intelligent speech or action. Here again he draws attention to the fact that while we do sometimes rehearse our words before speaking, or silently plan an action before performing it, in the large majority of cases no such inner processes are detectable. The exercise of intelligence consists in our manner of speaking or acting, and not in the presence of accompanying thoughts. In support of these facts, the argument is then adduced that the invocation of such thoughts would anyhow not account for intelligent speech or action. For the processes of thought must themselves be supposed to exhibit intelligence, and if they can do so only as the result of prior or simultaneous reflection, we again embark on an infinite regress.[2]

Ryle speaks of himself as being engaged in logical geography, the true location of concepts which we have a strong tendency to misplace. The misplacing does not consist in our using the concepts wrongly, but in our holding mistaken theories which lead us to give a wrong account of their use. Neither on Ryle's part, nor on Wittgenstein's, whose methods we have seen to be very similar, is there any suggestion that the concepts themselves may be defective, or that the beliefs into which they enter stand in need of justification. They both accept the validity of what Moore called the common sense view of the world; and seem to assume that there is no point in asking how it can be justified. Yet we have seen that the common sense view of the world is not immune from criticism, and even if it were, the question of its justification could still arise. We could have an interest in discovering how it achieved its security. Thus, Moore himself, while claiming to know for certain that the propositions which make up the common sense view are wholly true,

[1] cf. *The Concept of Mind*, p. 67.   [2] *Ibid.* pp. 30-1.

admitted that he did not know how he knew them to be true. This is one reason why so much of his work is devoted to the analysis of these propositions, especially those which express ordinary judgements of perception. The purpose of the analysis was not just to elucidate the meaning of this class of propositions, but to account for the knowledge which we were supposed to have of their truth. Whether or not it is counted as a form of analysis, this type of enquiry has a long philosophical history. It is one of the principal parts of what is traditionally called the theory of knowledge.

E The Theory of Knowledge

The theory of knowledge has three main purposes: to arrive at a satisfactory definition of knowledge; to determine what sorts of propositions can be known to be true; and to explain how these propositions can be known to be true. The first of these aims, as we have already noted, is relatively unimportant. It is of no great consequence exactly where we draw the line between knowledge and true belief. The second and third aims go closely together. For if one is not content to make merely dogmatic claims to knowledge, the range of propositions which one regards as capable of being known to be true will coincide with those which there can be shown to be sufficient justification for accepting; and in showing how we are justified in accepting these propositions, we shall also be answering the question how we can know them to be true.

The practice has most commonly been to start with propositions of such a sort that one can be certain, or virtually certain, of their truth, and then see what further propositions they can be supposed to justify. This procedure has its origin in Descartes's method of doubt. Descartes envisaged a malicious demon who had the power to cause us to mistake false propositions for true ones, and then sought to discover whether there was any proposition which one could not be mistaken in believing. His answer, as we have seen, is that I cannot be mistaken in believing that I exist, since my denial or even doubt of my own existence itself implies it. It might be objected that if the demon were all-powerful, he could cause us to be mistaken even about the validity of such a deductive argument. And if we are entitled to trust our intuition in this case, why not in others where we appear to face the alternative of accepting some proposition or falling into self-contradiction? This objection is, indeed, well-founded, in that Descartes does not allow the demon to be all-powerful. His power is limited by the role for which he is cast, since he is required to deceive a person who is already assumed to exist. He could still delude me into thinking that I do not exist when I do, if such a thought is possible, but not *ex hypothesi* into thinking that I exist when I do not. In short, Descartes assumed his own existence in order to infer it. Admittedly he assumed the existence only of his mind and not his body, and even so he may be held to have gone too far, in respect of what was strictly deducible from his avowed premiss. For he took himself to be a thinking substance, enduring through a period of time, and, as his critics have pointed out, this cannot be deduced from the occurrence of a momentary thought. Even if the substance is not credited with any temporal duration, its existence as an entity distinct from the thought is open to question. All that we are then left with is a momentary datum of consciousness.

Except that they did not confine themselves to the present moment, or even consistently to the experiences of a single subject, this attenuation of Descartes's 'cogito' was the starting-point of the classical British empiricists. Thus Locke, in his book *An Essay Concerning Human Understanding*, having defined an 'idea' as 'whatsoever is the object of the understanding when a man thinks',[1] raises the question how our minds come by the ideas which constitute 'all the *materials* of reason or knowledge', and answers that they all come from Experience. 'In that all our knowledge is founded; and from that it ultimately derives itself.'[2] Experience is said by him to have just two sources; Sensation, which yields us simple ideas of sensible qualities, such as '*yellow, white, heat, cold, soft, hard, bitter, sweet*';[3] and Reflection, 'the perception of the operations of our own mind within us', which yields such simple ideas as those of '*perception, thinking, doubting, believing, reasoning, knowing, willing*, and all the different actings of our minds'.[4] He then tries to show that all our ideas are formed out of these materials by the processes of combining them, comparing them or abstracting from them, and goes on to define knowledge as 'nothing but the

[1] John Locke. *An Essay Concerning Human Understanding*, Book I, Chapter I, Section 8.
[2] *Ibid*. Book II, Chapter I, Section 2.
[3] *Ibid*. Section 3.
[4] *Ibid*. Section 4.

perception of the connexion and agreement, or disagreement and repugnancy, of any of our ideas'.[1]

In his book *A Treatise Concerning the Principles of Human Knowledge*, and in his *Three Dialogues between Hylas and Philonous*, the two most celebrated of his philosophical works, Bishop Berkeley follows Locke in assuming that all our knowledge is founded on sense-perception, and in taking sense-perception to consist in our being presented with sensible qualities. But whereas Locke, inconsistently with his definition of knowledge, had credited us with the ability to know, with virtual if not complete certainty, that these simple ideas of sensation are caused by external objects, Berkeley took the bolder step of identifying what are ordinarily taken to be physical objects with collections of sensible qualities. This move was made partly in the interest of his theology, since, having argued that sensible qualities exist only so long as they are perceived, he avoids the paradoxical consequence that things like stars and trees and houses vanish out of existence when one ceases to perceive them, by assuming that they continue to exist as ideas in the mind of God. Had it not been for his desire to bring God into play, he might have been content with saying, as he also does, that for the table I write on to exist at times when I do not see and feel it, it is sufficient not only that 'some other spirit actually does perceive it' but that 'if I was in my study I might perceive it'.[2] This would have led him to the view, subsequently advanced by John Stuart Mill, that what we take to be physical objects are nothing more than 'permanent possibilities of sensation'.[3]

Both Locke and Berkeley treat one's own existence as a primitive datum. 'It being impossible,' in Locke's view, 'for anyone to perceive without *perceiving* that he does perceive,'[4] he holds that self-consciousness accompanies the reception of any ideas. He differs, however, from Descartes in holding that one's personal identity through time consists not, as Descartes thought, in the persistence of the same substance, which would, indeed, be completely unverifiable, but in the persistence of the same consciousness. Berkeley does treat the self as a spiritual substance, but differs

[1] *Ibid*. Book IV, Chapter I, Section 2.
[2] George Berkeley. *A Treatise Concerning the Principles of Human Knowledge*, Part I, Section 3.
[3] J. S. Mill. *Examination of Sir William Hamilton's Philosophy*, Chapter XI.
[4] John Locke. *An Essay Concerning Human Understanding*, Book II, Chapter XXVII, Section 9.

from Locke in not making it the content of an idea, his reason being that he does not wish to maintain that it exists only when it is perceived. Instead he says that we have a notion of our selves as well as of other spirits including God. It was left to Hume, a more radical and more consistent empiricist than either Locke or Berkeley, to identify the self with the series of its perceptions. He then faced the problem, which Locke had overlooked, of showing how different perceptions combine to form the same consciousness, and had to confess that he could find no solution to it. Reserving the term 'idea' for what are nowadays called concepts, he follows Locke and Berkeley in maintaining that all our ideas are derived from the data of sense which he calls impressions, and in opposition to Berkeley, he does not credit himself with any notions which are not ideas. The fact that we have no idea of our selves, or our minds, as distinct from ideas of our particular perceptions, is accordingly deduced by him from the fact that 'When I turn my reflexion on *myself*, I never can perceive the self without some one or more perceptions; nor can I ever perceive anything but the perceptions'.[1] But then, having concluded that it must be the composition of these perceptions that forms the self, he admitted, in an Appendix to his book, *A Treatise of Human Nature*, that he could not explain how this composition was effected. His difficulty was, in his own words, that 'there are two principles which I cannot render consistent; nor is it in my power to renounce either of them, viz. *that all our distinct perceptions are distinct existences*, and *that the mind never perceives any real connexion among distinct existences*'.[2] How serious this difficulty is on Hume's principles is a question to which we shall return, when we come to examine the problem of personal identity.[3]

Hume does not deny that perceptions do combine to form minds, though he is unable to explain how this happens. Neither does he explicitly deny that there are physical objects. 'Tis vain,' he says, 'to ask *whether* there be body or not? That is a point which we must take for granted in all our reasonings.'[4] Nevertheless, when he goes on to ask what reasons we have for believing in the existence of bodies, he finds that they are quite inadequate. The conclusion of

[1] David Hume. *A Treatise of Human Nature*, Appendix.
[2] *Ibid.*
[3] See below pp. 112–17.
[4] *A Treatise of Human Nature*, Book I, Part IV, Section II.

his argument is that both what he calls the vulgar and the philosophical beliefs in the existence of physical objects are confused and erroneous. With regard to the vulgar belief, he argues with Berkeley that the ordinary man identifies physical objects with the sensible qualities which he perceives, while also attributing to them a continued and distinct existence. The trouble is, according to Hume, that these views are inconsistent. Since the senses 'convey to us nothing but a single perception, and never give us the least intimation of anything beyond', the impressions which we receive from them cannot be representations of anything '*distinct*, or *independent*, and *external*';[1] neither is it possible that our impressions should have a continued existence, since it is a contradiction in terms to suppose that they exist apart from being sensed. The only question is how people are deceived into thinking that their impressions do have a continued and distinct existence. Hume's answer to this is that it is because of the 'constancy and coherence' which the impressions exhibit. Finding that what we take to be an impression of a physical object is succeeded after an interval of time by another impression which is very similar to the first, we imagine that the original impression has persisted throughout the interval. In the cases where, as we say, the object changes, there is sufficient regularity in the fragmentary series of our actual impressions to make it natural for us to supply imaginary impressions to fill in these gaps and contradictorily suppose that they actually exist. These relations of constancy and coherence are, indeed, of the first importance, though not, as Hume thought, just in accounting for an illusion. We shall see later on that they rather serve to justify the common sense belief in the existence of the physical world.[2]

What Hume calls the philosophical account of physical objects differs from the vulgar account in that it distinguishes them from perceptions. Realizing that their perceptions are 'interrupted and perishing' philosophers have assumed a 'double existence' of perceptions and objects, and attributed continued and distinct existence only to the objects. This is effectively Locke's position of which Hume says that 'it contains all the difficulties of the vulgar system, with some others, that are peculiar to itself'.[3] It is not

[1] *Ibid.*
[2] See below pp. 99–106.
[3] *Ibid.*

recommendable to reason since, being acquainted only with our perceptions, we have no basis for any inference as to the character or even to the existence of anything outside them, and such influence as it may have on our imagination is borrowed from the vulgar system. It is only because they naturally conceive of their perceptions as having a continued and distinct existence, only to discover that this is not consonant with reason, that philosophers invent duplicates of perceptions to which, under the guise of external objects, they attribute properties which the perceptions themselves cannot possess. In consequence, the philosophical system 'is loaded with this absurdity, that it at once denies and establishes the vulgar supposition'.[1]

We shall see later on that this exercise of the imagination, with which Hume credits, or rather discredits, philosophers, is a pretty accurate account of the procedure of common sense.[2] The question is whether it deserves the strictures which he casts upon it. We shall also have to consider whether the starting point which we have seen to be common to Locke and Berkeley and Hume is one that we are bound, or even entitled to adopt. What Hume has already shown is that if we do adopt it, we are going to have considerable difficulty in getting beyond it. This difficulty is of a kind that constantly recurs in the theory of knowledge. It illustrates the point, which I made earlier, that this branch of philosophy very largely consists in the advancing and the attempted rebuttal of a particular type of sceptical argument.

The aim of the sceptic is to demonstrate the existence of an unbridgeable gap between the conclusions which we desire to reach and the premises from which we set out. Thus, in the case of our belief in the existence of physical objects, he will claim that the only premises which are supplied to us are propositions which relate exclusively to our sense-impressions. But then, he argues, since the conclusion of a valid deduction can contain no reference to entities which do not already figure in its premises, there is no deductive passage from propositions of this sort to propositions which relate to physical objects. It must, therefore, be an inductive inference, one in which the conclusion goes beyond the premises, as when we advance to an empirical generalization on the basis of observing that it holds good in a number of particular instances.

[1] Ibid.
[2] See below pp. 99–106.

But, the argument continues, to the extent that this form of reasoning is legitimate at all, it can carry us forward only at the same level. As a generalization from past experience, it can enable us to predict the occurrence of future sense-impressions on the basis of those that we have already had, but it cannot lead us to a conclusion which we could not conceivably verify: it cannot justify a passage from the occurrence of sense-impressions to the existence of anything which is not an object of experience. But then, the sceptic concludes, if our belief in the existence of physical objects cannot be justified either by a deductive or by an inductive argument, it does not have any rational warrant.

It is clear that the same form of argument can be applied to other cases in which our access to the objects or events of which we claim to have knowledge can plausibly be represented as being only indirect. Let us suppose that we have been able to establish a sense in which we can properly be said to perceive physical objects, including human bodies. Then the question may be raised with regard to bodies other than one's own, whether one has any valid reason for believing that they are the bodies of persons who have experiences of the same kind as those that one has oneself. And again the sceptic will argue that there is neither a deductive nor an inductive passage from propositions which relate to the bodily states and behaviour of other persons to propositions which relate to their inner thoughts and feelings. There is no deductive passage, because descriptions of bodily states and movements and descriptions of mental states and processes do not logically entail one another, and there is no inductive passage, because the conjunction of the mental state of another person with what one takes to be its bodily expression is something that one can never be in a position to verify: all that one ever actually observes is the bodily expression. So here too, the sceptic concludes that since the influence to the mental life of others cannot be justified either deductively or inductively, it has no justification. And in the same way he will argue that we have no justification for believing in the existence of the objects, like protons and electrons, which figure in scientific theories, since here too there is an unbridgeable gap between them and what we take to be their observable effects.

Neither is the argument confined to the admission of different sorts of entity. It can equally be directed against the claim to know something of the past, including the character of one's own past experiences. Once more the starting point is that we have no direct access to the past; it is known to us only through the traces which it has left, the most important of them being our ostensible memories. But, even in the case of an ostensible memory of a recent experience, the connexion is not deductive. There is no self-contradiction in supposing the ostensible memory to be delusive. Neither is there any ground for an inductive argument, since there is no single instance in which one actually observes the conjunction of a present ostensible memory with a past experience. So again the conclusion is drawn that this belief, which we all hold, is not rational.

In this case also, the sceptical argument can be brought into operation at a further stage. Let us suppose that we do credit ourselves with some knowledge of the past. Then the question may be raised whether on the basis of this knowledge we can form any rational beliefs about the future. Again it is argued that our reasons for any such beliefs can at best be inductive since the past sets no logical limitations upon the future, but in this instance the inductive step cannot be impugned on the ground that it leads to an unverifiable conclusion. In favourable circumstances we shall be able to observe whether or not the future event occurs. The fact, however, remains that the conclusion is not yet verifiable, so that we have to find some present basis for maintaining it; and this can consist only in the existence of past or present connections which we project. But then, as Hume pointed out, we are assuming that the future will resemble the past in the relevant respect, and this assumption has neither a deductive nor an inductive warrant. It is not logically true and any attempt to justify it inductively must beg the question. This sceptical argument poses the problem of induction, to which I referred in passing earlier on.[1]

As I remarked in my book *The Problem of Knowledge*,[2] it is possible to characterize different philosophical standpoints by their acceptance or denial of different steps in the sceptic's characteristic form of argument. Thus, those who are known as naive realists deny the first step of all. They maintain that we perceive physical objects not through a screen of sense-impressions but directly, that we can under favourable circumstances have direct access to the experiences of others, that memory can yield direct knowledge of the past. In short, they deny that there is any gap to be bridged. In

[1] See above p. 45.
[2] pp. 85–90.

the case of the problem of induction the gap is abolished by the claim that we are capable of apprehending necessary connexions between events. These views are, indeed, independent of one another, so that it is possible to take a naively realistic line in any one of these cases, without being committed to it in all of them, and in fact it has more commonly been taken in respect of our knowledge of physical objects than in respect of the other targets of the sceptic's attack.

Reductionists accept the sceptic's starting point, but deny the second step in his argument. They represent the transition from evidence to conclusion as proceeding at the same level by bringing the conclusion down to the level of the evidence. Thus, they follow Berkeley and Mill in holding that statements about physical objects are translatable into statements about sense-impressions: they follow the pragmatists in construing statements about the past as referring only to present or future memories or other forms of record. In the same way they interpret statements about scientific objects, like electrons, as referring only to their observable effects. In the case where one seems to be speaking about the experiences of another person, they take what is known as the physicalist view that one is really referring only to his bodily condition or behaviour. It is again to be noted that one may take a reductionist line in any one of these instances without being logically bound to extend it to the rest.

What I call the Scientific Approach consists in accepting the first two steps in the sceptic's argument but denying the third. The existence of physical objects or of the experiences of other persons or of past events is represented in each instance as a probable hypothesis which one is justified in accepting because of the way in which it accounts for one's experiences. In the same spirit philosophers of this way of thinking may try to make a case for the acceptance of certain principles which will underwrite the attribution of at least a high degree of probability to some of our judgements about the future.

Finally there are those who accept all three steps in the sceptic's argument but deny that they entail a sceptical conclusion. Where this is not simply a matter of denying the sceptic the credit which he seems to have earned, the position most commonly taken is that in insisting that our beliefs be justified either deductively or inductively the sceptic is presenting us with a false dilemma. He overlooks the fact that these are not the only ways in which a proposition can be related to what we call its evidence.

The question which we have to answer in each instance is which, if any, of these approaches is correct. And in order to do this we have to give an account of the propositions which the sceptic puts in jeopardy. We have to determine exactly what their content is. It is for this reason that I am treating the attempt to solve the problems which arise in the theory of knowledge as an exercise in philosophical analysis. It is, however, to be noted that this is not simply a question of semantics. We are, indeed, unlikely to be content with an analysis of these propositions which is greatly at variance with what we intuitively take to be meant by the sentences which express them. On the other hand, we do wish to interpret them in a way that will give us some reason for holding some of them to be true. The difficulty, as we shall see, is to satisfy both motives. To discover whether it can be resolved, we need to go through this series of questions in detail. I shall begin with the analysis of propositions in which our claims to perceive physical objects are typically expressed.

IV The Problem of Perception

A What do we Perceive?

When we looked at the sceptical argument, which sets the stage
for the theory of knowledge, we saw that its first step was always to
assume that the evidence fell short of the conclusion. The gap had
to be taken to exist, before it could be argued that it was incapable
of being bridged. We remarked also that this first step was not
universally held to be undeniable. It has in fact been denied by
philosophers whom I characterized as taking the position of naive
realism. In most cases, indeed, this position is not very plausible.
It hardly seems correct to say that the particles which figure in
scientific theories are directly accessible to observation, nor, as we
shall see in due course, is it easy to give a clear sense to the claims
that we are capable of inspecting the minds of others, or that
memory affords us direct acquaintance with the past. On the other
hand, when it comes to the perception of the physical objects
which figure in the common sense view of the world, the naive
realist appears to be on very much stronger ground. The difficulty
in this case is rather to make sense of the sceptic's contention that
our access to these objects is not direct.

If naive realism is to be regarded as upholding in this domain, the
position of common sense, then, as Austin pointed out in the
polemical series of lectures which he entitled *Sense and Sensibilia*,
it must not be taken as implying that things like chairs and tables
are the only sorts of things that we see or touch or otherwise perceive. The ordinary man does, indeed, believe that he frequently sees
and touches the 'moderate-sized specimens of dry goods', as Austin
characteristically terms them, on which philosophers most commonly rely for their examples, but he also speaks of seeing, or in
some cases hearing or smelling, such very different sorts of things as
'people, people's voices, rivers, mountains, flames, rainbows,
shadows, pictures on the screen at the cinema, pictures in books or

hanging on walls, vapours, gases'[1] and of course many other sorts of things besides. In short, as Austin justly remarks, it is a mistake 'to try to represent as some single *kind of things* the things which the ordinary man says that he "perceives"'.[2] Even so, the solid, opaque, medium-sized objects, of which pieces of furniture serve as convenient examples, do constitute a very large proportion of the things that are ordinarily thought to be perceived, and they also share three very important properties with most of these other things. The properties in question are those of being accessible to more than one sense, being accessible, at least in principle, to more than one observer, and being capable of existing unperceived. Of the three, the property of being accessible to more than one sense is the least pervasive. Among the objects on Austin's list, it is not possessed by shadows and rainbows, which are accessible only to sight, or by voices, which can only be heard, and possibly not by pictures on screens, since it is arguable that what can be touched is only the screen and not the picture. Nevertheless the majority of things which are thought to be visible are thought also to be tangible. The other two properties belong to everything that is ordinarily said to be perceived, with the exception of mental images, bodily feelings and private hallucinations, if these are counted as objects of perception. It is also to be noted that they generally go together, in the sense that nearly everything that is thought to be perceptible by more than one observer is also thought to be capable of existing unperceived. The only exception that I can think of would be something that was discovered to have been the product of a mass hallucination. I conclude, therefore, that there is no serious objection to taking such things as chairs and tables as typical examples of what the ordinary man thinks that he perceives. If we can arrive at a theory of perception which deals satisfactorily with cases of this sort, it should not be too difficult to make it cover the whole range.

How then does the sceptic come to assert that the access to physical objects which we believe that we obtain from the exercise of sight and touch is not direct ? In the normal way, if someone were to say that he was seeing a table indirectly, one would probably construe his statement as a rather eccentric way of saying that he was seeing it reflected, in an ordinary mirror, perhaps, or through a

[1] J. L. Austin. *Sense and Sensibilia*, p. 8.
[2] *Ibid.*

periscope: if he said that he was touching it indirectly, one might take him to mean that he was in contact with it through some instrument, but clearly this is not what the sceptic has in mind, since these cases are exceptional, whereas he is contending that our perception of physical objects can only be indirect. What he is asserting is not, as in these construes, that one physical object is perceived through the medium of another, but rather that every physical object is perceived, if at all, through the medium of something else; an entity of a different sort. Our first task, then, is to make clear what he takes these other entities to be.

The view that our perception of physical objects is mediated in this way holds a very respectable place in the history of philosophy. I have been attributing it to the sceptic, because it marks the first step in the sceptical argument to which I have attached the theory of knowledge, but in fact it has been held by many philosophers who were not primarily sceptics, or even not sceptics at all. Thus, Descartes maintained that physical objects were perceived not directly but through the medium of what he called ideas. Locke, as we have seen, under Descartes's influence, referred to the objects by which he thought that perception was mediated, as simple ideas of sensation. Berkeley, following Locke, spoke indifferently of our perceiving ideas and perceiving sensible qualities. Hume took the same position, but substituted the word 'impression' for Berkeley's 'idea', reserving the word 'idea' for images or concepts. Kant, whose *Critique of Pure Reason* was a response to Hume's scepticism, spoke similarly of 'Vorstellungen' of which the favoured English rendering is 'representations'. John Stuart Mill took perception to consist in having sensations, and used the word 'sensation' to refer not only to such perceptual acts as those of seeing or hearing but also to what was seen or heard or otherwise sensed. In more recent times, philosophers who have wished to make a clear distinction between what they called acts of sensing, or states of acquaintance or awareness, and their immediate objects, have commonly followed Moore and Russell in characterizing these objects as sense-data. There have, however, been other locutions. Russell himself, regarding the notion of sense-data as being tied to that of mental acts, in the existence of which he came to disbelieve, preferred in his later works to use the term 'percepts' to refer to the data of the outer senses. In one of his early essays, Moore used the term 'sense-content' as an alternative to 'sense-datum', and I also used it, in my

Language, Truth and Logic, in a way corresponding to Russell's use of 'percept'. The Cambridge philosopher, C. D. Broad, advancing the theory that 'Whenever I truly judge that [a physical object] *x* appears to me to have the sensible quality *q*, what happens is that I am directly aware of a certain object *y* which (a) really does have the quality *q* and (b) stands in some peculiarly intimate relation, yet to be determined, to *x*',[1] used the term 'sensa' to designate the objects which fulfilled the function of *y*. This way of introducing sensa was also employed by Moore and Russell to introduce sense-data. More recently still, the American philosophers, C. I. Lewis and Nelson Goodman, have used the term '*qualia*', in a way that is reminiscent of Berkeley's reference to sensible qualities.

While there is a large measure of agreement in the ways in which these various terms have been used, they are not in all cases exactly interchangeable. It is not even true of them severally that they have been given a wholly consistent use. Thus, Locke employed the term 'idea' to refer to particular objects, to general characteristics and to concepts. The examples that he gave of simple ideas of sense were general characteristics, but he seems in fact to have conceived of the immediate data of perception as particular objects in which these characteristics inhered. For Berkeley, on the other hand, the things which we sense were complexes of qualities, though he thought of these complexes as constituting particulars. Moore began by using the term 'sense-datum' to refer indiscriminately to general characteristics and to the particular objects which exemplified them, but ended by confining its extension to particulars. Russell thought of sense-data as particulars but came to represent percepts as complexes of qualities. Since it is arguable that particulars can anyhow be constructed out of qualities and their relations, this divergence may not be very important, but it can have a bearing on the status which is assigned to the immediate data of perception.

One question which has been thought to arise concerning their status is whether or not they exist objectively, and here again there has been a divergence of opinion. Thus, as their choice of the term 'idea' indicates, Descartes, Locke and Berkeley agreed in making them subjective, in the sense that they denied them all three of the pervasive properties which we saw that common sense attributes to physical objects, including the two which are attributed to most of the other things that the ordinary man might say that he perceived.

[1] C. D. Broad. *Scientific Thought,* p. 239.

They took it to be necessarily true of ideas, in this usage, that they were not accessible to more than one sense, that they were not individually presented to more than one observer, and that they did not exist independently of being perceived. On the other hand, Moore and Russell, while they thought of sense-data as being, like Berkeley's ideas, the objects of acts of sensing, did not regard this as being incompatible with their existing unsensed. Unlike Moore, who wished to keep open the possibility of identifying some sense-data with the surfaces, or parts of the surfaces, of physical objects, Russell did confine each of them to a single mode of sensing and to a single observer, but his reason for this was that they were causally dependent upon the bodily state of the observer. That he did not regard them as constitutionally incapable of existing independently is shown by the fact that he did attribute independent existence to the objects to which he gave the name of 'sensibilia', describing them as objects 'of the same metaphysical and physical status as sense-data',[1] with the difference that they were not actually sensed. The same must have applied to the percepts which he substituted for sense-data, since he ended by identifying them with states of the observer's brain. Even so, he assumed that in their character as percepts, they were private to the observer whose mind they helped to constitute. In the same way, Hume thought of impressions as entering into mutually exclusive series, each of which constituted a different person, and held it to follow from their nature that they were 'fleeting and perishing'.[2] This cannot, indeed, be true of qualia, if they are treated as general characteristics; for it is in the nature of a general characteristic or, as philosophers now mostly say, a universal, that it can occur at many places and at many times. Nevertheless, the grouping of qualia which has been thought to furnish a perceptual datum has also been thought to be contained within the limits of a single sense-experience.

From this it appears that, for all the differences in detail, there has been a widespread agreement that the immediate data of perception do not enjoy what Hume called 'a continued and distinct existence'.[3] The suggestion is that when I look, or at any rate believe myself to be looking, at the table in front of me, what I primarily see is not the table at all but something else, which has the

[1] Bertrand Russell. *Mysticism and Logic*, p. 148.
[2] David Hume. *A Treatise of Human Nature*, Book I, Part IV, Section 2.
[3] *Ibid*. and see above p. 62.

impermanence and perhaps also the subjectivity of a mental image. In general, this view has been advanced as if it were an empirical discovery, with the implication that the naive realist who thinks that he does see the table is simply mistaken on a question of empirical fact. Thus, Professor Prichard, who thought it correct to say that we see colours, is supposed to have remarked of the ordinary man that when he sees a colour he 'straight off mistakes it for a body'.[1] In this way, all our ordinary judgements of perception are assimilated to the cases in which we misidentify what we perceive. It is as if we were constantly like the Eskimos who when they were first shown Flaherty's film about their lives rushed to harpoon the seals which they saw on the screen. But surely this is not a fair analogy. In the ordinary way, the ground for thinking that an object has been misidentified is that one's identification of it is not borne out by further observations. The Eskimos soon discovered that they were not destroying animals but defacing images. But what experience could reveal that we had constantly been mistaking colours, or ideas, or sense-data, for bodies? If bodies are not directly perceptible, there can be no chance for our senses to detect the masquerade. It follows that if the ordinary man is making any mistake at all when he thinks that he perceives physical objects without the mediation of other entities, it is a mistake of a different kind; a purely theoretical error. He must be misinterpreting not just some particular item but the general character of his perceptual experiences. But then what grounds do we have for thinking that this is so?

B The Argument from Illusion

The argument on which philosophers who have rejected the naive realist account of perception have mainly relied has come to be known, not altogether happily, as the argument from illusion. It is traditionally based on a set of empirical premisses, which can be sorted into four compartments. One of them brings together the instances in which an object is misidentified: these include cases like that of Flaherty's Eskimos and also cases in which one kind of physical object is confused with another, as when a figure in a wax museum is mistaken for a real person or vice versa. Secondly, there are the cases of total hallucination, the examples most commonly given being those of mirages, Macbeth's visionary dagger, and the

[1] See H. H. Price. 'Obituary of Harold Arthur Prichard', *Proceedings of the British Academy*, Vol. XXXIII.

pink rats which the drunkard sees, or thinks he sees, in delirium tremens. An example, not relating to sight, is that of the patient who feels pain in an amputated limb. The third class of cases points to the variations in the appearance of an object which may be due to perspective, the condition of the light, the mental or physical state of the observer, the presence of some distorting medium, or any combination of these factors. Here the stock examples are those of the large tower which looks small when seen from a distance, the round coin which looks elliptical when seen from an angle, the straight stick which looks bent when it is put in water, and the white wall which looks blue when it is seen through blue spectacles: the fact that objects appear mis-located when they are seen in mirrors also comes into this class. Once again, the examples are predominantly visual, but attention has also been drawn to such facts as that a coin feels larger when it is placed on one's tongue than when one holds it in the palm of the hand, and that water feels hotter or colder according to the temperature of one's fingers. Finally, the more general point is made that the way things appear to us is never just a consequence of their own nature. It is causally dependent also on their environment, on such factors as the state of the light, and on our own mental and physical condition. We tend to take notice of this only when our perceptual judgements are thought to have gone astray and we attribute the error to some abnormality in the environment or in ourselves. But the causal dependence of the way things appear to us upon these other factors obtains just as much in the normal cases in which our perceptual judgements are taken to be true.

It is to be remarked that of the facts assembled under these four headings, only those that come under the first two would normally be considered as affording examples of perceptual error or illusion. Rightly or wrongly, the causal machinery of perception is not commonly regarded as invalidating the belief that we often perceive things as they really are, nor is this belief weakened by the fact that the appearances of things vary under different conditions. We learn to account for such factors as perspective and the state of the light, in making our perceptual judgements, and find no difficulty in the idea that appearances are not always to be taken at their face value. The naive realist's assumption that we directly perceive physical objects is not understood to entail that we always perceive them as they really are, but only that we do so when the conditions are right. Of course if we make the assumption, which we saw that Broad made in introducing sensa, that 'whenever I truly judge that x appears to me to have the quality q, what happens is that I am directly aware of a certain object y which really does have the quality q',[1] we shall be able to conclude that at least in the cases where a physical object appears to us in any way otherwise than as it is, we are directly aware not of it but of something else; but why should we make this assumption? Why when a round object looks elliptical to me, because I am seeing it from an angle, or a red object looks purple in the evening light, should I have to be seeing anything that really is elliptical or really is purple? In the cases where someone undergoes a total hallucination, one may find it natural to say that something is genuinely seen, even if it is accorded no more than the status of a mental image, but where it is only a matter of variation in the appearance of a physical object, why should we dissociate the object from its appearance and treat what is in effect the appearance as the only perceptual datum?

In trying to answer this question, we must keep it in mind that it is not a question of fact, which could be settled by experiment, but rather a question of policy. If we are seeking a clear view of the facts which are supposed to verify our perceptual judgements, can we be satisfied with saying no more than that we perceive various sorts of things, including physical objects which sometimes appear to have properties that they do not really have? Surely we should at least attempt to analyse the distinction between the real and the apparent. It will then remain to be seen whether the result of this analysis supplies us with a good enough reason for distinguishing between direct and indirect perception in such a way that the perception of physical objects becomes indirect.

How then do we determine what perceptible properties a physical object really has? It may be objected that this is not a clear question since the word 'real' is used in many different ways.[2] It serves to contrast the natural with the artificial, as when we ask whether a woman's hair is really red as opposed to being dyed; the natural with the synthetic, as when we talk of real as opposed to cultured pearls; the genuine with the spurious, as one might say of a picture that it was a real Van Gogh; what comes up to standard with what does not, in the sense in which I should say that I was not a real

---

[1] See above p. 71.
[2] Cf. J. L. Austin. *Sense and Sensibilia*, Ch. VII.

bridge-player; what is designed for a practical purpose with what is designed for a mimicry of this purpose, as in the contrast between a real and a toy trumpet, which, as my small son pointed out to me, also makes real noises, though not of the same volume or range. We speak of real as opposed to affected or merely superficial emotions, of real as opposed to ostensible reasons, and we also contrast the real with the imaginary or the fictitious, which is not quite the same as contrasting it with the apparent. Etymologically, since the word 'real' descends from the Latin 'res', to be real is to be a thing, a usage which is preserved in our legal talk of real property. An extension of this usage in one direction yields the idea that not to be real is not to exist at all. An extension in the opposite direction yields the idea that not to be real is not to be a thing or a property or an action of the proper sort. It is because there are so many different standards of propriety, and correspondingly so many ways of being deficient, that the uses of the word appear so multifarious.

As an exercise in lexicography, this could well be taken further, but it has little relevance to our present purpose, since if there were any genuine doubt about the sense which we are attaching to the word 'really' in posing the question how it is determined what properties a physical object really has, it could easily be removed by giving examples. We are concerned with the analysis of such propositions as 'That small speck in the sky is really a very large star'; 'The penny looks elliptical from this angle but it is really round'; 'When I put on blue spectacles the curtains look blue to me but they are really white'. It is, indeed, true, as Austin has pointed out,[1] that there are cases in which the distinction between the real and the apparent, which these examples illustrate, does not apply so smoothly. We should, as he remarks, be hard put to say what was the real colour of the sun, or the real shape of a cloud, except in the rare case where it is clearly defined. There are things like chameleons which change their colour frequently, and things like cats or concertinas which do not preserve a constant shape. These difficulties, however, are not very serious. There are a great many things which do preserve what we judge to be the same real colour or shape over a considerable period of time and even in cases where this is not so, the distinction between real and apparent properties can still be drawn. For instance, we can contrast the colour which the

[1] J. L. Austin. *Sense and Sensibilia*, p. 66.

chameleon really displays on a given occasion with that which it only seems to display, and similarly we can ask what shape the cat really has, as opposed to a shape that it may only appear to have, at any given moment. This is because the distinction which we are considering applies also to the parts of things, and because physical objects, being extended in time as well as in space, have temporal as well as spatial parts.

How then is this distinction drawn? Evidently, since we are not able to inspect any physical objects in detachment from the various facets which they present to our perception, it must be drawn in terms of these facets, if it comes within the domain of perception at all. In fact, we denominate as the real colour of a physical object that colour which it looks, or would look, to a normal observer under the conditions which we take as standard. In general, the conditions taken as standard are those that are optimal, in that they make for the greatest possibility of discrimination. This principle applies also to our judgements of shape, together with the fact that the apparent shapes can be regarded as mostly forming a system of which what we judge to be real shape can be conveniently represented as the centre. In this case the question is further complicated by our having to correlate the data of sight with the data of touch, and by the existence of further and indeed over-riding criteria in the operations of measurement. Measurement plays a decisive part also in the determination of size, a process which especially in the case of distant objects like the stars may also draw upon scientific theories. It might be thought that our recourse to measurement, and to theory, constitutes an objection to my saying that the distinction between the perceptual properties that a physical object really has and those that it only appears to have must be drawn in terms of the different facets that it presents to us: and it is, indeed, true that an object like a star never actually looks to us as large as we believe it really to be. The fact remains, however, that our calculations are based upon apparent properties if not of the star itself, at least of photographs, and in making linear measurements we correlate the objects measured with the measuring instruments on the basis of their appearances. Moreover, our more sophisticated theories arise out of a simpler, more primitive, system in which the properties which physical objects are judged really to have are straightforwardly selected from those that they appear to have.

For our present purpose, we may confine ourselves to the simpler cases, and here what is of interest to us is not so much how the real properties are selected, but the very fact that they are selected. For it may well be thought that if appearances are considered purely in themselves, one is as good as another, and in that case it may be argued that we have no justification for discriminating between them as manifestations of reality. So Russell, having remarked, in his book *The Problems of Philosophy*, that 'It is evident ... that there is no colour which pre-eminently appears to be *the* colour of the table or even of any one particular part of the table – it appears to be of different colours from different points of view, and there is no reason for regarding some of these as more really its colour than others',[1] and having gone on to say that 'When, in ordinary life we speak of *the* colour of the table, we only mean the sort of colour which it will seem to have to a normal spectator from an ordinary point of view under usual conditions of light', concludes that 'the other colours which appear under other conditions have just as good a right to be considered real: and therefore, to avoid favouritism, we are compelled to deny that, in itself, the table has any one particular colour'.[2] But if neither the table nor any part of it, however small, has any one particular colour at a given time, it cannot, unless our eyes are constantly deceiving us, be identical with what we see: for even if the object which we see is multi-coloured, the same cannot be true of all its parts. And this indeed is the inference that Russell draws. Partly on this ground, which applies to the shape of the table as much as to its colour, and partly on the ground that our visual, tactual and auditory sensations are all causally dependent on our own bodily states, he concludes that 'The real table, if there is one, is not *immediately* known to us at all but must be an inference from what is immediately known'.[3] In fact, the upshot is that we know relatively little about the real table. From the character of the relevant sense-data we are supposed to be entitled to infer with a fair degree of probability that they are caused by an external object which bears some structural correspondence to them.

Deferring for the moment the question of the causal dependence of our perceptions on our own bodily states, let us see whether the rest of the argument is cogent. I think it clear that it is not. In the

[1] Bertrand Russell. *The Problems of Philosophy*, p. 9.
[2] *Ibid.* p. 10.
[3] *Ibid.* p. 11.

first place, no reason is given why we should not show favouritism, if showing favouritism consists in selecting only one of the colours or shapes which the object may appear to have as that which it really has. We could, indeed, have made a different choice but this is not to say that the choices which we do make are wholly arbitrary. On the contrary, we have seen that there are practical reasons for them. What Russell had in mind, no doubt, was that the appearances that we do not select are no less genuine than those that we do, but this does not entitle him to deny that those which are selected manifest the real properties of the object in question. If what we mean by saying that the object is really brown is just that it looks brown under such and such favourable conditions, then if it does look brown under those conditions it is really brown. Admittedly, this does not tell us what properties the table has independently of the ways in which it appears to us, but then it has yet to be shown that there are any such properties. So far as the argument has gone, we have as good a ground for identifying the table with its actual and possible appearances as we have for dissociating it from them. The theory that it can be so identified was, indeed, also advanced by Russell in his book on *Our Knowledge of the External World*, which was published only two years after *The Problems of Philosophy*, though for reasons connected with the causality of perception, which we shall presently consider, he subsequently reverted to his earlier view.

Can we say that the facts to which Russell draws attention at least make a breach in the position of naive realism? I think that we can, to the extent that they raise a problem which the naive realist does not attempt to answer. We think of the physical object as preserving its identity in the various guises in which it appears to us, but exactly how is this achieved? What is it that remains constant while its appearance varies? If the physical object is known to us only through its various appearances, in what way can we distinguish it from them? The naive realist ignores these questions, not because they imply the denial of any doctrine that he holds but because in treating the perception of physical objects as a primitive datum he has already gone beyond them. He has no convenient vocabulary by means of which he can refer to the appearances of things, independently of the things of which we take them to be appearances. But if we want to discuss the relation of physical objects to their appearances, we do need such a vocabulary, and it is just this that the introduction of terms like 'sensible quality' or 'sense-datum' has been intended to provide. We may, indeed, not wish to be committed to all the implications which their use has been made to carry. Exactly how any such term is to be construed in order to be acceptable is a question which we shall have to examine. All that I am now suggesting is that something of this sort is needed.

The point at issue here may be brought out more clearly if we examine Russell's claim that ordinary judgements of perception like 'This is a table' entail an inference, reserving for the moment the question what sort of inference it is: the suggestion then will be that we need to provide ourselves with the means of formulating the premisses on which such inferences are based. In Russell's case, as we have seen, the claim was supported, in traditional fashion, by the argument from illusion, but there is, I believe, a simpler and more effective way of establishing it. We need only consider the range of the assumptions which our ordinary judgements of perception carry. To begin with, there are the assumptions which we have seen to be involved in characterizing anything as a physical object like a table. It has to be accessible to more than one sense and to more than one observer and it has to be capable of existing unperceived. In addition, it has to occupy a position or series of positions in three-dimensional space and to endure throughout a period of time. It may, indeed, be argued that these are not straightforwardly empirical assumptions, but postulates of a conceptual system. They set the framework into which the results of our observations are most made to fit. The fact remains, however, that in particular instances they can fail to be satisfied. The Eskimos discovered that the images which they had mistaken for seals were not tangible: the presence of the snakes which the drunkard thinks he sees is not corroborated by other observers, and the fact that it is not so corroborated is taken as evidence that these visionary snakes do not have the capacity of existing unperceived. Similarly, we may discover in the course of further experience that what we had taken to be a physical object has not the requisite location in physical space or persistence through time. Part of the point of the argument from illusion is, indeed, that it calls attention to the fact that such mistakes are possible.

Neither is it only a question of the validity of these general assumptions. Our perceptual judgements are seldom indefinite, in the sense that we claim only to perceive a physical object of some sort or other. In the normal way, we identify it as a thing of some specific kind, and this brings in further assumptions, as, for example, that the object is solid, or flexible, or that it is not hollow. These further assumptions may relate to the purposes which the object serves, as when we identify something as a pen-knife, or a telephone: they may relate to its physical constitution, as in the identification of an object as an orange or an apple, which denies its being made of wax. They may presume on the deliverances of other senses, as when our descriptions of an object which we believe ourselves to be seeing or touching carries implications about the way in which it tastes or sounds or smells.

But now can it seriously be maintained that all this can fall within the content of a single act of perception? Can my present view of the table, considered purely in itself as a fleeting visual experience, conceivably guarantee that I am seeing something that is also tangible, or visible to other observers? Can it guarantee even that I am seeing something which exists at any other time than this, let alone something that is made of such and such materials, or endowed with such and such causal properties, or serving such and such a purpose? I think it evident that it cannot. But if these conclusions are not logically guaranteed by the content of my present visual experience, one is surely entitled to say that they go beyond it, and just this is what I take to be meant by saying that my judgement that this is a table embodies an inference. It embodies an inference, not in the sense that it results from any conscious process of reasoning, but just in the sense that it affirms more than can logically be entailed by any strict account of the experience on which it is based. What I mean here by a strict account is one that is tailored to the experience, in that it describes the quality of what is sensibly presented, without carrying any further implication of any sort. In the normal way, we do not formulate such propositions because we are interested not in the data as such, but in the interpretations which we have learned to put upon them. I cannot, however, see any logical reason why they should not be formulable.

If I am right on this point, the naive realists are wrong in so far as they deny that our ordinary judgements of perception are susceptible of analysis, or deny that they embody inferences which can be made explicit. This does not make it incorrect for us to speak of seeing and touching physical objects, in the way we ordinarily do: it shows only that the facts which verify our state-ments are more complicated than one might at first suppose. There is, however, another implication, if not of our ordinary way of speaking, at least of the common sense way of construing it, which can also be put in question. I take it to be the view of common sense that the physical objects which we perceive continue to exist on their own in very much the form in which we normally perceive them. This entails, for example, that whether or not anyone is looking at the table, it retains, in a literal sense, the colour and shape which it appears to us to have when it is observed under standard conditions. The question is whether this view is reconcil-able with the causal dependence of the way things appear to us both on their environment and on our own mental and physical states. It is often suggested that science tells us otherwise, or at the very least that it leaves us with no good reason to believe that things as they are in themselves are at all similar, except perhaps in respect of structure, to anything that we perceive. This point of view is put succinctly by Russell in his book *An Inquiry into Meaning and Truth*. Identifying the common sense position with naive realism he says: 'Naive realism leads to physics and physics, if true, shows that naive realism is false. Therefore naive realism, if true, is false; therefore it is false.'[1] I now want to consider whether this argument must be accepted.

C   The Causal Theory of Perception

The reason why physics is thought to falsify naive realism is also given by Russell in the passage of which I have just quoted the conclusion. 'We think,' he says, 'that grass is green, that stones are hard, and that snow is cold. But physics assures us that the green-ness of grass, the hardness of stones, and the coldness of snow, are not the greenness, hardness, and coldness that we know in our own experience, but something very different. The observer, when he seems to himself to be observing a stone, is really, if physics is to be believed, observing the effects of the stone upon himself.'[2] In the same way, the physicist Arthur Eddington, in his book *The Nature of the Physical World*, represents himself as sitting down to write at his 'two tables' one of which 'has extension, is compara-tively permanent, is coloured and above all is *substantial*, while the

---

[1] Bertrand Russell. *An Inquiry into Meaning and Truth*, p. 15.
[2] *Ibid.*

other is 'mostly emptiness', relieved by 'numerous electric charges rushing about with great speed',[1] the implication being that the two cannot co-exist. If the electric charges are what there really is, then the coloured substantial object is no more than an appearance, the effect on the observer's mind of a series of physical processes which starts with the electrical charges, continues through the intervening medium and ends in the observer's nervous system.

There are two strands to this argument. One is that science corrects the common sense picture of the physical world. The other is that the common sense picture is in any case unlikely to be accurate because of its causal provenance. I shall begin by trying to deal with the second of these theses.

A point to be noted is that this thesis depends, like the first, upon the acceptance of scientific theory: the conclusion that things are most probably not what they seem is derived from the scientific explanation of their seeming as they do. Accordingly, we should not allow the argument to lead us into a position where our acceptance of the relevant scientific theories would not be justified. For instance, we should not make it a reason for holding the sceptical view that we have no warrant for any of the hypotheses that we make about the character of physical events. This is not to say that the argument commits us to a belief in the existence of external objects, if calling them 'external' is taken to imply that they are merely inferred entities, inaccessible to our observation. The acceptance of the theories in question allows for some latitude in the interpretation that we put upon them; we may, for example, be able to construe them as relating to perceptual data. Our freedom is limited only to the extent that we have both to take account of the way in which the theories are established and to make our interpretation of them consistent with our having good reason to accept them.

Let us then take it to be proved that our perception of colour results from the impact of photons upon our optic nerves, setting aside for the moment the question how these references to photons or to optic nerves are to be interpreted. Why should this be thought to entail that the objects from which the photons emanate are not really coloured? How indeed is the word 'really' here to be understood? I suggested earlier that what is ordinarily meant by saying, for example, that the table is really brown is that it looks brown to normal observers under standard conditions, and clearly this is not

[1] Arthur Eddington. *The Nature of the Physical World*, p. xi.

in the least incompatible with any causal account of the way in which we perceive it. We must, therefore, assume that those who conclude that the table is not really coloured are using the word 'really' in something other than this ordinary sense.

How then are they using it? I think that it is easy to see what their intention is, though it is not so easy to draw out all its implications. They want to distinguish between things as they are in themselves and things as they can appear to us, and to count as the real properties of physical objects only those properties that they possess independently of our perceiving them. So what they mean by saying that the table is not really coloured is that being coloured is not an intrinsic property of the object or set of objects from which the light emanates which causes us to perceive a table. The reason why I have chosen to put it in this complicated way, rather than say more simply that colour is not, on this view, an intrinsic property of the table, is that if we think, as the theory requires, of the objects which enter into the common sense picture of the world as being processed by the machinery of perception, then words like 'table' are used to designate the results of the process rather than the material on which it operates. Neither would it have been sufficient for me to speak without qualification of the object or objects which cause us to perceive a table, for this would not have distinguished the object to which I wished to refer from the other objects, such as the photons of light or the elements of the observer's nervous system, which also enter into the causal processes. Even to speak as I did of the objects from which the light emanates is not sufficient, since this does not distinguish them from the sun or from other objects, like mirrors, from which the light might also be reflected. It might seem that this difficulty could be met by giving the spatio-temporal location of the objects which one is trying to single out, but for this we should need to identify their positions, which would not be possible if, as most causal theorists have maintained, the space which physical objects occupy is not observed by us, but only inferred. This is an important point to which I shall shortly return. For the present, I wish only to note the difficulty of finding any general formula for pin-pointing, among the causes of our sensations, the one that corresponds to the object which is said to be perceived.

The distinction which causal theorists attempt to make between things as they are in themselves and things as they appear to us is allied to the distinction which Locke drew between ideas of primary and ideas of secondary qualities. The ideas of primary qualities, according to Locke, are those of 'solidity, extension, figure, motion or rest, and number'[1]; they were supposed by him to be counterparts of the qualities of the objects which caused us to receive them. The ideas of secondary qualities, such as colours, tastes and sounds, were thought to be different, in that the qualities of which they were ideas were 'nothing in the objects themselves, but powers to produce various sensations in us by their primary qualities, i.e. by the bulk, figure, texture, motion of their insensible parts'.[2] So, on this view, to attribute solidity to an object is to say of it both that it is solid in itself and that it has the capacity of producing sensations of solidity in us, whereas to attribute colour to it is to say of it only that it has the capacity of producing sensations of colour in us, and not that it is itself literally coloured.

But if the reason for holding that colour is nothing in the object itself were that our sensations of colour are causally dependent upon other factors, such as the state of our nervous systems, then it could be objected that exactly the same is true of the sensations which Locke calls ideas of primary qualities. There has, therefore, to be some other ground for his distinction, if it is to be tenable. In fact, it would seem that Locke was simply following Newton: his list of primary qualities is a list of the qualities which Newton attributed to material particles. The question is whether he can be justified in thinking that these are the only qualities, as distinct from powers, that physical objects literally possess.

This question is made more difficult to answer by the fact that Locke, like some other causal theorists, is not wholly clear whether primary qualities are a selection of the apparent qualities of the objects which we perceive, or whether they are qualities of objects which we do not perceive at all, except in the sense that they cause us to have various sensations. Officially, he holds the second view but he frequently writes as though he held the first. Thus, when he speaks of the insensible parts of bodies, the implication is that they are insensible because they are minute. They are contrasted with the macroscopic parts of bodies which are in these contexts taken to be observable.

[1] John Locke. *An Essay Concerning Human Understanding*, Book II, Ch. VIII, Section 9.
[2] *Ibid.* Section 10.

On either view, there are difficulties. If the primary qualities are a selection of those that appear to characterize the objects which we perceive, the question arises whether these objects can be so truncated. Perhaps Berkeley went too far in objecting 'that those original qualities *are inseparably united with the other sensible qualities*, and not, even in thought, capable of being abstracted from them',[1] for physicists do seem capable of making this abstraction, but certainly if we divest an object of its colour it is hard to imagine its retaining its perceptible figure and extension; for how would these be demarcated? Moreover, since all the perceptible properties of physical objects are manifested to us under similar causal conditions, we would appear to have no motive for turning these objects into skeletons, except as an act of obeisance to science.

The second view is the one to which Hume was referring when he spoke of the philosophical system, and said of it that 'it contains all the difficulties of the vulgar system with some others that are peculiar to itself'.[2] His main objection, that we can have no good reason to believe in the existence of the objects which it postulates is, indeed, not immediately convincing. It seems open to the rejoinder that to outlaw any reference to unobservable entities would be unduly to fetter the liberty of science. The most that we can reasonably require is that the hypotheses in which such entities figure have consequences which are empirically testable. But this is to overlook the fact that the unobservable entities which are sometimes admitted into physical theories gain credit from their relation to objects which are thought to be observable and are thought to occupy positions in perceptible space. If we house every physical object in an external world, which is beyond the reach of observation, their spatial relations must accompany them, with the result that the space which they occupy itself becomes something of which the existence is only inferred. And then it is very hard to see how this inference can be justified. Indeed, I doubt whether the notion of a spatial system of which none of the elements can be observed is even intelligible. If we are able to think of unobservable objects as spatially located, it is only because we introduce them into a system of spatial relations which are predominantly observable.

Not only that, but the causal account of perception itself requires

---

[1] George Berkeley. *A Treatise Concerning the Principles of Human Knowledge*, Part I, Section 10.
[2] See above p. 62.

that physical objects be located in perceptible space. When my seeing the table is said to depend upon the fact that it emits photons which affect my optic nerves, the assumption is that the table is there where I seem to see it, not in a place which is known to me only by inference and never perceived by anyone. This is not to say that things are always where they seem to be. There are cases in which we allow the judgements of position which we should naturally make to be over-ridden by physical theory. For example, we believe the sun and the stars to be much further from us than they look to be. But the point is that the theories which lead to these conclusions only become established on the basis of the assumption that the physical objects in our immediate environment are where they appear to be.

Put succinctly, the decisive objection to the version of the causal theory which turns physical objects into unobservable occupants of an unobservable space is that if this were so we should have no means of identifying them, and if we had no means of identifying them, we should have no reason to believe that they played any part in the production of our sensations, or even that they existed at all. The point which the advocates of this position have overlooked is that physical objects cannot be identified in the first instance as the causes of our sensations: they have to be independently identi- fied before we can have any right to say that the causal relation holds. It is only because I can, through perception, independently establish the fact that the table is there in front of me, that I can subsequently explain my seeing it in terms of its effects upon me.

It follows that there must be a primitive account of perception which makes no reference to any causal relation between the per- cipient and the objects which he perceives. We do, indeed, have reason at some point to insert a causal clause in to our analysis of perceptual judgements. For instance, if someone had been induced by post-hypnotic suggestion, or by the artificial stimulation of his optic nerves, to believe that he saw such and such an object, whether it was really there or not, then the fact that it happened really to be there would not be thought sufficient in these circum- stances to entail that he genuinely saw it, just because the requisite causal relation between them would be lacking. Even so, this causal requirement can be laid down only at a later stage when we have already established our claim to have some knowledge of the physical world. It cannot operate from the start, because the objects to which it relates must be independently identified, and since they can be identified, at least in general, only through our perceiving them, there must be earlier stages in the analysis of perception in which it does not figure.

What then becomes of the argument that the causal conditions of perception make it improbable that we ever perceive things as they really are? The answer is that it too is out of order: it has no standing at the primitive level. Our criteria of reality have in the first instance to be framed in terms of the way things appear to us. We have nothing else to go by. Only when we have constructed at least an elementary picture of the physical world, can we theorize about it in a way that may make such an argument acceptable. If we do accept it, we should, to use Wittgenstein's simile, be throwing away the ladder up which we have climbed.[1] It will remain to be seen whether this is justifiable.

The same applies to Eddington's problem of the two tables. We shall have to consider in what way, if at all, the physicist's account of the world competes with that of common sense, and if they are found to be competitive, to decide which of them is to govern our conception of what there really is. The fact that the common sense view is lower down the ladder would not, as Russell suggested, necessarily condemn it. This would be so only if the relation between it and the physicist's view were that of logical entailment, which we shall see that it is not. The position is rather that common sense provides the data for physical theory, just as the common sense view of the physical world is itself a theory with respect to the immediate data of perception. Our first task then is to show how the common sense view can be evolved.

[1] L. Wittgenstein. *Tractatus Logico-Philosophicus*, 6.54.

V Construction of the Physical World

A The Elements

I have tried to show that there is an intelligible sense in which our ordinary judgements of perception may truly be said to go beyond the evidence on which they are based. They claim more than is strictly vouchsafed by the experiences which give rise to them. If this is so, then, as I have said, it ought to be possible to devise propositions which simply record the contents of these experiences, without carrying any further implications. The question is how these experiential propositions, as I shall call them, should be formulated.

This is a question on which we have already touched, in talking about the use which philosophers have made of terms like 'idea' or 'sense-datum', and we have seen that there has been some disagreement about the way in which it should be answered. Part of the reason for the difficulties which have arisen is that we normally do not attend to the character of our sensory experiences to any greater extent than is necessary for us to be able to interpret them successfully. In the ordinary way it is enough for us to be able to identify the object at which we are looking as a tree, or a book, or a match-box, or whatever it may be: we make no precise assessment of its size or shape or even of its colour; we may notice that the surface of the match-box is predominantly yellow, but most probably do not observe what shade of yellow it is. Thus, while it is possible to hold that my visual field at any given moment consists of nothing more than an array of colours it has to be admitted that I do not see these colours merely *as* colours, and to the extent that I do see them as colours, I do not discriminate them very finely.

Are we then to say that I am actually presented with the shades of colour which I do not consciously distinguish? The argument in favour of saying this is that it is logically necessary that any colour should be of some specific shade. The fact that I do not notice the difference in shade between two separate occurrences of the colour yellow in my present visual field does not entail that the difference does not exist. It may even be maintained that there have to be differences which I am incapable of detecting. For instance, it may happen that I cannot distinguish the colour of A from that of B, or the colour of B from that of C, but that I can distinguish the colour of A from that of C. It is then held to follow that the colour of B must really be different from that of both A and C, although the difference is too fine in either case for me to be able to observe it.

The objection to this realistic way of talking about appearances is that if we do not take what we notice, however cursorily, as a criterion for what appears to us, it is not clear what other criterion is available. We could try to appeal to physiology, but apart from the objection that we have first to decide what the appearances are before we can discover what states of our nervous systems are correlated with them, this would not yield a set of rules that we could practically apply. A better course might be to assess the visual data in terms of the judgements of colour, size and shape, that the observer would make if he fully exercised his powers of discrimination, together with any further refinements which these judgements might logically be considered to entail. This would, indeed, leave us for the most part in some doubt as to what the appearances really were, but it might be argued that this did not matter, since the doubt is one that generally exists.

I think that this course is feasible, so long as one is not pursuing it in the context of the theory of knowledge. If one is interested merely in constructing a language which will serve for the description of appearances, without claiming any priority for it over a language in which terms that refer to physical objects are allowed to be primitive, one is entitled to take whatever steps will enable one to deal most satisfactorily with the technical problems. An excellent example of this is supplied by Nelson Goodman in his book *The Structure of Appearance*, where he develops a system of which the basic elements are qualia of colour, qualia of place, and qualia of time. The places, as one would expect, are places in a visual field, and the times those that furnish the temporal order of experiences rather than the dating of physical events. Concrete particulars are constituted by a relation of togetherness which holds between qualia of these different types, and between qualia of one type and combinations of qualia of the other two. Thus a particular item in my present visual field may be characterized alternatively as a colour together with a place-time, or a colour-spot together with a time, or a colour-moment together with a place. The qualities of size and shape, which characterize these particulars, are then defined, and the ordering of colours and of places is achieved on the basis of a relation of matching by a method which could also be applied to data of other sorts, such as sounds. In this way the framework is set for a systematic description of visual appearances. To what extent, if any, a description of the physical world could be fitted into this framework, or into an extension of it which admitted the data of the other senses, is left an open question.

There are two reasons why I shall follow a different procedure. In the first place, I am mainly concerned not to organize appearances into a system but rather to show how they are capable of sustaining the interpretations which we put upon them. Secondly, I propose to make it necessary for anything to be an appearance that it be something of which the observer at least implicitly takes notice, and this induces me to treat as primitive a number of concepts which, from a purely logical point of view, it might be thought preferable to construct. Beginning also with the visual field, I add to the qualia of colour, not only qualia of size and shape, but also a set of patterns of which the description may be borrowed from that of the physical objects with which they come to be identified. Thus I shall speak of a visual chair-pattern, a visual leaf-pattern, a visual cat-pattern, and so forth, and I shall construe these terms as applying to any members of the range of visual patterns which would typically lead the observer to think that he was seeing the corresponding physical object. This is not to say that the character of the visual pattern is wholly determined by the identity of the physical object which it actually presents. If the object is camouflaged the pattern may be one that is associated with a different object: in the case of a puzzle-picture one and the same object may be responsible for patterns of different types; if the observer is undergoing an hallucination there may be no object which the pattern presents. Neither is it to say that the observer characterizes these patterns *as* patterns. He notices them implicitly, in the sense that it is his registering of them that governs his identification of the physical objects which he thinks he sees. They provide the main visual clues on which our everyday judgements of perception are based.

Both spatial and temporal relations hold between these patterns and between them and qualia of other sorts. Thus, a face-pattern encloses a nose-pattern; a cat-pattern may be spatially coincident with a quale of black; a bird-pattern may appear at successive moments at different points in a visual field. Spatial relations hold only between data of the same sense which are partners in the same sense-field, but temporal relations may hold between data of different senses. For instance, a visual bird-pattern may precede or follow an occurrence of a bird-note. It must be made clear that these descriptions are intended to be purely qualitative. The reference to a bird-note should not be understood as implying that the sound is caused by a bird. It serves only to characterize a sound of a distinctive type.

It has been argued, notably by Berkeley,[1] that the visual-field is originally two-dimensional and that we come to see things in depth only through the association of sight with touch. Against this, psychologists like William James have maintained that depth is as much an intrinsic property of our visual-fields as are length and breadth.[2] Since the arguments on which Berkeley relies are drawn from optics, whereas James takes his stand upon the way things actually seem, the issue between them is not a straightforward question of fact, but rather a disagreement over what is to count as primitive. Since we have chosen to adopt a psychological rather than a physiological criterion for determining what appearances are, we can side on this point with William James. This means that we can conceive of the spatial relations between qualia in three dimensions as being presented with the same immediacy as the qualia themselves. In the same way, I take the temporal relations of simultaneity and precedence to be directly given, with the consequence that the time at which a sense-field occurs is treated as having some duration. In both psychological and physical terms, this duration is likely to be short, but no general measure can be set. It is for the observer to judge in any given instance at what point an earlier datum passes out of the content of his present experience and into the domain of memory. In many cases the distinction will not be sharp.

At the most elementary stage, a quale is particularized simply by the recording of its occurrence. The primitive language-game, if I

[1] George Berkeley. *A New Theory of Vision.*
[2] William James. *The Principles of Psychology*, Vol. II, Ch. XX.

may so call it, consists merely in designating presented qualia, together, perhaps, with their spatio-temporal relations. It is these relations that set the limits of the sense-field in which the qualia occur. Indeed, since at this stage spatio-temporal relations do not extend beyond the presented field, except in so far as temporal relations may serve to correlate the data of different senses, we can actually define a visual or tactual sense-field as consisting of anything to which some designated quale is both spatially and temporally related. This makes the particular identity of the sense-field, and of the items in it, dependent on the context. We cannot exclude the possibility that the same configuration of qualia is presented on various occasions, but there can be only one such assemblage with which the observer is actually confronted when he records the occurrence of the items he picks out. If we wish to particularize qualia in a purely descriptive way, we have to proceed to a further stage at which we are able to conceive of sense-fields as having predecessors and successors. We can then take advantage of the empirical fact that complete repetition occurs only in short stretches of anyone's experience, and identify a sense-field by reference not only to its own character but also to that of its neighbours, and if necessary to that of their neighbours, and so on until we obtain a complex which is in fact unique. This method is not foolproof. It fails, for example, in the case where two different periods of unconsciousness are each interrupted briefly by qualitatively identical experiences. Such exceptional cases can, however, be provisionally disregarded. They will not be found to impede the progress of the argument. The resources which are needed to deal with them will become available to us only when we have constructed a physical system into which we can then re-interpret the elements on which it was based. I intend to show later how this is done.

B The Question of Privacy

When qualia are turned into particulars, whether by being located demonstratively or descriptively, I shall usually refer to them as percepts. In this I follow Russell, who also came to think of percepts as constituted out of qualities, and the term was used in much the same way before him by the pragmatists, Peirce and William James. There is, however, one important point in which I differ from Russell. Unlike him, I do not characterize percepts from the outset as private entities. It is obvious that qualia are not private entities, since they are universals which can be exemplified in anyone's experience. It might, however, be thought that privacy accrued to them when they were turned into percepts, in as much as their particularization has been made to depend on their location in sense-fields which are presented to a single observer. But the answer to this is that while the reference to a particular observer may occur in our explanation of the way that percepts come into being, it does not, and indeed cannot, occur in the primitive designation of percepts themselves. As I have tried to make clear, this is simply a matter of recording the presence of a set of patterns. Since persons do not yet come into the picture, there is no implication that the patterns occur in the experience of any particular observer, nor, therefore, that their concretion into percepts gives any one person a monopoly of them.

Not only, then, is it not necessary to characterize percepts as private from the outset; it would not be legitimate. The antithesis between what is private and what is public, in the sense which is here in question, comes into play only at a level where we have the means both of referring to different persons and of distinguishing between their inner experiences and the external objects which they perceive in common. I shall try to show later how this stage can be attained. At the level at which we are now operating the question of privacy or publicity simply does not arise.

Nevertheless, our experiential propositions do possess a feature which is the main target of the objections which Wittgenstein has raised against the possibility of what he calls a private language. The only criterion for determining the truth of these propositions is the observer's recognition of the patterns which he picks out. But what guarantee is there that he recognizes them correctly? He can appeal to his memory of previous occasions on which the same pattern, or what he assumes to be the same pattern, was presented to him. But how can he be sure that his memory is not playing him false? The answer is that he can at this stage have no better reason than his feeling sure. If he is satisfied with his judgement, that is all that can be asked for. As Goodman puts it, the identification of a presented quale is settled by the observer's decree.[1]

The objection then is that for anything to qualify as a language, it must consist of signs which are employed in accordance with

[1] Nelson Goodman. *The Structure of Appearance*, p. 134.

rules, and that this condition is not satisfied if the speaker is able simply to decree what is right: his decrees must be subject to some independent check. My answer is just to deny that this is a good enough reason for saying that the condition is not satisfied. The speaker of our primitive language can be assumed to have his habits of classification and these will constitute the rules. At the most primitive level there are indeed no checks, but they too can be supplied as soon as the observer starts to associate percepts over a wider range. He then may find that different decrees which he is disposed to issue come into conflict and consequently decide to rescind one of them. The decree which he rescinds may then be said to have constituted the infringement of a rule. Admittedly, he will still not be able to distinguish between the case in which he has been false to his habitual method of classification and that in which his experience is deviant, but this is a distinction for which there is no use at this stage. To make it, we should need the resources of the theory which we are engaged in developing.

This answer may appear more convincing, when it is shown that in this matter the speakers of what is deemed to be a public language are essentially in the same position. For, as I have argued else-where,[1] we too are obliged in the end to rely simply on our powers of recognition. When we are referring to what we conceive to be persistent objects, we may indeed have other specimens at hand by which to check our usage. Even when this is not possible, we may be able to compare our verdict with that of other speakers. But then the specimens must themselves be recognized. When other speakers are consulted, their signs or gestures have to be identified, if anything is to be learned from them. In the end we must simply decide that this is an instance of such and such a word or such and such another type of object. We do, indeed, have the advantage over the players of the primitive language-game that we command a much wider area within which our decisions can be cross-checked, but this is only a difference of degree. Even though we do not, as a rule, explicitly characterize the percepts which alone permit us to recognize physical objects or to receive any information from other people, our power to apply our language to the world depends on their being implicitly identified. Unless the primitive language-game were possible, our more sophisticated language-game could not be played.

[1] See *The Concept of a Person*, pp. 41-3.

A similar and equally unsound objection to our procedure is that the use of sentences which refer to percepts could not be understood by anyone who did not already understand the use of sentences which refer to physical objects. From this it is thought to follow that we are already pre-supposing the system which we are professing to construct. This objection gains some plausibility from the fact that I introduced percepts by whittling down our ordinary judgements of perception, and from the fact that my designations of qualia were largely borrowed from those of the physical objects which they are ordinarily taken to present. Nevertheless this plausibility is only superficial. In explaining, as opposed to defining, the use of unfamiliar terms, one is free to use any means to make oneself intelligible, and in devising a technical vocabulary, one is free to take account of the purposes which it is intended to serve. The objection would hold good only if I had so contrived my references to percepts that they logically entailed the assumption of the existence of physical objects, and this we have seen not to be the case.

But, it may be argued, even if the reference to percepts does not have this logical consequence, still our power to identify percepts does logically depend on our power to identify physical, or anyhow public, objects, and this is equally objectionable. The argument is that the qualia out of which percepts are constituted are supposed to be defined ostensively and that only what is public is ostensively definable. It is true that I have taken care not to characterize percepts as private entities, but equally I have not characterized them as public. The point that matters here is that I am allowing their character to be determined by the verdict of a single observer, independently of the way things seem to anybody else.

But why should it be thought that an object has to be public to be ostensively definable? If the reason is just that any use of language has to conform to some public standard of correctness, we are brought back to the previous objection, which I have already met. If it is rather that only a public object can be pointed to, in the way that I can point to my physical possessions but not to my thoughts, the simple answer is that to suppose that ostensive definitions require pointing is to take the word 'ostensive' much too literally. Not only that, but the view of the distinction between what is public and what is private which underlines this argument is altogether too naive. Objects are not given as either public or private. The distinction comes into operation only under the auspices of a theory in which a sense is attached to saying that different persons see and touch the same chairs and tables, books and trees and stars, see the same pictures in the cinema, even hear the same sounds, taste the same tastes and smell the same smells, but no sense is attached to saying that they similarly inspect one another's thoughts and feelings and sensations. I shall attempt later on to show how this distinction is arrived at.[1] For the present, I wish only to remark that it has no essential bearing on the way in which one learns to characterize the different parties to it. When we teach someone ostensively the name of what is classed in the theory as a public object we bring him into a situation in which we assume that he will have, let us say, a visual experience which is similar to our own, and that he will come to put a similar interpretation on it. If he subsequently seems to us to repeat the word that we have taught him in a way that we find appropriate, we infer that he has learned his lesson. When we teach someone the name of what is classed in the theory as a private sensation, we again rely on discovering him in a situation where we assume that he is having an experience similar to that which we should have under similar conditions, and we expect him to put a similar interpretation on it; for instance, sooner or later not to regard it, in the way small children are said to do, as a property of the stimulus, but rather as a state of his own. In this case also we infer that he has learned his lesson if he seems to us to repeat the word in a way that we find appropriate to our own experience; not indeed, normally, our experience of a similar sensation, but our observation of conditions in which it seems to us that the use of the word is called for. In either case there is the problem of drawing his attention to the right item in his experience. When it is a question of his having to select a percept from his visual field, the effect of our making a gesture may, indeed, be helpful, but even then it is not indispensable.

I shall be dealing later on with the problem of our right to attribute experiences to others.[2] The point that I now wish to make is that if there is a difficulty here, it arises just as much with respect to the perception of what are deemed to be public objects and events, as with respect to so-called inner states and processes. Those who maintain that inner processes stand in need of outward

[1] See below pp. 104–6.
[2] See below pp. 132–5.

criteria are justified in the sense that we need some observable evidence on which to base our belief that some other person is having such and such thoughts or feelings or sensations, but equally we need some observable evidence on which to base the belief that some other person is perceiving any physical object. If I have any philosophical reason for doubting whether another person has feelings similar to mine, or indeed any feelings at all, it will equally be a reason for doubting whether he perceives physical objects in the same way as I do, or indeed whether he perceives anything at all. The insistence on outward criteria does not avoid this problem, and the choice of percepts as a basis for the construction of the physical world does not worsen it.

The mistake which philosophers who have followed this procedure have too commonly made is that of assuming that if they start with percepts, they must also start with a percipient, to whom the percepts are exclusively attributed. Not only is this illegitimate for the reasons which I have already given, but it leads to insuperable difficulties. If the percipient is just the philosopher himself, which alone would seem to be warranted, he will be hard put to escape the conclusion reached by the German Idealist, Fichte, that 'the world is my idea'; a proposition which is simply false if taken as referring only to the speaker and contradictory if it is generalized.[1] If he tries, inconsistently, to assemble the data of a number of percipients, he falls foul of the objection that no one can be in a position to perform this synthesis. These difficulties are avoided by making percepts neutral, which is not to be confused with making them common. I shall, indeed, represent the theory out of which the physical world is constituted as being developed by a single observer. This Robinson Crusoe approach is not meant to be historical, but only to do justice to the fact that any knowledge of the world which anyone acquires is bound to be based upon his own experiences. It might seem, at first sight, as if this is to take the idealist position which I have just been condemning, but there are two vital points of difference. The first and most important is that the observer is not permitted to conceive of the data with which he works as private to himself. We shall see that this is eventually possible, but only when the theory has been developed and is allowed to transform its own origins. The second is that the observer is not identified either with myself or with any other

[1] See below pp. 126–7.

person. If I am asked who is then supposed to carry out the construction, my answer is that we can think of it as being carried out by anyone who disposes of the necessary percepts.

C Outline of the Construction

It is obvious that our observer can make no progress so long as we confine his attention to the contents of a single visual field. We may for the present continue to restrict his data to those provided by the sense of sight, but we need now to credit him with both memories and expectations. He is not, of course, in a position to prove that his memories are correct, but it is not required that he should be. It is not even necessary to postulate that his memories are in fact correct, but only that he holds the appropriate beliefs about his past experiences. If it is asked how these memories and expectations could be generated, a sufficient answer, except that he speaks of thoughts instead of percepts, has been given by William James. 'If the present thought is of ABCDEFG, the next one will be of BCDEFGH, and the one after that of CDEFGHI – the lingerings of the past dropping successively away, and the incomings of the future making up the loss. These lingerings of old objects, these incomings of new, are the germs of memory and expectation, the retrospective and the prospective sense of time. They give that continuity to consciousness without which it could not be called a stream.'[1] The implication is that sense-fields overlap in their contents, and that this makes it natural for the relation of temporal precedence, which is originally given as holding between members of a single sense-field, to be projected on to its neighbours on either side. If this relation is then conceived to hold between the members of these sense-fields and members of their neighbours, and if the exercise of memory endows it also with the power to bridge gaps in consciousness, one can come to conceive of the domain of temporal relations as being, if not infinitely, at least indefinitely extended. In the case of the past, this need not go so far as an actual belief in the existence of percepts that precede the earliest that are remembered. It is enough that this be treated as an open possibility.

The overlapping of sense-fields can also be regarded as facilitating the projection of spatial relations beyond the limits in which they are originally given. Thus a percept which appears at the right-hand edge of one visual field may in succeeding fields appear

[1] William James. *The Principles of Psychology*, Vol. I, p. 606–7.

at the centre and finally at the left-hand edge; the percepts on the left of the original field are not found in its successors, and fresh percepts appear upon the right. At the same time, the observer remembers that the percepts which have disappeared from view bore the same spatial relation to the surviving percept as it now seems to bear to the new arrivals. Accordingly, he comes to think of these successive sense-fields as spatially adjacent. The result, here again, is that any given visual field can come to be regarded as indefinitely extensible.

An important empirical fact, without which, indeed, the development of our theory would not be possible, is that the observer inhabits a predominantly stable world. What I mean by this, in physical terms, is that although things may change their perceptible qualities, they mostly do so gradually and very often by stages between which there is no perceptible difference, and although they may change their relative positions they mostly stay put, in the sense that there are many other things to which they bear constant spatial relations over fairly long periods of time. One result of this is that the process by which a percept appears at different positions in successive fields is often found to be reversible. Percepts similar to those that appeared on the former run occur in the same spatial relations as their predecessors stood to one another. From different angles of approach the members of the various series appear in different orders, but their qualities remain very similar, and the spatial relations within the series remain constant. This makes it natural for the observer to adopt a new measure of identity, according to which the corresponding percepts in these different series are not merely similar but identical. Not only that, but the fact that these percepts are recoverable, after longer lapses of time, and are then found to have much the same qualities, to stand in much the same spatial relations to one another, and to appear in much the same wider environment, leads him to think of them as having persisted throughout the interval. In this way, percepts which appear to him successively are conceived to exist simultaneously and to occupy permanent positions in an indefinitely extended three-dimensional visual space.

At this point the objection may be raised that we are assuming a greater degree of constancy among our observer's percepts than is justified by the facts of our experience. Even if we assume, in physical terms, that the objects in his environment are relatively static, and that their real qualities do not noticeably change, still they are going to look different to him, according as he sees them in different lights, or from different distances, or from different angles, or according as his own condition varies. How then can he naturally come to conceive of any single percept as persisting in each case?

To a considerable extent, I have already provided against this objection by the degree of generality which I have allowed into the original designations of qualia. The characterization of a quale as, say, a cat-pattern, leaves room for appreciable differences among the presentations which answer to it; in some cases, indeed, these differences will be greater than is consonant with ascribing identity to the percepts that display them. A more specific designation will then be needed. This will still allow for some variation in the percepts to which it applies, but not so much as to destroy the constancy of the pattern. The percept which is conceived to persist may be said to be standardized, in the sense that it constitutes a model which the actual percepts match more or less closely. From now on, I shall speak of these standardized percepts as visual continuants. There is then no reason why a visual continuant should not be regarded as subject to change. For instance, it may be spatially coincident with a quale of black at one time and with a quale of grey at another. It is to be noted that for our observer all changes are objective. He is not yet in a position to distinguish between the variations in appearances which are due to changes in the object and those which are due to changes in the environment, or in his spatial relation to the object, or in himself: indeed, he cannot as yet be credited with any conception of himself.

The next step is to allow for the possibility of movement. For this, we have to think of the observer as abstracting from the other qualities of percepts and considering only their extension. Then, since the extension of a percept is equivalent to the amount of space which it occupies, it becomes possible for him to think of places in detachment from their occupants. Not only the visual continuant, but also the place where it is, come to be regarded as permanently there. Since the place has to be identified as the meeting-point of a number of sensory routes, which are themselves sufficiently constant to be re-identifiable, the constituents of the observer's world have still to be predominantly static. Nevertheless a certain amount of movement can now be admitted. If a number of very similar percepts appear successively at neighbouring places, they may be deprived of their separate identities and treated as a single percept in motion. In the case where, as we should say, only the result of the displacement is observed, and not the actual process, it can be held either that the visual continuant has moved, or that it has ceased to exist and another one, closely resembling it, has come into existence at another place. The first of these hypotheses is the more likely to be adopted if the continuant is one of a kind that has frequently been observed to move. In other cases, the observer has no reasons for deciding the question one way or the other. He will acquire them only when he commands a much richer theory, in which causes are assigned for things coming into existence or ceasing to exist.

Among the visual continuants which the observer comes to posit there are some that are constructed on a different principle from the rest. The percepts which enter into their constitution do not regularly appear in a similar environment, except in so far as the visual continuants in question are seen to stand in constant spatial relations to one another. The peculiarity of these percepts consists first in their tendency to occupy similar positions in the sense-fields in which they figure and, secondly, in their pervasiveness; the qualia which they particularize are found in an unusually high proportion of sense-fields. It is on this account that they are transformed into persistent objects. These visual continuants are, in physical terms, those parts of the observer's body that he customarily sees. The acquisition of the concept of this body as a whole depends upon a fusion of visual with tactual and kinaesthetic data, and both accompanies and facilitates the identification of visual with tactual space.

Although the same general method serves for the construction of tactual as of visual space, there is the important difference that the tactual field is normally much less extensive than the visual, so that if our observer lacked the sense of sight, he would need to associate tactual qualia with kinaesthetic qualia of movement, and perhaps also with auditory qualia, in order to arrive at the conception of tactual places as permanently accessible. For one who is not so handicapped, we can take visual space to be primary, and then consider how it can be made to accommodate the data of touch. For this purpose we can take advantage of the double aspect of tactual percepts; in physical terms, the fact that they are felt both in the object which is being touched and, say, in the fingers which are touching it. Accordingly, the tactual percept comes to be located at the point of temporary coincidence of these different visual continuants. Since the visual percepts belonging to the observer's body are a relatively constant factor, the variations in the tactual qualia are ascribed to the differences in the other visual percepts. By this means the visual continuants of which they are members become endowed with tactual qualities. Once the association of visual with tactual qualities has been established in the cases where, as we should say, an object is both touched and seen, it is easily extended to the cases where the object is touched but not seen, and also to the cases where it is seen but not touched. The possibility of this last step depends on the fact that tactual, like visual, qualia are found to be reinstatable at the junction of relatively constant visual and tactual routes.

The association of visual with tactual qualities also permits the observer to round out the concept of his body. The parts of his body which he sees only in reflection are thought to be adjacent to the directly visible parts, rather than located separately in the place where the reflection is seen, because of their contiguity to them in tactual space. It is because of this contiguity and also because it is observed to be maintained when, as we should say, the body is displaced, that the various parts, which can still be represented as different visuo-tactual continuants, are also thought to constitute a single whole.

In speaking of the way in which our observer develops the concept of his own body, I do not mean to imply that he already conceives of it as his own. We have not yet given him any reason for distinguishing himself from the objects which he perceives. So far as he is concerned, at this stage, his body is just one among other visuo-tactual continuants. If it comes to assume a special importance for him, it is partly because it is the locus of kinaesthetic data, in a way the other continuants are not, but mainly because it is distinguished from the others by being what Peirce called the central body. Not only is it exceptionally pervasive, in the way we have already noted, but it supplies, as it were, the view-point from which the world appears to him.

At this stage we may suppose that the observer begins to make some simple causal correlations. He incorporates sounds and smells and tastes into his world-picture by tracing them to their apparent sources, this being partly a matter of locating the places of their maximum intensity, and partly one of noting the visuo-tactual conditions under which they are produced; and he also associates changes in the position or quality of one continuant with changes in the position or quality of another. In this way, the status of the central body is still further enhanced, because of the extent to which it is associated with changes in other things. In particular, it comes to be represented as the instrument through which the observer's desires for change are realized.

Having thus acquired some notion of the way in which the world works, the observer is at last able to take the first step towards drawing a distinction between his own experiences and the things which he perceives. The great majority of his percepts are interpreted objectively. The qualia which they particularize and the relations in which they stand are treated as qualities and relations of the rudimentary physical objects into which they have grown. There may, however, be some experiences which cannot be fitted into the general pattern. They are, perhaps, visual hallucinations, or dreams which the observer may be supposed to recollect, or even his day-dreams if these are sufficiently vivid to be mistakable for percepts. From his point of view, there is nothing amiss with these experiences as such. It is just that they do not noticeably concur with one another, nor do they fit into the general picture of the world which he has developed. He therefore distinguishes the various subsidiary accounts of the way things are, which these untoward experiences would lead him to give, from what we may call the main or central account, which is based on the general run of his experiences.

This is about as far as our Robinson Crusoe can be expected to go without a Man Friday to assist him. As an object of perception, Man Friday is just another visuo-tactual continuant. His importance to Crusoe and that of the other observers, whom we may now admit on to the scene, is that they also make sounds or marks or movements which Crusoe is able to interpret as signs. They share this capacity with the central body. What they do not share, so far as our original observer is concerned is the centrality of this body or its use as an instrument to realize his wishes.

In communicating with these other observers, our Crusoe finds that they appear to be giving information which very largely tallies with the course of his experience. In particular, he judges that it regularly corroborates his main account of the world. He also finds, however, that these people tell subsidiary stories which fit in neither with his main account, nor with his subsidiary accounts. In this way he acquires the idea of himself not only as an object represented by the central body, which figures in a main account of the world that the other makers of signs accept, but also as a teller of stories that they do not corroborate. From this he infers that the events which these subsidiary stories describe are events that exist only for him and correspondingly that the events which occur in the subsidiary stories that the others tell are events that exist only for them. The making of the private-public distinction thus goes together with the acquisition of self-consciousness and the attribution of consciousness to others.

In the final stage the private-public distinction is taken a great deal further. What happens is that the theory which I have been calling the main account of the world predominates over its origins. The objects to which I have been referring as visuo-tactual continuants are cut loose from their moorings. The possibility, which has already been accorded them, of existing at times when they are not perceived is extended to the point where it is unnecessary to their existence that they ever should be perceived, or even that there should be any observers to perceive them. Since the theory also requires that these objects do not change their perceptible qualities except as a result of some physical alteration in themselves, they come to be contrasted with the fluctuating impressions that different observers have of them. In this way the objects are severed from the actual percepts from which they have been abstracted and are even regarded as being causally responsible for them. A distinction is drawn between the main account of the world, as it is in itself, and any particular relation of it, with the result that all the observer's experiences, not only those that furnish the subsidiary accounts, but even those that furnish the main account are taken to be subjective. Thus the percepts out of which the theory grew are re-interpreted into it, and given a subordinate status. So far from being the only things that there are thought to be, they may be denied any independent existence, and treated merely as states of the observer. Whether they can be transmuted to the extent of being identified with physical states is a question which we shall have to consider later on, when we deal with the problem of body and mind. The point which now concerns us is that once the theory of the physical world has been developed, whether or not it has to allow room for objects or properties which are not classified as physical, we are entitled to let it take command, in the sense that it determines what there is. The fact that in doing so it downgrades its starting-point, in much the same way as a self-made man may repudiate his humble origins, is not a logical objection to this procedure. It may have a parallel, as we shall see, in the surgery which physics may be thought to practise upon commonsense.

D Phenomenalism

As I said before, my account of the way in which the common-sense theory of the physical world is developed is not meant to be historical. Young children, who very quickly assume the theory, do not elaborate it on their own; they are taught a language which already embodies it, and whatever may be logically possible, it is factually improbable that they would arrive at it otherwise. I have told a fictitious story, the purpose of which has been to highlight the general features of our experience that make it possible for each of us to employ the theory successfully. It is in order to throw these features into stronger relief that I have represented what is in effect a process of analysis as a process of construction. In its general outline, my description of this process has been very similar to Hume's.[1] The main difference is that whereas he found in the relations of 'constancy and coherence', which our 'perceptions' exhibit, a means of explaining how we are deceived into treating them as persistent objects, I have represented these relations not as accounting for a deception but as justifying an acceptable theory.

It is to be noted that while the position which I have taken has some affinity with Mill's view that things are permanent possibilities of sensation, it is not a phenomenalist position, in the sense in which this term is usually understood. I am not suggesting that physical objects are reducible to percepts, if this is taken to mean that all the statements that we make about physical objects, even at the common-sense level, can be adequately translated into statements which refer only to percepts. If the demand for an adequate translation requires that the statements referring to percepts set out necessary and sufficient conditions for the truth of the statements about a physical object which they are meant to replace, I think it unlikely that it can be satisfied. For the conditions to be necessary

[1] See above pp. 61–3.

it would have to be the case that the statement referring to the physical object could not be true unless they obtained, and for the conditions to be sufficient it would have to be the case that the statement referring to the physical object could not be false if they did obtain. But here there is, on the one hand, the difficulty that a visuo-tactual continuant may be represented by an indefinite variety of percepts in an equal variety of contexts, so that if the percepts in question had not occurred, some others would have done as well, and, on the other hand, the objection that any description of a particular set of percepts will be bound to leave open at least the logical possibility that the observer is undergoing some illusion.[1] But even if these difficulties could be met, there is another reason why I do not wish to adopt this position. The actual percepts that are presented to any observer, or even to the totality of observers at all times, are too scanty to answer to our conception of the physical world. It was for this reason, as we have seen, that Berkeley required an ever-vigilant deity to keep the world under observation, at times when other spirits were not being supplied with the necessary ideas. But apart from any other objections that there may be to the introduction of this *deus ex machina*, it takes us outside the boundaries of phenomenalism. If the phenomenalist thesis is to be at all plausible, it has to draw on possible as well as actual percepts, with the result that most of the propositions which render its account of the world will take the form of unfulfilled conditionals. They will state that if such and such conditions, which are not in fact realized, were to be so, then such and such percepts would occur. But apart from the obvious difficulty of giving a sufficient description of the conditions in purely sensory terms, I no longer think that such conditional statements are suitable to play this part. I shall argue later on[2] that conditional statements of this sort are best understood as belonging to a secondary system, which has an explanatory function with respect to a primary system of purely factual propositions: and from this it follows that they are not themselves equipped to function as primary statements of fact.

In the scheme which I have outlined, the need to have recourse to conditional statements is avoided by our treating the passage from percepts to physical objects, not strictly as a process of logical construction, but rather, in Hume's way, as an exercise of the

[1] See my essay on Phenomenalism. *Philosophical Essays*, Ch. VI.
[2] See below pp. 151-2.

imagination. The continued and distinct existence, not of percepts, but of the objects into which they are transmuted, is simply posited. Consequently, we are able to forsake phenomenalism for a sophisticated form of realism. Under the dominion of the theory which is erected on the basis of our primitive experiential propositions, the existence of visuo-tactual continuants becomes a matter of objective fact. If, as I shall advocate, we adopt this standpoint for judging what there is, these objects become the elements of our primary system.

Earlier on, I gave a list of the different ways in which philosophers have tried to meet the argument by which the sceptic professes to show, at various levels, that our claims to knowledge, or even to rational belief, cannot be justified. The course which we have followed is a variant of what I then called the scientific approach. It would, indeed, be somewhat misleading to say that we are representing the existence of physical objects as a probable hypothesis, since this description would ordinarily be taken to apply to propositions that lie within the framework of our general theory, rather than to the principles of the theory itself. Nevertheless, the difference is only a difference of degree. The theory is vindicated not indeed by any special set of observations but by the general features of our experience on which it is founded, and since these features are contingent, it could conceivably be falsified, in the sense that our experiences might in general be such that it failed to account for them.

E Common Sense and Physics

We have seen how the objects of perception come to be detached from any actual precepts and made causally responsible for them. The question which we have now to consider is whether this process can be carried further, to the point where these objects are stripped of all their perceptible qualities and left only with the properties which the science of the day attributes to physical particles. This step is certainly not forced on us, as some philosophers have taken it to be, by our having to reckon with the causal process of perception, since this can be taken to imply no more than that the states of different entities, which are alike generated out of percepts, can be systematically correlated. There may, however, be other reasons in favour of taking it. The unprocessed object, the thing as it is in itself, if we are to have any concept of it at all, is bound to be a creature of theory: the question is only what theory this should be.

To obtain a satisfactory answer, we have to try to get clear about the relation between the scientific view of the nature of physical objects and that which can be attributed to common sense. Were Russell and Eddington right in thinking that they are incompatible? It has been argued that they were wrong on the ground that the two views relate to different subjects. Thus Ryle has suggested that they are no more incompatible than an artist's picture of a landscape is incompatible with a geologist's description of the same area, or than the annual report of the activities of a college is incompatible with the entries relating to the same activities which appear in the college's accounts.[1] What is implied by these analogies is that physics differs from common sense only in being concerned with different aspects of the same things, but even if this is true it needs further explanation. For instance, it would be hard to say what aspect of a physical object can be taken to exhaust a physicist's interests in the way that an accountant's interest in the activities which he records is limited to their cost. The other analogy may come nearer the mark, in that the geologist is concerned with the physical composition of the objects which the artist paints. But then the question remains whether their having this physical composition is indeed consistent with their really being as the artist pictures them.

This question would present no difficulty if it could be shown that the statements which enter into scientific theories were logically equivalent to statements describing the observable states of affairs by which these theories would be verified; but I have already given reasons for concluding that this is not the case.[2] There is, however, a weaker thesis which for our present purposes would achieve the same result. It could be maintained, as I suggested earlier, that the factual content of a scientific theory consisted only in those propositions of our primary system that actually supported it, and that the theory itself belonged to a secondary system, the function of which would be purely explanatory. The entities which figured in any such secondary system, to the extent that they could not be identified with objects of the primary system, would be thought of

---

[1] See G. Ryle. *Dilemmas*, pp. 75–81.
[2] See above pp. 31–3.

simply as conceptual tools which served for the arrangement of the primary facts.

The distinction between primary and secondary systems is one that needs to be made on other grounds, and I shall have more to say about it at a later stage.[1] It does not, however, strictly require that the boundaries of the actual world be drawn so narrowly as I have now proposed. It could be consistent with a realistic view of the status of physical particles. The main argument in favour of adopting such a view would be that it is more consonant with the outlook of physicists themselves.

If one does hold a realistic view, there would appear to be just two forms that it could take, both of which go back in a way to Locke. The first of them consists in transferring all the perceptible qualities of things to the observer's account, leaving things, as they are in themselves, to be represented by the necessarily imperceptible objects of physical theory. The objection to this procedure, as we have already noted, is that these imperceptible objects, having been moved into the territory which the perceptible objects have been forced to abandon, are located in perceptible space, and it is not easy to understand how spatial relations can be thought to persist when their terms have been taken away from them. The second course would be to conceive of physical particles as being what Locke called the minute parts of perceptible objects, in which case their being imperceptible would not be a necessary part of their nature, but simply an empirical consequence of their being so minute. On this view, it has just to be accepted as an empirical fact that particles which are individually colourless compose coloured objects when enough of them come together, and since these particles are conceived to be in relative motion, it also has to be conceded that we are actually in error when we believe that the surfaces of physical objects are continuous. It is just that the gaps between their minute parts are too small for us to notice. These consequences make this position less agreeable to common sense, but do not, I think, prevent it from being tenable.

It may seem strange that I have represented the question as to what there physically is as being so much a question for decision. Why should not the opposition between a realist and a pragmatic view of the status of physical particles be taken to relate to an objective matter of fact? The answer is that if the problem were

[1] See below pp. 142–55.

treated in that way, we should have no procedure for solving it. Questions as to what there is can be treated as empirical only within the framework of a theory which supplies criteria for answering them. When, as in the present case, there is the threat of conflict between two different theories both of which we are inclined to accept, we must either find a way of blending them coherently, or else remove the competition by treating only one of them as determining the character of fact and the other as purely explanatory. If I have a slight preference for the compromise which is effected by the second form of Lockean realism, it is because it makes some concession to scientific orthodoxy, without doing any great violence to the more simple theory which is naturally developed out of our experiences.

VI Body and Mind

A Persons and Their Experiences

We have seen how the positing of physical objects leads to our drawing a distinction between the objects as they are in themselves and the experiences through which we come to know them. The objects are thought to retain their perceptible properties whether or not anyone is actually perceiving them. When percepts do occur they are treated as sensations which belong to the observer in the same way as the thoughts and images and feelings that do not supply material for the construction of the physical world. The question which we must now try to answer is how these various elements are brought together and how they are related to the body by which the observer is identified.

In saying that the observer is identified by his body, I may be thought already to be making an unjustified assumption. That we have to employ physical criteria for the identification of other people will hardly be disputed, but it may well be denied that this applies also to our identification of ourselves. Descartes is not the only philosopher, much less the only person, to have believed that in being self-conscious one is aware of a spiritual substance which is housed contingently and perhaps only temporarily in the body.[1] This view may not be tenable, but it surely deserves to be examined. We are not entitled to dismiss it without a hearing.

My answer is that I am not dismissing it without a hearing. All that I have so far assumed is that self-consciousness is not a primitive datum, or in other words that the observer's experiences are not intrinsically marked as his own. They are distinguished as his experiences only by contrast with the external world and with the experiences of others who also inhabit it. But then to arrive at these

[1] Cf. René Descartes. *Discourse on Method*, Part V.

contrasts he must, as we have seen,[1] distinguish the central body from other physical objects, and in particular from those other objects which are also the sources of signs. It is, as I said, his ability to interpret these signs as corroborating his main account of the world but not as corroborating his subsidiary accounts, and also as giving subsidiary accounts which he cannot corroborate, that leads him to think of the central body as sharing with other bodies the property of being the focus of an independent series of experiences. His own experiences are thus initially characterized as those of which the central body is the focus. Once this point has been reached, it may be possible to proceed to a more sophisticated theory in which the attachment of experiences to a body, or to a particular body, is not conceived to be necessary, or even to a theory in which they are assigned a different sort of owner. Whether any such theories are tenable remains to be seen. All I am now saying is that our starting point does not exclude them.

Before we come to these theories, there is, however, a step in the argument that needs further explanation. In what way exactly are experiences allocated to the body which I have spoken of as their focus? In the case of bodily sensations, there is no problem, once the observer has carried out the synthesis of visual and tactual space. But bodily sensations, though they are always or nearly always present, make up only a small fraction of the whole range of one's experiences. Why should the observer's percepts be associated not only with the objects which they manifest but also with the central body? Why should his thoughts and images be taken to be members of the same series of experiences as his percepts?

These questions are not easy to answer, mainly, I think, because there are several different factors at work. I suppose that the reasons why the observer associates his percepts with the central body are chiefly causal. He notices that tactual percepts occur only when the objects to which the tactual properties are assigned are in contact with some part of this body; indeed, as we have already remarked,[2] there is a way in which they are also located in the body. The same double location is characteristic of percepts which belong to the sense of taste. When it comes to the data of the other senses, the causal connexion is not quite so obvious, but it is not very hard for the observer to correlate variations in these

[1] See above pp. 102-3.
[2] See above p. 102.

data with movements of the body, to note that the appearance and disappearance of visual percepts systematically coincide with the kinaesthetic sensations of having his eyes open or shut, to discover that he can cut off most of his auditory data by stopping up his ears. He may come to realize that these are not the only conditions that are necessary for the percepts to occur, but he remarks that they are constantly necessary in a way that nearly all the others are not. For instance, if two other persons are speaking, it is necessary for his auditory data to occur not only that his ears should be functioning but also that their lips should move, but whereas the movements of the lips are only respectively necessary for each series of data, the use of his ears is necessary for both. Another relevant fact is that the part played by his body is found to a greater extent to be under his control. Thus, the presence of light is a constant condition of the occurrence of his visual percepts, but it is not normally connected with his wishes in the way that the opening or shutting of his eyes, or the displacement of his body, is discovered to be.

It is also of importance that the observer's identification of himself goes together with his identification of other persons and with their identification of him. He takes the signs which emanate from these other bodies as a ground for attributing experiences to the persons with whom he now associates them, and he realizes that these persons take the signs which emanate from the central body as a ground for attributing experiences to him. Seeing himself, as it were, through their eyes, he regards the central body as belonging to him in the special way in which their bodies belong to them, and he thinks of his body not only as a contributory cause of his percepts but also as the medium through which his entertainment of them, and indeed of his experiences in general, is made known to others.

Finally, the association of his percepts with his body is reinforced by the fact that many, if not all, of them are sensibly compresent with bodily sensations. Much of the time, indeed, these sensations are not explicitly attended to, but it is arguable that even when they do not obtrude themselves upon one's notice, they are usually present in the form of a relatively constant background to more interesting items of experience. Moreover, even if we allow that some percepts are not accompanied in this way by bodily sensations, it is very probable that they will be sensibly continuous, at one or more removes, with percepts which are so accompanied. Because of this it might even be possible actually to define the attachment of a series of experiences to a particular body in terms of the location of the bodily sensations with which the members of the series are sensibly compresent or sensibly continuous.[1] It is, however, doubtful whether the empirical generalizations on which this definition would depend are sufficiently well established to make this step desirable.

However this may be, it is these relations of sensible compresence and continuity that chiefly explain how thoughts and images are brought together with percepts to form a single series of experiences. The difficulty which Hume found in his acknowledgment that 'all our distinct perceptions are distinct existences', between which he was unable to discover any 'real connexion',[2] is met by an appeal to the empirical facts. It is indeed true that our distinct perceptions are distinct existences, in the sense that they are logically independent: one can describe the character of any one of them in a way that does not entail anything about the character of the others. But from this it does not follow that they are not factually connected. What unites them in the main is that either they are experienced together, or if they occur at different times, they are separated by a stream of experience which is felt to be continuous. In talking of the relations of sensible compresence and sensible continuity, I am referring just to these familiar features of our experience.

I shall argue presently that this answer to Hume is satisfactory so far as it goes, but clearly it does not go all the way, if only because it is not in fact the case that all one's experiences do form a sensibly continuous series. There are gaps in consciousness of which we have to take account. When I wake from what I take to have been a dreamless sleep—and the fact that I do so take it is sufficient to break the sensible continuity, whether or not it really has been so—I have no doubt that I am the same person as went to sleep so many hours before; but what is it that unites my present experiences with those that I had then? The obvious answer that they are joined in memory turns out not to be correct. It is, indeed, through memory that I discover my self-identity over this period of time, but it cannot be memory that produces it. The reason why

---

[1] See my *The Origins of Pragmatism*, pp. 270–3.
[2] David Hume. *Treatise of Human Nature*, Book 5, Appendix.

it cannot is that if we make the assumption that the experiences which I think that I recall cannot fail to have been my own, we are reasoning in a circle; and if we do not make this assumption, the link is not established; the experiences in question might never have occurred, or they might belong to a different biography. It would appear, therefore, that we must again have recourse to the fact of bodily identity. My present experiences and those that occurred before the interval of unconsciousness belong to the same series because they are alike compresent with percepts which are associated with the same body. This does not preclude the possibility of paranormal occurrences which might lead us to say that two different persons inhabited the same body or that the same person inhabited different bodies at different times. The fact that the claims of memory are not in themselves sufficient to bridge a gap in sensible continuity does not mean that they carry no weight at all. In general the two criteria of memory and bodily identity work together. If the results to which they lead conflict only occasionally, one's memory is adjudged to be at fault. We shall, however, see that if they were radically divergent, there might be circumstances in which the criterion of memory could be allowed to prevail, not perhaps to the extent of our being able to dispense altogether with the physical criterion, but at least to the point where we could allow the possibility of there being something other than a one to one relation between different series of experiences and the bodies to which they are attached.

But now it may be objected that this whole account of the way in which identities are established is unnecessarily elaborate. Surely I do not have to trouble myself about the relation of my experiences to my body or even about their relations to one another in order to discover that they are my own. The very question whether they are mine seems ridiculous and out of place. I may be in doubt as to what I perceive or what I feel, but I cannot be in any doubt as to their being *my* perceptions and *my* feelings. The suggestion that this headache might not be mine at all but somebody else's is quite nonsensical.

This is true, but the reason why it is true is that when the reference is to my present experiences the personal pronoun functions as a demonstrative. The absurdity of saying that this headache might not be mine is just the absurdity of saying that this headache might not be this one. If the experiences were identified purely descriptively and not demonstratively, the question would not have to be absurd. It is quite legitimate to ask whether an experience of such and such a sort is one that I am having. This becomes clearer when the experience is located in the past or in the future. Admittedly, the question is usually cast in a form which makes it appear to relate to the character of the experience rather than to the identity of the owner. One asks 'Shall I have such and such an experience?' rather than 'Will such and such an experience be mine?' Nevertheless, the two formulations are equivalent. In each case the answer will be 'yes', only if a future experience of the relevant kind is related to those that I am now having in the way that I have described.

The position changes in the same manner if the personal pronoun is replaced by a description of the person. It then becomes possible to attach a good sense to saying that one can be in doubt or mistaken about one's own identity. It is in this sense that people who have lost their memories can be said not to know who they are. This is a matter not only of their not knowing their names but also of their not knowing facts about their past by which they could be identified. Of course they still know that they are themselves, but this is to know nothing more than that they still exist as persons to whom a demonstrative can be used to point.

B   Are There Mental Substances?

This is not, however, the only objection that can be raised against our procedure. Surely, it may be said, we obtain a much simpler theory, and thereby avoid a great many difficulties, if we take the personal pronoun just to refer to a single persistent mental entity. Why should not the unity of a person's experiences, whether they are simultaneous or successive, be held to consist in their having a common relation to this entity rather than a variety of relations to one another? Have we not, indeed, been tacitly making this assumption all along? I have spoken of the relation of sensible compresence as holding between elements which are experienced together: of the relation of sensible continuity as holding between elements which are felt to be continuous. But surely this implies the existence of a subject who has the experiences. If something is felt, surely there must be something to feel it, call it a mind, or a soul, or a self, or what you will. As Bradley put it, in criticism of one of Mill's disciples. 'Mr Bain collects that the mind is a collection. Has he ever thought who collects Mr Bain ?'[1]

This argument is plausible but, I think, fallacious. As I have already suggested,[2] there is no reason why percepts should not be presented as spatio-temporally related, and no reason why temporal relations should not similarly hold between experiential data of different types. The question, therefore, is whether the character of being an item of experience is one that can accrue to a quale through its relation to other qualia or whether it must consist in a relation to a subject which is conscious of these elements and distinct from them. The ground for taking this second view is, presumably, that the elements have to be identified : they are brought under concepts and they give rise to judgements which usually go beyond them. Accordingly, there must be an agent to carry out these tasks. But the answer to this is that in so far as these judge-ments are made explicitly, they can be taken to consist in the occurrence of thoughts which are compresent or continuous with the items in question: when they are not explicit the existence of the appropriate behaviour, which here may be understood to include not only physical movements but also the occurrence of subsequent thoughts, can serve as the criterion for their being tacitly made. I draw no radical distinction here between the thoughts that are contained in the production of sounds or visible marks, and those that consist in what Ryle has called 'silent soliloquy',[3] and I admit that in either case there is a serious prob-lem about the way in which these sounds or marks, or their mental counterparts, can come to refer beyond themselves. This is, however, a problem that arises in any event. If we bring in a mental agent, we have to explain how he contrives to endow a sign with meaning, and if we can say what this endowment consists in, there would seem to be no reason why we cannot ascribe it to the signs without the assumption that they draw it from this source. I think that it in fact consists in the interpretation of one sign by another and in the inter-relation of the utterance of these signs with other forms of behaviour,[4] but it may be disputed whether an explanation of this kind can be made to work without the help of

---

[1] F. H. Bradley. *Ethical Studies*, p. 39.
[2] See above p. 92.
[3] G. Ryle. *The Concept of Mind*, p. 47.
[4] See *The Origins of Pragmatism*, IV.B.

some semantic concept, such as that of truth. The point remains that if we do have to make use of such a concept, there again seems no reason why it should be thought to require a reference to an enduring mental agent.

But what of our possession of self-consciousness? Who *does* collect Mr Bain? Because I am able not only to be aware of my present feelings, but also to be aware that I am aware of them, and perhaps even aware that I am aware that I am aware of them, and because this series can be prolonged indefinitely, at least without doing any violence to grammar, if not to psychology, there is a temptation to think of one's self as a set of Chinese boxes, each surveying the one which it immediately encloses. The need to supply this series with an upper term has led some philosophers, notably Kant, to postulate a self which is always a subject and never in its turn an object of consciousness. It is to this 'transcendental' self, as Kant called it,[1] that the task is assigned of processing the raw material of experience, so that a world emerges in which one's everyday self, or selves, can find a place. In Kant's system, the transcendental ego stands outside this world. Its labours make our experiences possible, but because it is not a possible object of experience, it is not itself in space or time.

Clearly there can be no empirical evidence for the existence of any such entity. It is postulated on the assumption that if the world, as we know it, is our construction, we must be both in it and outside it. In it, as objects which are constructed, but outside it as subjects which perform the construction; for it would be contradictory to suppose that such subjects constructed themselves. But here the metaphor of construction is misleading. I have employed it as a means of referring to the derivation of concepts and not to suggest that we bring into existence the things to which the concepts apply. To construct our selves, in this sense, is merely to find out the features of our experience which make it possible for the concept of a self to be satisfied, but these features exist, independently of our bringing them to light. I have, indeed, argued that persons, like other physical objects, are the products of theory, but this does not entail either that they cannot themselves develop the theory in which they figure, or that the theory cannot consistently provide for the existence of objects which are

[1] See in his *Critique of Pure Reason* the chapter on the 'Deduction of the Pure Concepts of the Understanding'.

independent of the persons who develop it. There is circularity in that the theory is presupposed by the account of its own development, but this is unavoidable. As I said earlier,[1] we must have some standpoint from which to survey the world and we cannot prise off the world, or any part of it, from our conception of it. Kant's attempt, therefore, to put the transcendental ego outside the world as we know it is bound to be a failure. This ego becomes, as William James said, 'simply nothing'.[2] It is an invention that does not explain but merely pays tribute to the relativity of things to our description of them.

Let us return then to the facts. We have still to account for the apparent duality of subject and object in the phenomenon of self-consciousness. The first point to be noted is that the self as such is not an object of acquaintance, not because it lies too deeply hidden but rather for a logical reason. When Hume said that he could never perceive his self without one or more perceptions,[3] or indeed perceive anything but the perceptions, he was not merely drawing attention to an empirical fact. Though this may not have been entirely clear to him, he had hit upon the logical point that nothing would count as one's discovering oneself apart from any perceptions. What happens when one is self-conscious is that one claims some present or past experience as one's own, where its being one's own is a matter of its being related to other experiences and to one's body in the ways that I have described. The making of the claim itself consists in the occurrence of a thought or the utterance of a sign which is intended to refer to the experience in question. There is no need, therefore, for any duality but the duality, or multiplicity, of particular experiences. The use of a personal pronoun or a proper name to refer to oneself suggests that there is some constant object which it names; some object which is distinct from the body, since the expression 'I' and 'my body' are not simply substitutable; rather, my body is grammatically represented as one of my possessions. But grammar is not always a safe guide to the facts. In fact, the use of the personal pronoun or the proper name commits us to no more than is strictly necessary for the establishment of one's self-identity; and for this we have seen that the occurrence of experiences which are

---

[1] See above p. 49.
[2] See William James, *The Principles of Psychology*, Vol. 1, p. 365.
[3] See above p. 61.

suitably related to one's body and to one another can be taken to be enough.

If this is correct, I have shown that the postulation of mental substances is not needed to explain self-consciousness. I have not shown that they do not exist. But now if we ask what other grounds there could be for believing that they do exist, we find that there are none. Not only that, but the part which these substances are supposed to play has simply not been written for them. Exactly how are these substances related to the experiences which they are supposed to own or to the bodies which they are supposed to occupy? What criteria are there for their identity? Would it make any noticeable difference to me if I kept my memories and my physical continuity, but woke every morning with a different soul? How do I know that this does not actually happen? Without any answers to such questions, we have no concept to evaluate. As William James put it, 'The spiritualists do not deduce any properties of the mental life from otherwise known properties of the soul. They simply find various characters in the mental life and these they clap into the soul, saying "Lo! behold the source from which they flow".'[1] But an entity which is neither observable nor fulfils any explanatory function can have no interest for us.

C Vagaries of Personal Identity

If we reject the idea of there being mental substances, are we then committed to denying the capacity of persons to exist apart from their bodies? The belief that human beings survive their corporeal death has been widely held, and while many of those who hold it also hold that their bodies will at some time be restored to them, others believe that they will continue to exist in a different body, and others still that they will enjoy a disembodied existence. The question that I now wish to consider is not so much whether there is any good reason to hold any of these beliefs as whether the situations which would be required to verify them are logically possible.

The main problem here is that of the relative weight of the criterion of memory and that of bodily continuity in determining personal identity. I remarked earlier on that these criteria normally worked together, but that it was at least conceivable that they should radically diverge, and I added that there might then be

[1] *Ibid.* p. 397.

circumstances in which it would seem reasonable to give preference
to the criterion of memory. The idea that there could be such
circumstances may become more acceptable if we first consider an
intermediate case in which there is still some physical continuity.
Let us suppose that medical science has advanced to the point
where it is possible to transplant not merely hearts but brains.
There may be physical grounds for believing that this would never
be feasible but surely the hypothesis is not logically contradictory.
If this were to be done, should we not have a strong motive for
saying that the person whose brain had been transferred to a
different body continued to exist in that body ? On the assumption
that memories are causally dependent on the brain, it would surely
seem to the person in whose body the brain was now located that
he was the same person as the one from whose body it had been
taken, and if, as well as identifying himself with this person, he
also, as might be expected, displayed the same character, we might
very reasonably accept his claim. On the other hand, we should
also have a motive for denying it, in that one of the two persons in
question must be supposed to have died, and it appears more
natural to say that this is the brain-donor rather than its recipient.
This motive would be greater if there had been a significant
disparity between the two persons before the operation; if, for
example, the recipient of the brain were a young girl, and its
donor an elderly man. In that case, we might prefer to say that the
girl had inherited the old man's personality, rather than that he
continued to exist in the form of a young girl. Whether she would
be able to see it in this way is more doubtful, but I suppose that
she might if the social pressures were strong enough.

Now that we have embarked upon science fiction, let us imagine
a more complicated case. There is reason to believe that each of the
hemispheres of the brain is capable of sustaining the exercise of
memory. Suppose then that a person's brain were removed and
that its hemispheres were severally transferred to two other bodies
from which, as in the previous example, the brains had also been
removed. The result would be that each of the persons who
occupied these bodies would believe himself to be identical with
the brain-donor. Could these claims be accepted ? The difficulty
here is that these persons would not themselves be identical, so that
if we were to accept their claims, we should be violating what
is taken to be the necessary principle that things which are

identical with the same thing are identical with one another. What might happen, if such operations became frequent, would be that we should modify our conception of personal identity, so that persons came to be thought capable, like worms, of being divided into discrete parts, each of which functioned as a replica of the original. It would still not be true that the recipients of the hemispheres were severally identical with the donor, but they would be identical with him collectively. Alternatively, we again might find it more natural to say that the donor had ceased to exist and that two other persons had inherited his personality.

If such fictions are at all credible, it is because they trade on the not too far-fetched hypothesis of brain-transference. It would be more of a simple fairy story if we just supposed that a person's memories and character were transferred from one body to another, without there being any physical explanation. Yet it would seem that this too is logically possible and, what is more, that it would raise exactly the same problems about personal identity. There are, indeed, those who argue that if we have the option, in these examples, of saying that the same person successively occupies different bodies, it is only because the bodies are not totally different: the transference of the brain assures at least some physical continuity. It is, however, hard to see why this should be thought essential. The person who claims identity with the previous owner of the brain does not do so on the ground that this brain has been transferred to him, or rather, as he would say, remained in his possession: he does so because of his memories. Indeed, he may not even know what operation has been performed on him. He awakes, as from a period of sleep, to find that he occupies a different body. Again, we are not obliged to tell the story in this way, rather than by saying that one person has mysteriously inherited another's memories, but again it would seem a legitimate choice, especially if the person whom we allow to have survived does not also have memories of a different existence and his previous body is no longer animate.

There may be those who are inclined to protest that this cannot simply be a matter of choice. Either the person in question really has survived in another body, or there has been a transfer of memories from one person to another. We may not be able to discover which is the right answer, but one of them must in fact be true and the other false. But to speak in this way is to miss the salient point that these would be circumstances in which our usual criteria of identity did not yield an unequivocal answer, and until we had decided on the rules that were to be followed in such cases, there would not be any basis for a true or false judgement of identity. To say that it must be either true or false that the same mental substance survives in the other body is again to show the emptiness of this concept. For how could this possibly be determined except by the use of the very criteria which our examples put in question?

In admitting the possibility that the criterion of memory might in certain circumstances over-ride the criterion of bodily continuity, I have not so far implied that it would operate on its own. The persons to whom these unusual changes have been attributed are still identified by their bodies at any given instant. The only rule which has been relaxed is that which requires a person to occupy one and the same body throughout the whole period of its existence. We have yet to consider the suggestion that there might conceivably be persons who existed, or at any rate continued to exist, without occupying any bodies at all.

At first sight, there might appear to be no doubt that such a state of affairs is logically possible, however improbable it may be that it ever in fact occurs. One can imagine oneself waking to find oneself deprived of any bodily feeling or any perception of one's own body; one can imagine oneself seeming to wander about the world like a ghost, intangible to others and only occasionally visible and after a time not visible at all, a spectator of a world in which one does not participate. Of course such fancies trade on one's actual sense of one's own identity, a sense which we have seen to be established through an identification with one's body. It is much less easy to imagine oneself having any such experiences before one came to occupy a body, or spending one's whole existence in a disembodied state. Yet if it is not logically necessary that persons should be embodied, these other variations ought also to be possible. It might be argued that it was essential to the concept of a person that one should come into existence in possession of a body, so that the most that would make sense would be the notion of surviving as what might be called an after-person. But if there could conceivably be disembodied spirits, the fact that it would not be correct to call them persons would not perhaps be of very great importance.

Is anything of this kind conceivable? There is, indeed, the difficulty that if there were temporal gaps in the consciousness of these spirits, the occurrences of memory-experiences would not be sufficient to bridge them; for again, these ostensible memories might be wholly delusive, or they might lay claim to past experiences which in fact belonged to a different series. This difficulty might, however, be met by making the assumption that the experiences which kept the different spirits in being were sensibly continuous. A more radical objection is that the notion of a series of experiences, existing as it were on their own, is not intelligible.

This objection is not easy to evaluate, so long as it relies merely on an appeal to intuition; for on a question of this kind, an appeal to intuition may well yield different answers according to the different preconceptions of those to whom it is addressed. There is, however, one argument which goes some way to sustain it. Our judgements as to what can exist are made in the light of a theory in which objects are ordered in a single spatio-temporal system. This theory may be flexible enough to allow for there being objects which are not located in space, but at least they must be located in time. But now the way in which we arrange things in an objective temporal order is by first assigning temporal positions to physical events, originally by correlating sequences of percepts which are obtained from different points of view, and then by applying scientific laws such as those concerning the velocity of light and sound. Any other occurrences, which are not regarded as physical, are then dated in terms of their temporal relations to these physical events. Moreover, since the theory is neutral as between different observers, the existence of these relations is required to be generally testable. It follows that no series of experiences can be admitted into the system unless at least some of its members are physically manifested.

If this argument is sound, it limits the freedom of our imagination to people the universe with spirits, but I do not think that it removes it entirely. To obtain this result, we should have to regard it as a necessary truth that only experiences which are associated with the bodies in the normal way can have physical manifestations, and while I believe this to be in fact the case, I cannot see that it is logically necessary. I am inclined, therefore, to conclude that the objections to the idea of there being disembodied streams of consciousness are in the end scientific rather than purely logical.

Some explanation has, indeed, to be found for the phenomena which have been attested by the Society for Psychical Research, but the evidence of the causal dependence of all our experiences upon the condition of our bodies appears to me to carry the greater weight.

D Physicalism

There are some philosophers who would make very short work of the speculations in which we have been engaging. These are the materialists, or physicalists as they are now more often called, who deny the existence of mental as opposed to physical events. They do not of course deny that people think and feel and act and perceive things through their senses, but they believe that all these processes can be described in purely physical terms.

The strongest version of this theory is that in which it is maintained that propositions which would ordinarily be construed as referring to mental states and processes are logically equivalent to propositions which refer only to people's overt behaviour. In recent times this position has been taken by Rudolf Carnap[1] and in a less consistent way by Gilbert Ryle,[2] and in Carnap's case at least it was the outcome of a verificationist theory of meaning. Since the only way in which we can test the truth of the propositions in which we attribute experiences to others is through observation of the ways in which these other persons behave, in a sense of the term 'behaviour' which includes their physical demeanour and their verbal responses as well as other sorts of acts, it is inferred that this is all that these propositions can legitimately be taken to refer to. The same consideration does not, indeed, apply to the propositions in which one attributes experiences to oneself, since here one is not restricted to observation of one's own overt behaviour; one can test these propositions by actually having or failing to have the relevant experiences. It is tempting, therefore, to do what I did in my *Language, Truth and Logic*, which was to combine a mentalistic analysis of the propositions in which one attributes experiences to oneself with a behaviouristic analysis of the propositions in which one attributes experiences to others.

[1] See Rudolf Carnap, *The Unity of Science*.
[2] See G. Ryle, *The Concept of Mind* and my essay 'An Honest Ghost' in *Ryle. A Collection of Critical Essays*. Edited by Oscar P. Wood and George Pitcher.

This is, however, a temptation that should be resisted, since the result is self-contradictory. The contradiction arises because the mentalistic analysis is supposed to hold good not only for me when I talk about myself but for anyone who refers to his own experiences. But if the only sense that I can attach to saying that any other person has experiences is that he behaves or is disposed to behave in such and such a fashion, then I cannot consistently allow that he means anything different from this when he attributes experiences to himself. The contradiction can be avoided only by someone who is prepared to believe that he is the only person in the world of whom it is meaningful to say that he has experiences, in a sense which is not exhausted by references to his behaviour, and then only when he says it. If one is not prepared to take this ridiculous position, and if one still adheres to the view that the propositions in which one attributes experiences to others are open only to a behaviouristic analysis, one will therefore be driven to extend this analysis to the propositions in which one attributes experiences to oneself.

I have no doubt that this view is false, if only for the reason which Ogden and Richards gave in their book *The Meaning of Meaning*, that it obliges one to feign anaesthesia,[1] but, as is quite often the case with philosophical falsehoods, it has borne some useful fruit. In particular, it has served to draw attention to the fact that many terms which might be thought to have a purely mentalistic meaning do also carry references to overt behaviour. This is most obviously true of terms which refer to the emotions, but it can apply also to the attribution of motives and beliefs. Intelligent thought and action, as we have seen that Ryle truly maintains,[2] do not necessarily require the occurrences of inner processes. Nevertheless, these inner processes do sometimes occur. People do have thoughts which they keep to themselves, and to say that they are having such thoughts is not exactly equivalent to saying that they are disposed to speak or act in such and such a fashion. Neither is it even plausible to equate having sensations or percepts with any form of overt action. One may be disposed to report their occurrence, but this does not follow logically from the fact that they occur, neither does it entail it, since the reports may be false. No doubt if one is writing a man's biography one will take

[1] C. K. Ogden and I. A. Richards. *The Meaning of Meaning*, p. 23.
[2] See above p. 57.

more interest in what he has overtly said and done than in his private thoughts and sensations, but this is not to say that these did not exist.

An attempt has been made to salvage this theory, at least with respect to one of its weakest points, the treatment of sensations, by making what may be called an open provision for the existence of inner processes. Thus, Professor Smart has suggested that 'When a person says, "I see a yellowish-orange after-image", he is saying something like this: "*There is something going on which is like what is going on when* I have my eyes open, am awake, and there is an orange illuminated in good light in front of me, that is, when I really see an orange"'.[1] The point of this non-committal formula is that it leaves the way open for the empirical discovery that what is in fact going on in these circumstances is some process in the brain.

As it stands, the suggested rendering of the claim to see an after-image is absurdly inadequate, since all manner of things are likely to be going on inside the claimant, let alone elsewhere. No doubt if some trouble were taken the formula could be made a little more precise, but any whole-hearted attempt to diminish its vagueness would be likely to frustrate its purpose. For instance, if we were to take what might seem the obvious step of requiring that what was going on inside the man should be causally respons-ible for his seeing an after-image, we should be making a reference to the man's experience, which is exactly what Smart wishes to avoid. Even as it is, he does not really avoid it. For what is it that links the man's seeing a yellowish-orange after-image with the presence under the stated conditions of an orange in his neigh-bourhood, except that in both cases an orange quale occurs in his visual field? It is true that the list of circumstances is not sufficient to entail that the man does really see the orange, but that is just a further defect in the analysis.

The straits to which Smart is put in his endeavour to avoid referring to anything like percepts are shown by his account of what is meant by the sentence 'This is red'. He says that it means 'something roughly like "A normal percipient would not easily pick this out of a clump of geranium petals though he would pick it out of a clump of lettuce leaves"'. The idea is that seeing colours

[1] J. C. C. Smart 'Sensations and Brain-Processes', *Philosophical Review*, LXVIII.

consists in discriminating between physical objects. But apart from the fact that there are any number of reasons for which one might pick an object out, this analysis simply puts the cart before the horse. Geranium petals and lettuce leaves are not presented to us as collections of colourless atoms; they are differentiated by their perceptible qualities, including their colour. I do not judge my scarf to be red because I associate it with geranium petals rather than with lettuce leaves. I associate it with geranium petals rather than with lettuce leaves, because the lettuce leaves look green to me and the geranium petals and the scarf look red. To suggest that it is the other way round is merely disingenuous.

A more prudent theory, which has recently come into fashion, is one that does not attempt to explain away the occurrence of experiences, or to maintain that our descriptions of them are logically equivalent to descriptions of physical events, but still claims that they can be factually identified with states of the central nervous system.[1] On this view, to have such and such an experience *is* for one's brain to be in such and such a state, in the way in which lightning *is* an electrical discharge, or temperature *is* the mean kinetic energy of molecules. The identity is not an equivalence of concepts, which could be discovered *a priori*, but something which is established on the basis of empirical research. The obvious objection that experiences and processes in the brain have quite different sorts of properties is met with the answer that what is identified with the process in the brain is not the experience as such but the having of it. A thought is not spatially located, at least in any straightforward sense, but this does not make it impossible to identify the thinking of the thought with a process that does have spatial properties: an after-image is not located in the brain, but this does not prevent the seeing of it from being a process which takes place there. If someone were to inspect my brain, he would not thereby come to have my thoughts or percepts, but he could, on this view, be said to witness the events which consisted in my having them.

This theory depends on the empirical hypothesis that there is a correlation between a person's experiences and events which take place in his brain. This hypothesis may not be acceptable to those who wish to deny, in the interest of free-will, that human thoughts

---

[1] In fairness to Smart, it should be said that he also holds this conclusion.

and actions are physically determined, but we shall see later on[1] that this is not a question that can be decided, one way or the other on *a priori* grounds. It is for us to discover how far we are capable of subsuming events of all kinds under causal laws: beforehand, we have no right to assume either that all events must be determined or that some cannot be. In the present instance, the science of physiology has not in fact reached the point at which it can be said to have established that there is a one to one correlation of the sort that identity-theorists postulate. There is very strong evidence of a general dependence of mental occurrences upon the functioning of the brain, but it has still to be shown that the correspondence is so exact that from observation of a person's brain one could itemize his experiences in every detail. For the sake of the argument, however, let us assume that this would be possible.

It is to be remarked that if there were known to be such an exact correspondence, we should on the face of it have just as good ground for saying that the brain was dependent on the mind as that the mind was dependent on the brain. If predominance is given to the events in the brain, rather than the other way round, the reason is that they fit into a wider explanatory system. We think of the world as a whole as being governed by physical laws, which account for the functioning of our brains, as for other physical events. We also think of mental events as having physical as well as mental causes and effects. To the extent that mental events obey laws of their own they are an anomalous feature of the overall picture. This anomaly can, however, be removed if there is a set of physical events to which the mental events exactly correspond: for then they can be allotted the causal roles which the mental events appear to play. A mentalist might object that these physical events would not be sufficient for the purpose if the mental events did not accompany them, but if in fact they always do accompany them, he will be unable to make the experiment that would prove his case, and so can safely be ignored. Then, mental events having been rendered causally otiose, the physicalist, in his pursuit of uniformity, proceeds to eliminate them altogether by reducing them to their physical counterparts.

But what exactly does this final step come to? At first sight, the fact, if it is a fact, that mental events are perfectly correlated with events in the brain points rather to their being distinct than their

[1] See below pp. 231–2.

being identical: it might indeed be argued that if they were not distinct it would not even make sense to talk of their being correlated. This would, however, be to mistake the character of what is being proposed. Not only must it be conceded that the two series of events are logically distinct, it might also be conceded that they are empirically distinct, to the extent that their existence can be independently established. Obviously there are ways of finding out that someone is having an experience other than by examining his brain, just as there are ways of finding out what the temperature of a body is other than by investigating the properties of molecules. In both instances, the judgement of identity, if it is made at all, is the outcome of a theory. In the case of mental and physical events, the suggestion is that as a result of our accepting the hypothesis that mental events are causally parasitical upon processes in the brain, we shall come to think of them as identical. A person's having such and such an experience and there being the corresponding process in his brain will no longer be counted as separate events.

But if this is the thesis, it is either not very interesting or not very plausible. It is not very interesting if it merely forecasts that after a scientific advance which has not yet been made, people, though still speaking about their experiences in the old way, will conceive of them as events which are more knowledgeably described by the use of physical predicates. It is not very plausible if it implies that our descendants will give up accounting for their own and other persons' behaviour in terms of their conscious sensations, purposes, and reasoning, and rely instead only on the notion of their making such and such responses as the result of the stimulation of their central nervous systems. For one thing, it is not very likely that they would normally be in a position to know what was going on in the central nervous system except by an inference from the experiences with which these physical processes were correlated by their theory. It is even very doubtful whether in the case of an apparent conflict, the voice of one's own experience would not continue to carry the greater conviction. I find it hard to imagine someone who seemed to himself to be feeling great pain, but on being informed that his brain was not in the condition which the theory prescribed, decided that he was mistaken in believing that he felt any pain at all. He might be persuaded that it was wrong to use the word 'pain' in these circumstances, since it had ceased to stand only for a sensation, but he would still be the best authority as to what he felt.

E One's Knowledge of Other Minds

It is, indeed, the fact that we do make such extensive use of psychological explanations that supplies what may well be the solution to the stubborn problem of our knowledge of other minds. This problem has provided a happy hunting ground for the sceptic, because both horns of his characteristic dilemma look solid. On the one hand, as we have seen, the relation between propositions which ascribe experiences to another person and propositions which describe his overt behaviour is not, in general, a relation of logical equivalence. On the other hand, the argument that because I know that such and such experiences accompany my own behaviour, I am therefore entitled to infer with a high degree of probability that similar behaviour on the part of other people is accompanied by similar experiences of theirs does not seem sufficiently strong for the purpose. Not only may one doubt the propriety of generalizing in this way from a single instance, but it may even be questioned whether an inductive argument of which the conclusion could not possibly be verified, at least by the person who relies on it, is legitimate at all.

The acceptance of physicalism would undercut the problem by equating experiences with events in the brain, which are publicly observable. The difficulty is, however, that this identification is the outcome of what is assumed to be a perfect correlation. It therefore requires that there be very good evidence that this correlation universally obtains. But if one has no good reason to believe that any person other than oneself does have experiences, this evidence will be wanting. To suppose that it could consist merely in the observation of other people's brains would simply be to assume the hypothesis that it is incumbent on the physicalist to establish.

An attempt has been made to escape between the horns of the sceptic's dilemma by maintaining that the relation between experiences and the behaviour by which they are believed to be manifested is quasi-logical. The argument is that we learn to use words like 'pain' in situations in which some person, oneself or another, is behaving in a way that is generally recognized as an expression of pain; we learn the use of the word 'thought' in relation to the acts of speaking or writing which are said to be its expression, and in relation to the play of feature, the furrowed brow, the abstracted air, which sometimes precede these acts: we learn to ascribe motives and intentions to ourselves, and to other persons, when we are observed to be acting in such and such special ways. From this it is held to follow that the inner experiences and their outward manifestations are not just contingently correlated. The behaviour is a criterion for the existence of the experience. In particular cases, the relation may not hold; we may be deceived by some pretence; we may be mistaken in our diagnosis. But to suppose that it did not hold in the main would be to make not merely a factual but a conceptual error.

This argument has persuaded many good philosophers but, as I said earlier,[1] I do not find it at all convincing. I see no reason why the meaning of words should be indissolubly tied to the contexts in which they are originally learned. No doubt a child's use of the past tense is originally linked to the exercise of his memory. He speaks of an event as past only when it seems to him that he remembers it. This does not prevent him from being able quite soon to draw a logical distinction between past events in general and the very small fraction of them which he remembers; and once this distinction has been made he can come to understand that even when he does remember an event, his remembering it is not a necessary condition of its being past. In the same way, it may well be true that I should not have learned to use the word 'pain' in the way I do, if I had not, on occasions when I was feeling pain, behaved in a way that others took to be the expression of it. Nevertheless, this does not in the least prevent me now from taking the word to refer, in my own case, not to my behaviour but only to the sensations by which the behaviour is caused, and I see no reason why I should not be able to make the same distinction when I attribute pain to others. Of course, I should be puzzled if someone regularly claimed to be in great pain and yet exhibited none of the signs which it is ordinarily thought to produce. I might judge that he was using the word 'pain' incorrectly, but this is certainly not the only course open to me. I could also judge, perhaps truly, that the accepted hypothesis about the effects of pain had met with a contrary instance.

The right answer to this problem, I now think, is the one recently

[1] See above p. 54.

given by Professor Putnam in an essay entitled 'Other Minds'.[1] He argues that 'our acceptance of the proposition that others have mental states is both analogous and disanalogous to the acceptance of ordinary empirical theories on the basis of explanatory induction'.[2] The main point of difference is that the theory that other people besides oneself have mental states is one that has no serious rival; in this respect it is like the theory that there are physical objects. What we establish inductively, on the basis of our knowledge of our mental states and our observation of other people's behaviour, is a set of special hypotheses about their mental states: the alternatives to these hypotheses are hypotheses which account for the same behaviour in terms of different mental states rather than hypotheses which deny to others any mental life at all. Thus, the similarity of our theory about other minds to ordinary empirical theories consists in the fact that the special hypotheses which presuppose it do seem to us to explain human behaviour. The advocates of the traditional argument from analogy were right to the extent that part of what makes these hypotheses acceptable is that the connexions which they postulate are found to obtain in one's own experience. They were, however, wrong in treating the attribution of minds to others as if it were like the attribution of some special feature, which one could observe in oneself but could not observe in them. Thus, one might imagine there being a firm taboo against our ever seeing one another unclothed, and in that case my knowing that I had a hidden birth-mark would not entitle me to infer with any great degree of confidence that the same was true of everybody else. Consequently, if the inductive reasoning which leads me to attribute consciousness to others were of this order, it would, indeed, be a very weak foundation on which to erect so strong a belief. But these cases are not parallel. My attributing consciousness to others is not just a matter of my accepting, on the strength of a doubtful analogy, the generalization that two different series of events, one mental and one physical, habitually go together. It is a consequence rather of my accepting a whole body of theory which enables me to account for the behaviour of others by crediting them with conscious thoughts and sensations and emotions and purposes. My ability to entertain

[1] Hilary Putnam. 'Other Minds', *Logic and Art*, Essays in honour of Nelson Goodman.
[2] *Ibid*. p. 82.

this body of theory does depend on my having learned from my own experiences what these mental states are like, but my justification for accepting it is that it has been found, in Putnam's words, to have 'genuine explanatory power'.[1]

Of course none of this puts the sceptic out of court. If he is able to persuade himself that he has been cast into a world in which only he is conscious, there is no way in which he can be refuted. He will not even be at a disadvantage in accounting for the appearances, since he can believe that everything is and will continue to be as if other people had minds, though in reality they do not. All I can say is that this is not a theory which I myself find it necessary or useful to adopt, and if anyone else adopts it with regard to himself, my possession of my own experiences enables me to know that it is false.

There is a parallel here with the problem of our knowledge of the past, where indeed the sceptic's position is even stronger, since no one has present access to a past event. It is true that some philosophers have spoken of memory as making us directly acquainted with the past, but all that this comes to is a declaration that they trust their memories. The fact remains that the occurrence of a memory-experience is always logically consistent with the non-existence of the previous event of which it purports to be a memory. As Russell puts it: 'There is no logical impossibility in the hypothesis that the world sprang into being five minutes ago, exactly as it then was, with a population that "remembered" a wholly unreal past.'[2] This is not a theory that I should expect anyone seriously to hold, but a not dissimilar theory has been held. The critic Edmund Gosse related in his book *Father and Son* that his father, a member of the sect of Plymouth Brethren, held firmly to Archbishop Ussher's calculation, on the basis of biblical evidence, that the world had been created in the year 4004 B.C. In face of the abundant scientific evidence which suggested a considerably earlier date, he reasoned that God had endowed the world with delusive appearances of much greater antiquity in order to test men's faith. Once more this is not a position that can be refuted. The hypothesis that everything is and will continue to be as if the world had existed for many millions of years will fit the

---

[1] *Ibid.* p. 83.
[2] Bertrand Russell. *The Analysis of Mind*, p. 159.

available facts just as well as the hypothesis that the world really has existed for many millions of years. If most of us prefer the realistic hypothesis, it is because it is simpler, besides supplying the goods in which the other trades.

VII Facts and Explanations

A The Problem of Induction

The account of the world which we have so far given is founded on what I have taken to be the primitive elements of our experience, but it is also the product of theory. Physical objects have been introduced by what is at least in part a method of postulation. The ascription of consciousness to persons other than onself has been defended on the ground that it is entailed by the most satisfactory explanations that we can give of their behaviour. The realistic view of the past which we all naturally take has been shown not to be demonstrably true, but to be acceptable as a simpler hypothesis than one that makes us all the victims of a vast delusion. The sceptic has been left in this citadel, a pocket of resistance which the invaders are unable to reduce but feel entitled to ignore. We hold fast to our theories because we find that they work, even though they do not satisfy the sceptic's standards of proof.

Admittedly, there is a circularity in our procedure. The special theories which we hold about the behaviour of physical objects presuppose the validity of the general principles which enter into our conception of those objects, such principles as that they are accessible to different senses and to different observers, and that they are capable of existing unperceived; but equally these principles are themselves consolidated by the success of the theories which presuppose them. In the same way, our general disposition to attribute consciousness to others and our general belief in the existence of the past are both pre-supposed and sustained by the special hypotheses that we accept about the connexions of people's mental states with their behaviour, or about the particular course that history has taken. Again, this circularity is inescapable. We cannot stand in the void, and there is nothing exterior to our system by which it could be justified. There are, indeed, the facts by which our hypotheses are tested, but although there is a sense in which they are set over against our theories, there is also, as we have seen, a sense in which they are conditioned by them.

This is not, however, all that there is to be said. Even if the framework of our system is allowed to stand, at least provisionally, for want of any serious alternative to it, a question may still be raised about the propositions which are fitted into it. I said a moment ago that we hold fast to our theories because we find that they work. But even on the assumption that we are entitled to accept historical testimony, at least when it represents a large measure of agreement, the most that we can claim is that our theories have been found to work in the past. What assurance does this give us that they will continue to work in the future?

The philosophical problem which this question raises is technically known as the problem of induction. It was first clearly posed by David Hume in his book *A Treatise of Human Nature*. The assumption from which Hume starts is that we can have reason to believe in the existence of any matter of fact, which we do not currently observe or remember, only if we know it to be connected in a law-like fashion with something that we do remember or are currently observing. He makes this point in a later work by saying that 'all reasonings concerning matters of fact seem to be founded on the relation of cause and effect'.[1] This is, however, misleading, in that his argument applies to all forms of factual inference and not merely to those that appeal to what would ordinarily be counted as a causal relation. He then attempts to show that no inference of this sort can be rationally justified, with the consequence that once we go beyond the immediate data of perception and memory, we have no good reason to believe in the truth of any empirical proposition.

As usual with sceptical arguments, the first step is to show that the inference which is being put in question is not deductive. Speaking, as he does, in terms only of the relation of cause and effect, Hume reasons that since every effect is distinct from its cause, it cannot be logically contained within it. Put more generally, the point is that if two events are distinct, there cannot be any logical contradiction in affirming the existence of either of them and denying the existence of the other.

The second step in the argument is to deny that events can be connected by any relation of necessity which is not a logical

[1] David Hume. *An Enquiry Concerning Human Understanding*, Section VII.

relation. Another way of making this point would be to say that there is no such thing as natural necessity. When we say of two events which are not logically connected that each necessitates the other, we are indeed implying that events of the kinds in question invariably go together, but in going beyond that and representing the connexion between them as necessary, we can, in Hume's view, be doing no more than testifying to the strength of our tendency to associate them.

If these two first steps in the argument are valid, there is nothing in the nature of any two distinct events, considered in themselves, which would entitle us to infer from the occurrence of either one of them to the occurrence of the other. Consequently, the argument continues, if we are to have any good reason for making such an inference it can only be that we have observed events of the type in question to be constantly conjoined in the past.

But is this a good reason? From the fact that every event of the type A, which has so far been observed, has been found to stand in the spatio-temporal relation R to some event of the type B, it surely does not follow that this is true of all A's whatsoever, or even that it will be true of the next A to be observed. In predicting even that the next A will also stand in the relation R to some B, we are going beyond our evidence. How is this step to be justified?

Hume's answer is that it can be justified only if we are entitled to adopt a principle which yields us the assurance that what has held good in the past will hold good in the future. As he formulates it in his *Treatise*, the principle is 'that instances of which we have no experience, must resemble those of which we have had experience, and that the course of nature continues always uniformly the same'.[1]

The question then is what justification there can be for accepting this principle, and Hume argues that there cannot be any. He begins by claiming that it is not a logical truth. 'We can,' he says, 'at least conceive a change in the course of nature; which sufficiently proves that such a change is not impossible.'[2] But even if the principle is not certain, might it not be shown to be probable? Hume's answer to this is that since judgements of probability must themselves be founded on past experience, any attempt to

[1] David Hume. *A Treatise of Human Nature*, Book I, Section VI.
[2] *Ibid.*

confer probability on the principle would be viciously circular. As he puts it, 'probability is founded on the presumption of a resemblance betwixt those objects of which we have had experience, and those of which we have had none; and, therefore, it is impossible this presumption can arise from probability'.[1]

But if the justification for all our factual inferences depends on the assumption that 'the course of nature continues always uniformly the same', and if this assumption itself cannot in any way be justified, then it follows that we have no good reason to trust any of these inferences; and this indeed is the conclusion that Hume drew. He admitted that he was not able to adhere to this sceptical position, outside his study. Like the rest of us, he allowed himself to be guided in the practical conduct of life by what he called his natural beliefs, but he did not claim that this was rational; indeed, even to speak of the beliefs on which he acted as natural beliefs, with the implication that they were shared by the generality of people over some period of time, was to make an inference which he could not rationally justify.

B   The Primary System

This is not a conclusion which many people would be willing to accept, but the argument is impressive and has not been found at all easy to answer. Let us, then, examine it in detail. The first step, which consists, as we have seen, in claiming that there can be no logical connection between distinct events, must, I think, be conceded, but it needs to be carefully explained if the valid point which Hume is making is to become clear. To begin with, logical relations neither hold nor fail to hold between events as such, but only between descriptions of events. Let us, therefore, consider the proposition that descriptions of distinct events are logically independent of one another. To discover whether this proposition is true we have to know both what sort of descriptions we are dealing with and what is meant by saying that two events are distinct. Hume does not say what he means by distinctness, in this usage, but a reasonable definition would seem to be that two events are distinct if and only if they have no common part. But then, if we accept this definition, we have to admit that not all descriptions of distinct events are logically independent. On the contrary, most of the descriptions that are ordinarily given of any

[1] *Ibid.*

particular event will probably be found to contain an implicit reference to some other distinct event, to which it is implied that the event in question is, or under suitable conditions would be, causally related. The reason for this is that our descriptions of events very often associate them with familiar kinds of physical objects, which are at least partially defined in terms of their origins or their causal properties. Thus it might be held to be logically necessary for anything to be an oak that it should have sprung from an acorn, for anything to be a table that it can bear certain weights, for anything to be a camera that it can be used to take photographs, and similarly for any number of examples. This simply reflects the fact that we take at least as much interest in the way things come into being and in the uses to which we can put them as we do in the perceptible properties by which they are immediately recognized.

These facts, however, must not be taken to imply that causality is a logical relation, in any more interesting sense than that we may choose to refer to objects or events in terms which incorporate the causal properties that we attribute to them. To the extent that we do this, we safeguard propositions which assert causal connections from any possible refutation, but the security which they enjoy is only verbal. Magnets cannot fail to attract iron, because anything that did fail to attract iron would not properly be called a magnet. What has happened, here, as in many other cases, is that we have become so confident of a causal generalization that we have built it into the definition of a term. This is not, however, to say that the generalization itself was logically true before it was treated in this way. To see that it was not we have only to coin a new term which applies to anything that has the appearance and physical constitution of a magnet, but does not include the property of attracting iron as part of its definition, and then ask whether all the things which satisfy this term also have the property of attracting iron. Even if they all do have this property, they will have it as a matter of fact and not as a matter of logic. The proposition that at least one of them lacks it will not be self-contradictory. The point to note is that when a term incorporates a causal property as part of its definition, the connection of this property with the other properties which enter into the definition of the term will in general be not logical but purely factual; and it is with connexions of this sort that Hume's argument is concerned.

The trouble, then, with most of our ordinary descriptions of events, from Hume's point of view, is that they range too widely. They are not closely tailored to the events which they describe. To meet his demands, we have to limit ourselves to what I have elsewhere called intrinsic descriptions.[1] The definition which I there gave was that a description of a particular subject S at a time t is intrinsic to S at t if and only if nothing follows from it with regard to the state of S at any time other than t or with regard to the existence of any subject S' which is distinct from S. From this definition, together with our definition of distinctness, it follows immediately that all intrinsic descriptions of distinct events are logically independent of each other.

This seems too easy. Any sentence can be made to express a true proposition if we define its terms in such a way that the proposition is deducible from the definitions. At this point, the interest shifts to the definitions themselves. Why should they be adopted? In the present case, the real question at issue is whether we can accept the underlying assumption that intrinsic descriptions are all that we need to give an account of everything that happens. The belief that it should be accepted is the core of the atomism which Russell and other modern empiricists have inherited from Hume.

I think that this position is tenable, so long as we are concerned only with what, following Ramsey, I have called the primary system.[2] It will be remembered that we are taking this to consist, not in an account of the primitive data of perception, but rather in the theory which is first developed out of them. If we think of the physical objects which this theory introduces as being replaceable by the series of events which constitute their histories, the propositions of the primary system may be cast in a form in which they serve to state that such and such observable properties are located at such and such particular places at such and such particular times. If atomic particles, as I have suggested,[3] can be regarded as minute parts of physical objects, the propositions which affirm the presence of these particles at particular places and times will also be included in the system. Generalizations of these propositions are also admissible, provided that these are generalizations of fact. This means that they can refer indefinitely to

[1] See my *Probability and Evidence*, p. 6.
[2] See above p. 33.
[3] See above p. 110.

actual events, or at least to what are asserted to be actual events, but cannot be construed as referring to merely possible events. The system can also contain numerical expressions, though, as was pointed out earlier,[1] the numbers which record the results of actual measurements will always be rational and finite, and it can contain logical operators like those of negation, conjunction, and disjunction, which are what is technically known as truth-functional, in the sense that the truth or falsehood of the propositions which they help to form is entirely dependent on the truth or falsehood of the propositions on which they operate.

It would appear that this system meets the requirement of atomicity. From the fact that some observable feature is exemplified at some particular place and time, nothing logically follows about what is or is not to be found at any other place or time. There is, however, a difficulty about the identification of these places and times. They cannot be identified simply in terms of the features that occur at them because the same feature may be repeatedly exemplified. It is, indeed, practically safe to assume that different occurrences of the same feature can be distinguished by there being some differences in their respective neighbourhoods: for, unless the world is mirrored in space, or its history exactly and infinitely repeats itself, there is bound to be some difference if we extend the neighbourhood far enough. Alternatively, we may secure identification by anchoring the whole system at any given moment to some feature which is identified demonstratively; or by relating everything to one or more objects, like the fixed stars, or events, like the founding of the city of Rome, that can be presumed to be unique. The demonstrative method guarantees uniqueness, but it has the great disadvantage of making the whole system egocentric, in as much as every spatio-temporal reference is tied to the context of the speaker. I therefore prefer to identify by landmarks, even though this has the consequence that uniqueness of reference is only practically and not logically guaranteed.

Whichever method we choose, there will be some sacrifice of atomicity. Unless it is itself one of the landmarks, the identification of an object, or an event, will always involve at least an implicit reference to something other than itself. The sacrifice is, however, not very serious. The reasons why it is not are, first, that the relations of objects or events to the landmarks by means of which they

[1] See above p. 32.

are situated will always be contingent, and, secondly, that the choice of landmarks will be to some extent a matter of convenience; it will not in any case depend upon there being any logical relation between their qualities and the qualities of any objects or events from which they are distinct. The result is that even if the process of identifying an element in the system carries some reference to other elements, there will be no two elements of which it can be said that they are necessarily related, and this is as much as Hume's argument requires.

A more troublesome question is whether our primary system is equipped to give an account of everything that happens. The world which it is capable of describing approximates to the world of common sense, but it is much more austere. The objects in it do not have dispositional properties; neither do they stand in causal relations to one another. The reason for this is that causal laws are in part dispositional, in that they cover not only actual but also merely possible correlations; they lay it down that under such and such conditions, which may or may not in fact be realized, such and such events invariably would, or would not, occur. I shall, indeed, be arguing that while a particular causal statement always invokes some generalization, these generalizations need not amount to laws; they may be no stronger than statements of tendency. For our present purposes, however, the result is the same, since in the cases where the causal statement rests on something weaker than a law, it always contains a hypothetical element: it implies that one event would not occur unless another event stood in such and such a spatio-temporal relation to it. So once again we travel beyond fact into possibility; we are speaking not just about what does or does not happen, but about what would or would not happen under conditions which may not be realized. But possibilities are the concern of what I have called the secondary explanatory system. The primary system is limited to the domain of actual fact.

It may be objected that this is to conceive of fact too narrowly. In the ordinary way, no sharp distinction is drawn on this score between dispositional and occurrent properties; it is considered to be as much a matter of fact that a glass is brittle as that it actually breaks. It is not, after all, as if our primary system were not itself the product of theory. I admit that this is so and I admit that both the decision to treat only categorical statements as strictly factual and the choice of the boundary line between categorical and hypothetical statements are somewhat arbitrary. The limits which I have set to the primary system will be justified only if I am able to develop a secondary system which will account satisfactorily for everything which they exclude, and this I hope to do presently, at least with regard to the physical world.

I make this reservation, because there are special difficulties about mental events. They can be introduced into the primary system through the bodies with which they are correlated, but they can appear in it only in a very attenuated form. This is due to the fact that apart from the attachments which are needed for their identification, the elements of this system are not supposed to refer beyond themselves, whereas it has plausibly been taken to be an essential characteristic of mental states and processes that they do refer beyond themselves. A thought is not just a visual presentation in the mind's eye, or an unvoiced series of sounds; to the extent that it consists in images, the images operate as signs. An emotion is not just a pang, but something directed towards a real or imaginary object: one is angry with someone over something which may or may not have occurred; one hopes for something that may or may not be realized. This common feature of mental states is technically known as their intentionality. The question is whether it is irreducible.

One point which is clear is that it cannot simply be reduced to the properties of a series of occurrences in the primary system. Even if it is possible to analyse, say, a man's ambitiousness in terms of his thoughts and his behaviour, not only do we have to deal with the objection that his thoughts must be significant and his behaviour something more than just a set of physical movements, but a reference to his actual thoughts and actions will not be sufficient. His being ambitious is also a matter of what he would say or think or do under a variety of conditions. In short, as in most uses of natural language, our talk of mental states straddles different systems: the conditional way of speaking is fused with the categorical. It is, however, possible to separate them, and if our account of conditional statements is satisfactory in general, there is no reason why it should not apply to the conditionals which are involved in the descriptions of mental states and processes. A much more serious problem is that of finding a way to **deal with the intentionality of thought, which includes any** problem of this sort that may seem to be presented by action, since what makes an action more than a set of physical movements is just the interpretation which the agent and others put upon them. The problem arises in so far as thinking consists in the use of signs, and the difficulty is to explain how any sign acquires a meaning.

If we do not think of signs as intrinsically meaningful, which is a way of denying any explanation, and if we do not evade the difficulty by conceiving of meanings as abstract objects to which signs stand in some undefined relation, it would seem that we are bound to agree with Peirce that 'the meaning of a thought is altogether virtual'.[1] As what Peirce calls a mere feeling, a thought is devoid of meaning. It owes its meaning only to the actual or possible interpretation which it receives from further thoughts. This view may seem to be supported by the fact that a criterion for establishing that somebody has understood a sign is found in the answers which he gives to further questions, but it faces a very strong objection. If the interpreting thought is itself without meaning, how can it bestow meaning on the thought which it interprets? How can the mere accumulation of signs, none of which is meaningful in itself, endow the whole collection with meaning? It seems that something more is needed, and the obvious place to look for it is in the connexion of thought with action.

The question then is how this connexion is to be made. In my book, *The Origins of Pragmatism*,[2] I have sketched a theory, according to which a thinker's disposition to assent to a given sentence is treated as part of a pattern of actual or hypothetical behaviour which as a whole constitutes his belief in such and such a proposition; the truth-conditions of this proposition are then taken to determine the meaning which he attaches to the sentence. There is, however, the difficulty that if this account is not to be circular, the behaviour in question cannot be held to consist in anything more than the person's making or being disposed to make certain physical movements, neither can his assenting to the sentence be held to consist in anything more than his making a positive response to an uninterpreted set of noises or marks, and it is doubtful whether this gives us sufficient material for a satisfactory analysis of belief.

[1] C. S. Peirce. *Collected Papers*, V, 289.
[2] Ch. iv, Section D.

Since I am not sure that this difficulty can be met, and have not been able to devise a theory which does not raise it, I remain uncertain whether our Humean scheme can accommodate mental events. If we have to modify it to make room for their intentionality, we shall incur a further loss of atomicity, and also have to allow a blurring of the distinction between the actual and the possible; the description of certain events in the primary system will contain a reference to intentional objects which may or may not exist. I hope that this conclusion can be avoided but for our present purposes we can afford to leave the question open, since it does not affect the first step in Hume's argument. Even if an event which consists in someone's forming an intention cannot be adequately described without reference to the action which he intends, still the intention can be frustrated; its existence does not entail that the action will occur. Even if a desire cannot be adequately described without reference to its object, its existence does not carry the existence of the object with it: it is not logically necessary that the desire should be realized. We are, therefore, able to maintain the principle that there is no logical connection between distinct events.

C Necessity and Law

Can there be a necessary connection which is not logical? This has been a subject of some dispute, but it is still not altogether clear what the dispute is about. The difficulty lies in understanding what those who believe in such necessary connexions take them to be. The examples on which they rely are instances of the exercise of causal properties. They maintain that this is not just a matter of two states of affairs being constantly conjoined, but rather that objects, or events, are endowed with a force which, under suitable conditions, compels the occurrence of such and such effects. Against them, the followers of Hume remark that no such forces are observable; and what is more that they do not know even what would count as our observing them. The only domain in which it is at all plausible to suggest that we can observe anything of this sort is that of our own actions and the effects of other things upon us; but even if we do have what may be described as a feeling of necessity in these cases, and it is not at all clear to me that we do, it has still to be shown that there is anything in the actual causal processes to which this feeling corresponds. What is true is that we do not in general have any doubt of our command over our own bodies, or of their reactions to certain stimuli. One does not have to work out how to move one's arm; a single experience may be enough to convince a child that some object is hurtful. Even so, the only relations that appear to be detectable in such situations are spatio-temporal: the decision to reach for something is simply followed by the movement of one's arm; the child's coming into contact with the hurtful object is simply followed by his feeling of pain. It is still unclear in what the additional agency can be held to consist.

This question is anyhow less important than it might appear, since even if there were something in these or other situations which a term like 'force' or 'agency' could reasonably be taken to name, its presence would make no difference to the general argument. What we are seeking for is some assurance that a relation which has hitherto been found to obtain between events of such and such different sorts will continue to make its appearance in further instances. But now so long as this relation is something which is observable in particular cases, it makes no difference to the question what its nature is taken to be. Let us consider the example in which an object imparts motion to another and let us suppose, for the sake of the argument, that what is observed is not just that the objects are first in spatial contact and then that they change their relative positions, but that one of them forces the other to move. If there is any doubt whether, on another occasion, when the same two objects or two objects of the same sorts are in contact in similar circumstances, they will again be found to change their relative positions, there must be at least an equal doubt whether one will again force the other to move. And the same would apply to any other example, including examples of human action. If there is any doubt whether my decision to reach for something will simply be followed on a future occasion by my arm's moving, there must be at least an equal doubt whether it will force my arm to move. Consequently, nothing is gained by bringing in a relation of agency, which anyhow appears to be mythical. If it be objected that its being a necessary relation guarantees that it will hold in similar instances, the answer is that in that case those who invoke it cannot be limiting themselves to describing what is discoverable in a particular situation. What they are doing is building into their description the assumption that events of the same sort will in similar circumstances always be found to be similarly related; and this is an assumption which they have yet to justify.

The upshot of this argument is that if the idea of natural necessity is to serve any purpose, it must not be viewed as a relation which can be observed to connect particular events, but rather as a relation which holds conceptually between events of different kinds. The suggestion must be that we can somehow apprehend the truth of the general proposition that one state of affairs necessitates another. Since this necessitation is not supposed to be logical, and since to say that the existence of something, under such and such conditions, is necessary is equivalent to saying that its non-existence, under those conditions, is impossible, this theory relies on an undefined notion of factual possibility.

But can such a notion be accepted? I do not believe that it can. We do, indeed, contrast causal with logical possibility. A state of affairs the description of which is not self-contradictory may still be said to be impossible on causal grounds. It is not logically but causally impossible that cats should breed with mice or that steam-engines should run without fuel. But here the difference consists not in the use of different concepts of possibility but rather in an implicit reference to different sorts of laws. To say that a state of affairs is impossible is, I believe, in either case to say that there is some law which excludes it. A necessary state of affairs will then be one that is required by law, in the sense that its negation is excluded, and a possible state of affairs one that is neither required nor excluded. The difference, then, between logical and causal possibility is just that what is logically impossible is excluded by the laws of logic, and what is causally impossible is excluded by the laws of nature. But if this is correct, it must be a mistake to try to found the notion of causal law on that of natural necessity, for the notion of necessity of any sort itself presupposes the notion of law.

A further objection is that even if the notion of natural necessity could be taken as primitive, it would not be of any assistance in dealing with the problem of induction. If on the basis of the fact that all the A's hitherto observed have been B's, we are seeking for an assurance that the next A we come upon will be a B, the knowledge, if we could have it, that all A's are B's would be quite sufficient; to strengthen the premiss by saying that they not only are but must be B's adds nothing to the validity of the inference.

The only way in which this move could be helpful would be if it were somehow easier to discover that all A's must be B's than that they merely were so; and perhaps this is what its advocates believe. But how can they possibly be right? It would, indeed, be easier, if being a B were included in the definition of an A. To revert to a previous example, we have no difficulty in discovering that magnets must be attractors of iron, so long as we refuse to apply the term 'magnet' to anything that fails to be so. We have, however, seen that this manoeuvre leaves things just as they were; the empirical generalization that the property of attracting iron is bound to accompany the other properties of magnets still remains to be established. And how is this to be achieved? It is no good claiming that empirical hypotheses of this or any other sort are known to be true by intuition. For not only is the appeal to intuition simply a mask for the fact that one is making an otherwise ungrounded claim to knowledge, but in cases of this kind there is no reason why one's intuition should be trusted, unless the hypothesis is found to agree with the observable evidence. But then, if it is a matter of evidence, it must be easier to discover, or at least find some good reason for believing, that such and such an association of properties always does obtain, than that it must obtain; for it requires less for the evidence to establish.

It would seem, then, that the idea of natural necessity does nothing to help us justify our acceptance of what we believe to be laws of nature, nor does it serve to explain the character of these laws. We must, therefore, look for some other answer to these questions. Let us begin with the attempt to show what natural laws are. The principal reason for which philosophers have ascribed necessity to them is that they have not seen how they could otherwise explain the way in which they differ from mere generalizations of fact. Is this a genuine distinction, and if so, how can we account for it?

I think that it is a genuine distinction. One common way of bringing it out is by remarking that generalizations of law entail unfulfilled conditions, whereas generalizations of fact do not. For example, let us suppose that a meeting is held at which some motion is passed unanimously with no abstentions. Then it will be a true generalization of fact that all the persons present at the meeting voted in favour of the motion. Given the characters and opinions of the persons in question, this may not be wholly accidental, but the generalization still falls short of being a generalization of law. We can infer with regard to anyone you please that if he was present at the meeting, he voted in favour of the motion, but we cannot infer with regard to anyone you please that if he had been present he would have voted in favour of the motion, for among those who were not present there might very well be some whose characters and opinions were such that if they had been present, they would have voted against it. On the other hand, if we consider the generalization that all those present at the meeting were warm-blooded, we think that we can safely infer with regard to anyone you please not only that if he was present he was warm-blooded, but that if he had been present he would have been warm-blooded. It being a generalization of law that all men are warm-blooded, we can extend it to merely possible cases in a way that we cannot extend the generalization of fact.

I hope that this example throws some light on the nature of the distinction which we are examining, but it does not take us very far because the notion of an unfulfilled conditional itself stands in need of explanation. Not only that, but there seems to be no satisfactory way of explaining it except by reference to laws, so that once again we are in danger of turning in a circle. The reason for this is that nearly always the truth of a conditional statement, whether its antecedent is fulfilled or not, is held to depend not just on the truth-value of its components but on the existence of some connexion between them. If conditionals were supposed to be truth-functional, they would be taken to be true in all cases except that in which the antecedent was true and the consequent false, from which it would follow that the falsity of the antecedent would be sufficient for their truth. Thus, on this interpretation, the conditional statements 'If I strike this match, it will light' and 'If I strike this match, it will not light', will both be true, just so long as I do not strike the match. But this is certainly not how we ordinarily reason. So far are we from taking 'If p then q', in its most common usage, as being merely equivalent to 'Not-p or q', that even the truth of both 'p' and 'q' may not be sufficient for the truth of the conditional. Suppose that a doctor says to his patient 'If you go on drinking at this rate you will be dead within a year' and that the man, who does go on drinking, is killed in a motor accident to which his drunkenness in no way contributed, we should not conclude that the doctor's prediction had come true.

The reason why we should not is that the implied connexion between the man's drinking and his death would not have been established.

The conclusion which I wish to draw from these examples is that conditional statements of the most common sort perform a double function: they have both a narrative and an argumentative aspect. Assuming, for the sake of simplicity, that both 'p' and 'q' are statements of the primary system, we may say that the factual content of 'If p then q' is limited to the denial of its being the case that p and not-q. Beyond this, the conditional arranges 'p' with 'q', in that it offers what is asserted by 'p' as at least a partial explanation of what is asserted by 'q', or represents it as a circumstance in which, on the basis of facts which the speaker is tacitly assuming, what is asserted by 'q' might be expected to occur. For this purpose it need not be implied that either 'p' or 'q' is actually true. On the contrary, in the case of unfulfilled conditionals, the implication is rather that 'p' is false. In its argumentative aspect, the conditional invites us to suppose that p, and then to derive 'q' only in the story which this supposition originates. In the case where 'p' is known to be false, the conditional is thus frankly an excursion into fiction, but it is fiction with a moral. Its point is to draw attention to the facts in the background which favour the truth of 'q' on the supposition of 'p' and to the generalizations which combine with these facts to link the two propositions. These generalizations may but need not take the form of universal laws. Very often we advance a conditional on the basis of nothing stronger than a statement of tendency. This applies especially to the field of human conduct, where our comparative lack of success in lighting upon universal laws leaves room for what may easily develop into rather idle speculation. I doubt, for example, if there are any true or false answers to such questions as what the result of the Second World War would have been if Hitler had not invaded Russia, or whether some other person would have discovered the law of gravitation by the end of the seventeenth century, if Newton had not existed. One party to such a dispute stresses one set of facts, another another; the generalizations on which they respectively rely are weak: supposition is added to supposition. In the end we are left to decide which piece of fiction seems to us to have the greater verisimilitude.

With this account of conditionals, let us now return to the

distinction between generalizations of law and generalizations of fact, which I believe can be explained on similar lines. As I see it, the distinction does not lie in the characters of the generalizations themselves, but rather in our attitude towards them. Because generalizations of law entail unfulfilled conditionals, it might be thought that they had the greater factual content, but this would be a mistake. On the purely factual side, the most that can be expected of any generalization is that it holds in every instance in which its antecedent is satisfied, and this is equally achieved by a true generalization of fact. In either case, also, if we believe the generalization, we believe that it applies to all actual instances. It is only when it comes to imaginary instances, or instances not known to be actual, that a difference arises.

To show how it does arise, let us suppose that I am concerned with a generalization to the effect that everything that has the property f also has the property g. Let us call this generalization H and let there be some object O which I believe to have the property f. Then, if I believe H, I shall ascribe g to O, whether I take H to be a generalization of law or merely one of fact. However, if I am treating H only as a generalization of fact, my belief that it does cover O will be vulnerable to the information that O has such and such other properties, in a way that it would not be vulnerable if I were treating H as a generalization of law. For an illustration, we may revert to our previous example but imagine this time that the meeting has yet to be held. Then my belief that all those who attend it will vote in favour of the motion may not withstand the information that someone with whose views the motion conflicts or someone who has been bribed to oppose it has declared his intention to be there. On the other hand, no information of this kind would affect my belief that all those who attend the meeting will be warm-blooded. If they are human, I count on their being warm-blooded, no matter what opinions they hold and no matter what other properties they can be imagined to possess, unless one carries one's imagination so far as to deny them the physical properties on which warm-bloodedness depends.

This is not to say that we always have more confidence in the propositions that we treat as generalizations of law than in those that we treat as generalizations of fact. If anything, we tend to have more confidence in generalizations of fact, if we believe them at all, since we commonly come to believe them only when we also believe

that all their instances have been checked and discovered to be
favourable. This does, however, go with our regarding the
association of properties in their case as accidental, in the sense
that it is not an association that we are willing to project into the
unknown. In the case of a generalization of law the association is
thought to be projectible, not indeed over every imaginable set of
circumstances, but at least over every set of circumstances in
which it would not conflict with what is regarded as being a more
fundamental law. Since the distinction can also be represented as a
difference in the range of properties which we can imagine to be
added to the antecedent without ceasing to be disposed to associate
it with the consequent, it emerges as a difference of degree, rather
than a difference in kind. In between purely accidental generalizations, which we would not project any further than they have been
discovered to obtain, and fundamental physical laws, with which,
so long as our experience conforms to them, we require that all our
speculations should be consistent, there are generalizations, such
as those relating to personal habits or to social customs, which
we project with fairly considerable reservations, and generalizations of law in which our belief is resistant to all flights of fancy but
those that would bring them into conflict with more fundamental
laws. From this point of view, it does not matter whether the
fundamental laws are causal or statistical. At other levels, we are
disposed to think of generalizations of tendency as being explicable
in terms of universal laws, even when the universal laws have not
been discovered. It can, however, also go the other way. For the
fundamental laws to be statistical, it would be required first that we
should think of the statistics as remaining constant however other
circumstances were varied, and secondly that we should not expect
to find any further reason why this should be so.

It may be objected that we have not avoided the circularity
which we have seen to be involved in explaining laws in terms of
conditionals, since to say that we are disposed to treat different
sorts of generalizations in different fashions is itself to make a
conditional statement. Moreover, we cannot simply define a
natural law as a true generalization which we are willing to project
in the way I have described, since we have to allow for there being
natural laws which have not yet been discovered. We can characterize them as true generalizations which we should treat as
generalizations of law, if we came to believe them, but this is again

to rely upon a conditional. I acknowledge this objection, but think that it can be circumvented. We can take advantage of the fact that our account of conditionals follows the same lines as our account of laws. To speak of our disposition to project generalizations over undetermined or imaginary instances, is itself to make a similar projection, which can be explained in the same fashion. All that we need as a starting point is a number of instances in which the disposition is actually exercised.

The idea which I have been developing is that we explain an event not only by associating events of its kind with events of another kind which are believed in fact to stand in constant relations to them, but also by projecting this generalization over unknown and fictitious instances. The generalization may then be explained in its turn by being derived from another generalization or from a theory which ranges more widely, again over both actual and imaginary cases. There are weaker forms of explanation, in which we rely in the first instance only on statements of tendency, but they too are held to be projectible, though to a smaller extent. It may be asked why we should not be simply content with the arrangement of facts, without bothering to speculate about the hypothetical consequences of fictitious events, but the answer to this is that these speculations guide us in our dealings with the largely unknown future. Being uncertain as to what will actually take place, we have to provide for various possibilities. We therefore need a more extensive explanatory system than one that simply deals in generalizations of fact.

D Theory and Observation

In giving an account of natural laws, I have said nothing about our reasons for believing in them. The doubt which Hume raised has not yet been removed. On the contrary, we have found ourselves obliged to concede the first two steps in his argument. What now of the third? Is it true that the only reason we can have for believing that events of two different kinds are universally connected, or even that the connexion will be found to obtain in a single further instance, is our knowing that they have been constantly conjoined in the past?

This proposition needs to be interpreted. If it is taken as implying that the only way in which we can legitimately arrive at a universal hypothesis is by generalizing from observed instances, it arbitrarily disallows a great deal of our actual practice. It would be going too far to say that such simple inductive procedures never occur in science, but they play a very much smaller part than the advancing of theories which connect events in ways that have not previously been noticed or thought to be significant. Another very important feature of scientific method is that one theory evolves out of another. Kepler did not start by observing that the planet Mars moved in an elliptical orbit around the sun and then make the inductive inference that this was true of all planets at all times. The data which he had assembled about the apparent positions of Mars at different times accorded with Ptolemy's geocentric system very nearly as well as with the heliocentric system of Copernicus. He thought that the Copernican system explained the facts better and he made various assumptions to bring it into line with them: these assumptions were then subsequently verified. Newton did not observe bodies, on which no forces were acting, continuing in their states of rest or of uniform motion along straight lines. There are no such bodies. Having taken from Galileo the idea that one should explain the motions of bodies in terms of the changes of these motions, he laid down the principles that would govern these changes in an ideally isolated system. In short, he set up a model to which he assumed that the facts would conform. The supersession of Newton's theory by Einstein's theory of relativity was the outcome of an experiment which appeared to yield the paradoxical result that the velocity of light remained constant with respect to a number of bodies which were moving relatively to each other in the same direction as the light. Einstein's solution of this problem did not consist merely in the substitution of one set of empirical generalizations for another, but rather in the adoption of a different system of geometry for describing the physical world, in a radical revision of the concept of simultaneity, and in the enthronement of the proposition that the velocity of light is constant as an axiom of physical theory. In this and in other ways his conclusions ran counter to common sense. They gained general acceptance because they provided a means of accounting systematically for a number of facts for which Newtonian theory could give only *ad hoc* explanations. The terms in which they accounted for them were, however, a long way removed from the perceptual level. This is, indeed, an instance of a general tendency for scientific explanations to become more abstract, as their range is extended There is only a remote and devious connexion between the terms of contemporary quantum theory and any observable event.

But when all this is said, it is still required of theories that they fit the facts. The notion of fitting the facts may itself be elastic, but at least some operative sense must be given to a failure to fit them. If a theory is to have any explanatory value, it must be empirically testable, and this means that some boundary must be set to the range of observable situations with which it is held to be consistent. But then Hume's question can be revived, in a more general form. It may, indeed, be incorrect to say that the only reason we can have for accepting a theory is that it has been found to fit all the available facts. Of two theories which equally fit the facts one may be thought superior to another on the ground that it is simpler, or more far-reaching, or that it explains the facts more systematically. But even if it is not sufficient that a theory fits the facts in order for it to be acceptable, it is eventually necessary. I say 'eventually' because a theory which is otherwise attractive may be provisionally accepted even though there are some facts which it cannot yet accommodate. It will not, however, be thought wholly satisfactory until it does succeed in accommodating them. And this is all that we need to be able to pursue Hume's argument. What ground can we have for believing that a theory which has fitted all the facts that have come under our observation will continue to fit those that have not yet done so?

It is worth stressing the point that this question does still arise, since it has been suggested, notably by Professor Popper,[1] that once it is realized how little part the process of generalizing from observed instances actually plays in science, the problem of induction disappears. The choice, which we have seen that Popper makes,[2] of a criterion of falsifiability for delimiting scientific statements goes with the contention that scientific progress is made by putting forward theories and trying to falsify them. There is, therefore, no inductive step to justify. A theory, or a hypothesis, is retained so long as it resists our attempts to falsify it. If it is eventually refuted, it is discarded or modified and another theory adopted in its place. The greater the range of falsifying

[1] See Sir Karl Popper, *The Logic of Scientific Discovery* Part I and *Conjectures and Refutations*, Ch. 1.
[2] See above p. 27-9.

instances to which a theory is exposed, the richer it will be in content; and the richer it is, the greater its explanatory value.

Popper does not like to say that a theory is confirmed by passing the tests to which it is subjected, because he associates talk of confirmation with the inductivist approach that he rejects, but he does say that it is corroborated. He also allows for degrees of corroboration, as is implied by his saying that 'the better a statement can be tested, the better it can be ... attested by its tests'.[1] And, indeed, it appears reasonable for him to speak in this way. For what would be the point of testing a theory if it did not gain credit in proportion to the number and variety of tests which it had passed? It would not be contradictory to believe that a hypothesis which had once met with a contrary instance was thereby rendered immune from any further refutation. In practice, we conclude, no doubt in the light of our past experience of the fortunes of hypotheses, that if it has failed once it cannot any longer be relied on. But then we are making an inductive inference. It is an inductive step to assume that a theory which has passed a variety of tests is a better guide to the future than one that has not been tested or one that has been tested and found wanting. And if we do take this inductive step, then it seems legitimate to ask how it can be justified. Not only that but Popper's concept of corroboration encounters the same major difficulty as does the inductivist concept of confirmation. Earlier on,[2] I referred to Hempel's paradox according to which every state of affairs, however seemingly irrelevant, which is consistent with a hypothesis, equally confirms it. If this paradox calls for a rebuttal, as I think it does, then we have also to explain why every state of affairs, however seemingly irrelevant, which fails to falsify a hypothesis, does not equally corroborate it.

This problem is allied with what seems to me another objection to the exclusive emphasis on falsification. If a hypothesis gains credit only through withstanding our attempts to falsify it, we ought to lose interest in any circumstances which serve to test it as soon as we can discover that they cannot furnish a counter-example to it. This would mean, for instance, that if we were testing the hypothesis that people suffer from malaria only when they have been bitten by an anopheles mosquito, and there were someone of whom

[1] *Conjectures and Refutations*, p. 267.
[2] See above p. 28.

we knew that he had been so bitten but did not know whether he had malaria, we should take no further interest in him. Since he cannot be discovered to have the disease without the mosquito's having bitten him, his case cannot falsify the hypothesis. But surely this would not be in accordance with scientific method. The experimenter in such a case would wish to know whether the man had caught malaria and if he discovered that he had, he would regard the hypothesis as having been confirmed. We do require hypotheses to be confirmed; and not every situation which merely fails to refute a hypothesis is therefore regarded as confirming it. This still leaves the question whether such an attitude is rational. But then we return to the problem of induction.

VIII Order and Chance

A The Uniformity of Nature

An assumption which we have seen to be made by Hume is that inductive reasoning would be justified if only we were entitled to adopt the general principle that 'Instances of which we have had no experience must resemble those of which we have had experience and that the course of nature continues always uniformly the same'. The problem, as he saw it, was that this principle, which we may call the principle of the uniformity of nature, did not appear to be logically demonstrable, and that to try to support it on the basis of factual evidence would be to beg the question, since the use of factual evidence would rest on the principle which it was designed to justify.

Other philosophers have assigned the same part to the principle but taken a different view of its status. Thus Kant argued that our ability to order events objectively in time depended on the assumption that they were subject to causal laws.[1] Since he believed that the ordering of events in time was one of the necessary conditions of their being accessible to our understanding, he concluded that what he called the law of universal causation was bound to apply to everything that was capable of falling within our experience. John Stuart Mill, on the other hand, regarded the principle of the uniformity of nature as an empirical generalization which was justified inductively by the more specific generalizations of law, which it was itself used in establishing.[2] He saw that this reasoning was circular but denied that the circularity was vicious. The position as he saw it was that the general principle and the more specific laws needed and received mutual support. This was, indeed, the only point on which he seriously disagreed with Hume. No more than Kant did he question the assumption that an

[1] See *Critique of Pure Reason*, Second Analogy.
[2] J. S. Mill. *A System of Logic*, Book III, Ch. XXI.

assurance of the general uniformity of nature was both necessary and sufficient to justify inductive reasoning.

But is this assumption true? The trouble is that it is not at all clear what it should be taken to imply. It can hardly be supposed that when Hume spoke of the course of nature as continuing always uniformly the same he meant to exclude the possibility of there ever being any change. The proposition that 'there is nothing new under the sun' is not literally in accord with our past experience. What we must take him to have meant is that the changes which undoubtedly do occur are governed by constant laws, so that they are in principle foreseeable. Similarly, if there were a law of universal causation, a sufficient knowledge of the antecedents of any event would enable us to predict its occurrence. There may still be surprises in store for us because we neither know all the relevant facts, nor have we yet discovered all the laws which govern them; but if we at least knew that there always were such laws, we should be entitled to feel some confidence that the generalizations which we had so far found to hold without exception would continue to apply to further instances.

But now we encounter the difficulty that if the principle of the uniformity of nature is taken to imply no more than that every event comes under some valid generalization, it is, indeed, true, but trivial. If no restriction is set upon the form and complexity of the generalizations, or upon the choice of the terms which enter into them, we can always adjust them to any finite series of events. It is like our ability to draw a curve through any finite series of points. We may come to grief when we try to extend the curve to points which have not yet been supplied to us, but once they have been supplied, we can always make it fit them retrospectively. If we have complete freedom in the coinage of predicates, we can cause any two events to share a common quality just by introducing a predicate which is so defined that its extension covers them both. Even if we outlaw such devices, and restrict ourselves to predicates which are such that their different instances accord with our intuitions of resemblance, their failure to reproduce themselves at all frequently, or to reproduce themselves in the same combinations, would not prevent the things to which they applied from falling under universal generalizations. To illustrate this, let us take the extreme case of a world in which the only recurrent pattern is that of spatio-temporal relations. No other property is ever found in more than one instance. This is the most heterogeneous world that it is possible to imagine, but it is also completely orderly. For if only one event of type A and one event of type B ever occur, and the instance of A stands in the spatio-temporal relation R to the instance of B, it will be true that every instance of A stands in the relation R to some instance of B; and the same will apply to any other pair of unique events. It may, indeed, be objected that these trivial generalizations would not be laws, but that is beside the point. To speak of the uniformity of nature is to speak of the regularity which it actually displays; and this is not affected by the distinction between those generalizations that we are and that we are not disposed to extend to imaginary instances.

Nevertheless, the objection does give the clue to what is amiss. If the principle of the uniformity of nature is to be of any use to us, we have to avoid making it either too weak or too strong. To illustrate this difficulty, we need only consider the attempt to fit inductive reasoning into a deductive mould by treating the proposition that nature is uniform as the major premiss of a syllogism, which has the proposition that all hitherto observed A's have been B as its minor premiss and the proposition that all A's are B as its conclusion. Let us take as an example the false proposition that all swans are white, and let *n* be the date at which the first black swan was observed. Then the syllogism will run: Nature is uniform. All swans observed before *n* are white. Therefore, all swans are white. Since the conclusion is false, one of the premisses must be false, if the syllogism is valid. But *ex hypothesi* the minor premiss is true. Consequently, it is false that nature is uniform. Since we do not draw this inference, it follows that the syllogism is not thought to be valid. The uniformity of nature is not so rigidly conceived as to be at the mercy of an exception to what has so far seemed to be a true generalization. On the other hand, we do not want to conceive it so elastically that it becomes consistent with anything whatsoever; for then it cannot authorize us to expect any one thing to happen rather than any other. What we want is a backing for just those hypotheses that we are actually disposed to project. But where are we to find a general principle that will secure this for us?

One thing which should be clear is that we are not going to achieve complete security. There is no acceptable principle that is going to guarantee us against error. Even if we follow John Stuart Mill in making such special assumptions as that the determinants of every event lie in its immediate spatio-temporal neighbourhood, we are not going to put it out of the power of nature to surprise us.[1] The most that we can hope for is to find some general assurance that the hypotheses which we are disposed to project can, under favourable conditions, at least be shown to be highly probable. But before we consider whether even this hope can be realized, we need first to examine the concept, or concepts, of probability.

B Statements of Probability

1 *The Calculus of Chances*

Whether or not it is correct to say that there is more than one concept of probability, or that the word 'probability' is used in different senses, it can at least be said that statements of probability fall into three distinct classes. This can best be shown by examples. Consider the statements that the probability of throwing double-six with a pair of true dice is 1/36, that the probability that such and such an unborn infant will be a boy is 51 per cent, and that it is probable that the economic union of Europe will lead to political union within the next half-century. The first of these statements is an example of what is often called a statement of *a priori* probability; it relates to the mathematical calculus of chances. The second is a statistical statement; it is concerned with the actual frequency with which some property is distributed among the members of a given set. The third is an example of what, following Russell, I call a statement of credibility; it implies that we have reason to feel at least more confident than not that such and such an event will come about. Statements of credibility, which may of course relate to the present or the past as well as to the future, may be based upon statistical statements, but they are not themselves statistical. It is only by a roundabout procedure, such as that of assimilating them to betting offers that we are able to express them in numerical terms.

It is important also to distinguish statements of my first class from statistical statements. The temptation not to do so is increased by the fact that they could be interpreted in a way that

<hr />

[1] Cf. G. H. von Wright. *The Logical Problem of Induction*, Ch. IV.

would make them statistical. Thus, we might define a true die, or an unbiased coin, in physical terms, as one which was made of such and such materials, and had its centre of gravity in such and such a place, and in that case the truth of such a statement as that the probability of throwing heads with a true coin is $1/2$ would depend upon the actual results that were obtained with coins which met these physical requirements. This is not, however, the way in which such statements are usually interpreted. More commonly, what is meant by saying that a die is a true die or that a coin is unbiased is just that it yields results which are in accord with the *a priori* calculus of chances, and the consequence of this interpretation is that statements which assign probabilities to these results turn into mathematical truisms. On the understanding that a coin has two faces and that when it is tossed one of them will fall uppermost, to say that there is a probability of $1/2$ that an unbiased penny will come up heads is to say no more than that one is the half of two.

The mathematics is by no means always so simple as this, but the principle remains the same. Thus, when it is said that the probability of throwing heads three times in succession with a true coin is $1/8$, what is meant is that among all the possible three-term sequences of the two alternatives of heads and tails, the sequence consisting of a succession of three heads stands to the total in the ratio of 1 to 8. If we generalize this and say that the probability of throwing heads n times in succession is $1/2^n$, what we are saying is that among all the possible n-fold sequences of the kind in question, the sequence consisting of n heads stands to the total in the ratio of 1 to 2^n. It is obvious that the value of $1/2^n$ grows smaller as n increases, and this is all that is implied by saying that a long run of consecutive heads or tails, or a long run of red or black, or even or odd numbers at roulette, is very improbable. The notorious Monte Carlo fallacy consists in assuming that because the odds against an even number's coming up ten times in succession are over a thousand to one, there is equally little chance of the tenth spin yielding an even number, if the previous nine have done so. This reasoning is fallacious because the odds in any given instance are simply based on the proportion of even numbers in the total, and this is not affected by previous results. The point to be remembered is that these are not statements of credibility. To say that the odds against a sequence of ten even numbers are over a thousand to one is to say no more than that this sequence is one of more than a thousand that are mathematically possible. To say that the odds in any given instance do not change is just to say that the proportion of even numbers in the total remains constant. In either case, it is simply a matter of counting abstract possibilities.

Since the calculus of chances is a branch of pure mathematics, it does not in itself yield any conclusion about the likelihood of actual events. We can use it only to infer that if certain ratios obtain within a class of actual events, then certain other ratios must obtain as well. The application of the calculus to games of chance depends on the empirical assumption that the objects which are used in them behave in a way that accords with the mathematical distribution of chances. This does not mean that their behaviour is not causally determined, though it is essential to the interest of these games that the determining factors, if they exist, should be so complex that the result of any particular coup is not practically foreseeable. Neither does it mean that their behaviour is not designed. On the contrary, dice are normally constructed in such a way that in sufficiently long sequences of throws each face will come up about as often as any other: playing cards are so manufactured and the processes of dealing them so organized that in a sufficiently long series of deals each possible combination of a given number of them appears with approximately equal frequency. It is a statistical question whether these intentions are actually fulfilled. In itself, the calculus of chances is independent of statistics, but it is only by relying on statistical assumptions that we can draw any practical conclusions from it.

This is a point which is too often overlooked. In particular, it is often assumed, quite unwarrantably, that if things were left to themselves, they would be equally indulgent to all the logical possibilities. Thus, I have heard it advanced as an argument in favour of the hypothesis that the world was deliberately created, that the actual distribution of atoms, so far as we know it, is very improbable. That is to say, it is very different from what it would be if there were a tendency in the course of time for every atom to occupy any one position as frequently as it occupied any other. But the answer to this is that, antecedently to any experience, we have no reason to expect atoms to behave in this way, rather than in any other, including the way in which they actually do behave. So long as we remain in the realm of purely *a priori* possibilities, we can make no inference at all about what is actually likely to happen. The same applies to the card-guessing experiments, where much is made of the fact that some performers obtain results which, for some time at least, are consistently better than the mathematical chances. Antecedently to experience, we have no reason to expect that the average proportion of successful guesses, which results from the enumeration of all the logical possibilities, either will or will not be attained in any actual experiment. If it is found to be the case that most people do succeed in about this proportion of attempts, then what is remarkable about the superior performers is just that they are a little better than the rest of us at guessing the identity of cards which are concealed from them. The fact that their results are also 'better than chance' is not in itself of any consequence.

2 *The Frequency Theory*

When it comes to statistical statements, the first point to note is that they always relate to classes. Even when the statement appears to be about an individual, there is always a tacit reference in it to some class to which the individual belongs. Thus, in the example which I gave, the statement that there is a probability of 51 per cent that such and such an unborn infant will be a boy is to be understood as referring to the proportion of male births in some class of cases of which this particular one is a member. The statement is, indeed, not fully explicit until this class is specified.

When the class in question is finite, and its extension is at least approximately known, the statement that there is a probability m/n that any one of its members has a given property can be interpreted straightforwardly as stating that the property is in fact distributed among the members of the class in the proportion m/n. This is not, however, always so. If I make the statistical statement that the probability of throwing heads with the penny which I take out of my pocket is $1/2$, I am not taken to be implying that the penny will in fact be tossed an even number of times; nor will my statement be held to be falsified if it is in fact thrown only twice and comes up heads each time. The reason for this is that my statement is construed as being at least partly hypothetical; it refers to the results of possible as well as actual tosses. Neither does the straightforward interpretation serve in the cases where we do not intend to imply that the extension of the class is finite; for no meaning is attached to saying that a property is distributed in the proportion m/n among the members of an infinite class.

The usual way of dealing with these more complicated cases is to invoke the notion of limiting frequency. The distribution of a property among the members of a class is said to have the limiting-value m/n, if, in the course of listing them successively, there comes a point after which the proportion which has the property, counted from the start, does not differ from m/n by more than an arbitrarily small amount. The probability that any given member has the property is then identified with this limiting value. Thus, to say that there is a probability of $1/2$ that if I toss this penny it will come up heads is, on this interpretation, to say that if I were to toss the penny repeatedly, there would come a point in the series of tosses at which the distribution of heads in the total would attain the limiting value of $1/2$. Since all that is required is that the limit, once reached, should be indefinitely maintained, this allows for the possibility that the series is infinite.

The frequency theory of probability, as this interpretation of statistical statements is usually called, has also been made to carry the requirement that the series on which it operates be randomly ordered. What this is most commonly taken to imply is that they satisfy the very strong condition of being indifferent to place-selection, in the sense that every sub-series which is formed by such methods as selecting every nth member, or, in the example of coin-tossing, every member following a throw of heads, attains the same limiting-value as the main series. The purpose of this is to rule out artificial arrangements which would endow the series with more than one limiting-value with respect to the distribution of the same property. For example, an infinite series of tosses which conformed to the pattern heads, tails, heads, tails tails, heads, tails tails tails, and so on indefinitely with each occurrence of heads being followed by an increased number of tails, would tend to the limit of 100 per cent tails. We could, however, arrange the series in such a way that the heads and tails alternated, since there is an infinite number of both, and in that case the limiting-value of the proportion of tails would be not 100 per cent but 50 per cent. Incidentally, the fact that in the first arrangement the proportion of tails does tend to the limit of 100 per cent makes it clear that 100 per cent frequencies, in this sense, are not to be

identified with universal generalizations. For a universal generalization admits of no exceptions, whereas a 100 per cent frequency
can accommodate an infinite number of them, as this example
shows.

A disquieting feature of statistical statements, to which I have
already drawn attention,[1] is that when they are interpreted in this
way they are not falsifiable. So long as the series is not known to be
complete, its failure to reach a predicted limiting-value at any
given stage will always leave open the possibility of its reaching it
later on. If we are to operate with the frequency theory we are,
therefore, obliged to make light of this possibility. We must decide
to count a statistical statement as having been at least provisionally
falsified, if the frequency which it attributes to the incidence of
some property in such and such a total population is markedly
different from that with which the property has been found to
occur in a sufficiently large sample. This decision has the support
of the so-called Law of Large Numbers, according to which it is
very improbable that the frequency of a property in a large sample
will fail approximately to match its frequency in the population
from which the sample is drawn, and becomes increasingly
improbable the larger the sample. It is, however, to be noted that
this law, belonging as it does to the calculus of chances, is a
probability statement of my first class and not a statement of
credibility. The logical truth which it expresses is that among all
possible samples of the large size in question the proportion of
those in which the frequency of a property fails even approximately
to match its frequency in the population from which they are
drawn is very small. What it does not state is that it is at all
improbable, in the way of credibility, that the sample which we
actually possess is one of the deviant minority. This does not
invalidate the decision to count a statistical statement as false if it
runs counter to the law of large numbers, since this decision can
always be revoked if subsequent evidence goes to show that we
have been relying on a deviant sample. Nevertheless, it does mean
that when we infer from the character of a sample to the character
of a population, which exceeds the sample by an unknown amount,
we are relying not only on the law of large numbers, but also on a
principle of fair sampling, which is not logically demonstrable. We
are assuming that our observations are not biased or at least that if

[1] See above p. 29.

they are biased the bias will extend to the further instances over which we intend our statement to be projected. In the case of most statistical statements, the range of this projection will be fairly narrow. We think of current statistics as providing a guide to the immediate rather than the indefinite future. Even so, a principle of fair sampling will still be assumed; and there appears to be no way, free of circularity, in which it can be justified.

We have already remarked that statistical statements, if they refer to individuals at all, refer to them only as members of classes. A consequence of this is that, so long as we remain within the confines of the frequency theory, the question how probable it is that a given individual has such and such a property may not have any one true answer, since the individual may belong to various different classes in which the property occurs with different limiting-frequencies. An example which often figures in the literature of this subject[1] is that of a Swede called Petersen who is known to have made a pilgrimage to Lourdes, the question being how probable it is that he is a Protestant. If we consider him as a member of the class of contemporary Swedes, the answer will be that he very probably is a Protestant: if we consider him as a member of the class of those who make pilgrimages to Lourdes, the answer will be that he very probably is not a Protestant. It looks therefore as if we have reached a contradiction, so long as we interpret the question as genuinely relating to this individual case. This is not, however, an interpretation which is allowed by the frequency theory. If we adhere to this theory, we have to interpret the two apparently conflicting answers as being no more than restatements of the facts that Petersen is both a Swede and a pilgrim to Lourdes, that a high proportion of Swedes are Protestants and that a high proportion of such pilgrims are not Protestants. Since these facts are clearly mutually consistent, the contradiction vanishes. Unfortunately, the question which we were trying to ask about Petersen vanishes with it.

This result is unsatisfactory, in that we do often wish to arrive at a unique estimate of probability for an individual case. For instance, I might be interested in the statistics of longevity through being concerned with my own chances of living to a ripe old age.

---

[1] See e.g. Carl Hempel. 'Inductive Inconsistencies' *Logic and Language: Studies Dedicated to Rudolf Carnap* (1962), and my own *Probability and Evidence*, I.2.

If that were so, I should not think it rational to make a random choice among the many classes of which I am a member and estimate my chances according to the average duration of life that obtained within that class. Even if the classes were restricted to those exhibiting a frequency which I felt justified in projecting, I still should not be indifferent between them. I should pick the one that was defined by the greatest number of predicates, on the ground that I should thereby minimize the risk of overlooking any factor that bore upon my special case. But while this may be a rational policy, it is not one that can be justified, or even formulated, within the terms of the frequency theory. If the assignment of such and such a probability to an individual case is taken to imply no more than that there is such and such a frequency in some class to which the individual belongs, no sense can be attached to saying that the choice of any one class yields a better estimate of probability than that of any other. So long as the respective frequencies have been correctly assessed, there can be nothing to choose between them. If we are to justify, or even be able to interpret, the making of such a choice, we have to find some way of relating statistical statements to statements of credibility.

3   The Logical Theory and Statements of Credibility

When it comes to statements of credibility the first problem is to decide how they should be analyzed. It has often been assumed that they too are elliptical, in the sense that when they state that some proposition is probable, what they are really stating is that the proposition is probable, relatively to such and such evidence. This is the view held by those who take the concept of probability in this usage, to be a logical concept, whether, like Keynes,[1] they regard it as covering all probability-statements, or whether, like Carnap[2] and Russell,[3] they treat statistical statements as falling under the different concept of proportional frequency.

The consequence of treating probability as a logical relation is that the statements which are construed in this way become analytic, in the sense that the answer to the question whether and to what extent one proposition probabilifies another will depend

[1] J. M. Keynes. *A Treatise on Probability*, Part I.
[2] Rudolf Carnap. *The Logical Foundations of Probability*.
[3] Bertrand Russell. *Human Knowledge: Its Scope and Limits*, pp. 343–4.

only on the content of the propositions and on a decision to assign them initial probabilities. Thus, in Carnap's system of inductive logic,[1] the different possible distributions of truth-values among the primitive propositions of the system represent different possible states of the universe which the system portrays. Some of these state-descriptions, as Carnap calls them, will have the same structure, in the sense that they represent the properties which the system admits as occurring with the same frequencies, though they do not assign them to exactly the same individuals. In a finite universe, there will be a finite number of these possible structures. The decision is then taken to treat the descriptions of these possible structures as being equally probable on no evidence, or in other words, antecedently to any experience. As a result of this decision, each state-description is assigned an initial probability or, in Carnap's terms, an initial degree of confirmation, which is inversely proportional to the number of possible structures multiplied by the number of state-descriptions which exhibit the same structure as it does. Since every proposition is equivalent to the disjunction of the state-descriptions in which it comes out true, and since the probability of a disjunction is equated with the sum of the probabilities of the propositions which it disjoins, it follows that every proposition which can figure in the system is assigned some definite measure of initial probability. Since also the probability which one proposition bestows on another is taken to depend on the extent to which they come out true in the same state-descriptions, it is then easy to prove that their relation is uniquely determined by their initial probabilities. What is left to experience is the accumulation of evidence: everything else is laid down *a priori*.

Since Carnap's system is intended only to provide a model on which one might eventually pattern some practical system of betting on the course of future experience, it is not an objection to it that it fails to provide a satisfactory analysis of statements of credibility. What may be objectionable is the arbitrariness of the special principle of uniformity which is concealed in the decision to treat all possible structures as equally probable. Nevertheless, if we are looking for an analysis of statements of credibility, there is a strong objection to construing probability, in this sense, as a logical relation. The difficulty is of the same sort as that which

[1] *Op. cit.*

arises when one tries to apply the frequency theory to an individual case. Just as the probability of an event, in terms of frequency, may be different according as it is assigned to different classes, so the logical probability of a proposition may be different according as it is related to different items of evidence. Suppose now that we are interested in the truth of some proposition 'p', for which we have the evidence of the propositions 'q' and 'r', and that we have correctly estimated the probability of 'p' relatively to 'q', relatively to 'r' and relatively to both 'q' and 'r', the result being different in each case. Have we any reason, on the logical theory, to prefer one of these estimates to another? The answer is that we can have none. According to the theory, the propositions which express these different estimates are all logically true. But how then can we have any ground for deciding between them?

The answer which the proponents of the logical theory have made to this objection, which I first put forward fifteen years ago,[1] is that we have to adopt the methodological rule that the probabilities to go by are those that are relative to the total evidence. As it stands, this rule is somewhat obscure, since we are not told what the total evidence is to be taken to consist in; but perhaps we can construe it as an injunction always to try to maximize the evidence. The rule might have to be subject to certain restrictions on the score of morality and also of economy, but with these provisos it seems to be in accord with common sense. If we ask what reason there is for adopting it, the obvious answer is that by doing so we put ourselves in a better position to estimate what is actually likely to happen. But what the proponents of the logical theory have overlooked is that this is not an answer which they can consistently give. If the statement that 'p' is likely to be true is construed as an elliptical way of saying that 'p' is highly confirmed by some other proposition 'q', or some other set of propositions, '$q, r, s \ldots$', then any true statement of this kind must be as good as any other. One cannot say that one or other of them comes nearer the mark, because there just is no mark for them to hit. On this basis, the rule that we are to maximize evidence appears entirely arbitrary: its purpose cannot even be expressed.

[1] See 'The Concept of Probability as a Logical Relation', in *Observation and Interpretation*, Proceedings of the Ninth Symposium of the Colston Research Society at Bristol University. The essay is reprinted in my *The Concept of a Person*.

In order to express it, we need to be able to speak of probability, or likelihood, in what G. E. Moore, in his *Commonplace* Book, called 'an absolute sense', the sense in which, as he puts it, 'When you say that something is probable what you are saying is merely something as to what it's reasonable to expect'.[1] This is surely, as Moore claims, an extremely common use of the term, though perhaps not one to which we at all times adhere consistently. Thus, when something which was considered probable is known not to have happened, we are inclined to say in retrospect that it *seemed* probable rather than it *was* probable, though the fact that it did not happen does not imply that it was not reasonable to expect it. This is because we characterize propositions as probable or improbable when we do not feel ourselves to be in a position to characterize them as true or false; when ascriptions of truth or falsehood can confidently be made, ascriptions of probability are thought to lapse. This may be the reason why some philosophers have held that words like 'probably', at least as they occur in statements of credibility, play only a performative role. On this view, to say that '*p*' is probable is merely to express something short of complete confidence in the truth of '*p*', and to encourage others to feel the same. This is, however, to overlook the fact that we can talk significantly of what would be the case if such and such a state of affairs were probable, without in any way implying that the state of affairs may actually obtain; and at least to pay too little attention to the fact that we can dispute whether a statement of credibility is justified. Admittedly, any evidence which goes to show that it is reasonable to believe '*p*' will also be evidence which goes to show that '*p*' is true, but the two conclusions can be distinguished, at least in principle. Indeed, they must be distinguished if we are to allow for the possibility that some propositions which it is reasonable to believe will turn out to be false. Of course, we do not know which they are. If we did, it would not be reasonable to believe them.

In spite of the vacillations in ordinary usage, I therefore think it better to construe the assertion that '*p*' is probable as an assertion that it is reasonable to believe '*p*' rather than as a qualified assertion of '*p*'. This procedure also has the advantage that the injunction to maximize evidence can be given the justification which it failed to obtain from the logical theory of probability. For clearly if we are

[1] *The Commonplace Book of G. E. Moore*, ed. Casimir Lewy, p. 403.

considering whether it is reasonable to believe that p, we want so far as is practicable to take account of every factor which has any bearing on the question whether 'p' is true. The best position is that in which we have at our disposal some generalization of law, which together with the facts that are known to us enables us to deduce 'p' or alternatively 'not-p'. In such a case it is clearly essential not to overlook any fact which would make the law inapplicable. If we are reduced to relying on a statement of tendency, there is a corresponding need to take account of any fact which either strengthens or weakens the tendency of the existing evidence to be associated with the object of our enquiry. It is for this reason that when we apply the frequency theory to an individual case, we have to assign it to the narrowest class for which there is a projectible frequency. We have seen that this rule cannot be justified within the terms of the frequency theory, the reason being that it is not a rule for estimating chances as the theory portrays them. It represents a precaution which we need to take in using statistics to forecast what will actually happen in an individual instance.

In talking of such rules as being justified, I am of course assuming that it is reasonable to trust the generalizations which they are designed to safeguard. But this, it may be objected, is just what Hume's argument puts in question. Neither have we done anything so far to meet it. All that has emerged from our discussion of probability is that we are justified in projecting our hypotheses if we are entitled to assume that the instances which have conformed to them are not deviant; and this comes to no more than the triviality that we can rely on our samples if we can assume that they are fair. Can we really go no further than this?

C The Problem of Confirmation

Let me say at once that I do not think that we can. We have already seen that it is vain to look for a guarantee against error, and we now find that the search for an assurance that we have at least a very good chance of being right leads only to the result that we simply take our stand on what we think it reasonable to believe. The demand for a proof that what we think to be reasonable really is so leaves us at a loss, because we do not know even what would count as such a proof. This is not to say that our standards of rationality are not subject to criticism. It is open to anyone to suggest that some different method of choosing our hypotheses would serve us better. But how is this claim to be tested except by adopting this method and seeing how it works? And if it is found to work, and we consequently adhere to it, we shall again be taking our past experience as a guide to the future. What else do we have to go by?

The position may become clearer if we consider how we do justify our beliefs. Let us suppose that the proposition in question relates to some particular event which I cannot claim either to perceive or to remember. Then if I am asked what reason I have for accepting it, the best way for me to answer will be to adduce some other proposition or set of propositions with which I believe it to be connected either by a universal generalization or at least by a strong generalization of tendency. If those whom I am trying to convince accept these other propositions and also accept the generalization, I need go no further. If they do not accept them, or do not accept the generalization, then I have to try to justify them in their turn. If the proposition which is questioned relates to some particular event I shall proceed in the same way as before. If it is the generalization that has to be justified I may be able to show that it is derivable from some wider generalization or some theory which my interlocutors accept. Otherwise I can do no better than show that it accords with all the available evidence.

The fact that a proposition is accepted does not, indeed, entail that it is true. All the same, the propositions which we seriously put forward as being true are bound to be identical with those that we accept. To admit that they may still not be true is, in practical terms, to admit that we may have occasion to reject them. Consequently, the conclusion that a belief has been justified is always subject to revision. It can survive the discovery that one has accepted a false proposition, and even the discovery that the belief itself is false; for the acceptance of a false proposition can still have been justified if it depended on its connexion with true propositions by a true generalization of tendency. It can survive the discovery that a universal generalization on which one has relied is false, provided again that the generalization holds sufficiently widely for it to entail a strong generalization of tendency which is true. On the other hand, it would not survive the discovery that the argument lacked a substantial basis of truth.

The question now arises whether it is sufficient that the propositions which are used in justifying a belief should actually be true, or whether it is also necessary that we should have good reason to believe that they are true. The advantage of making it sufficient that the propositions in question actually be true is that we then have a definite criterion for deciding when our beliefs are justified. The disadvantage is that we are not required to know, or even to have any ground for believing, that the criterion has been complied with. On the other hand, if we insist on our having a good reason to accept any proposition which is used to justify another, we run the risk of embarking on an infinite regress, since whenever we give a reason for any belief we shall have to give a reason for the reason and so *ad infinitum*. We can put a stop to the regress only by making special rulings such as that any confident judgement of perception or memory is *prima facie* justified, or that the acceptance of a generalization is justified, at least provisionally, if we have evidence of such and such strength in its favour. This will still leave Hume's argument unmet, but there is no help for that. The kind of assurance that he asks for is simply not available.

The difficulty is, however, not just that Hume's argument remains unmet; but that the notion of evidence is itself not clear. I have already referred on one or two occasions[1] to Hempel's paradox, according to which every state of affairs which is logically consistent with a given hypothesis equally confirms it. This conclusion is highly counter-intuitive but it is hard to see how we can avoid it. To use Hempel's example, the proposition that all ravens are black is ordinarily taken to be equivalent both to the proposition that all non-black things are non-ravens and to the proposition that everything is either not a raven or black: and it would seem perverse to deny that equivalent propositions are equally confirmed by the same evidence. But then, as we have seen, the proposition that all ravens are black is going to be confirmed not only by instances of black ravens but also by instances which similarly satisfy these other propositions, that is, by anything other than instances of non-black ravens. It is, however, to be noted that the idea of confirmation which is here at work is that of going through a finite set of instances. The generalization is progressively confirmed in the sense that the number of instances which are found to be favourable is an increasing

[1] See above pp. 28 and 158.

proportion of the total. But from this point of view the propositions which generate the paradox are not equivalent. They are concerned with different sets of things.

But how does this idea of confirmation apply to open generalizations, where it is not assumed that the number of instances is finite? For clearly, if the total number of instances is infinite, the proportion of those found to be favourable will not increase; however many are examined, there will be an infinite number left. The answer is, I think, that it applies only indirectly. Open generalizations are confirmed in this way through the confirmation of the generalizations which are derived from them by restricting their antecedents to a finite number of instances. It is, indeed, true that the validity of an open generalization carries with it the validity of any generalizations which are equivalent to it. If this does not apply to its confirmation, it is because the way in which it is confirmed does nothing for its equivalents. In confirming the truth of some finite set of propositions to the effect that this and that and the other non-black thing is a non-raven I obtain nothing which implies even that any raven exists.

It has been suggested[1] that the generalization that all non-black things are non-ravens is not confirmed even by positive instances, on the ground that the property of being a non-black thing is not projectible. I no longer think that this will serve as a solution to Hempel's paradox, because it does not cover enough examples. For instance, the property of being invertebrate and that of possessing kidneys are considered equally projectible; yet it would seem strange to set about confirming the generalization that invertebrates lack kidneys by examining animals that have them and finding that they are vertebrate. Nevertheless, the point is important because of its bearing on another difficulty which has recently been raised by Nelson Goodman,[2] though in effect it goes back to Hume. The difficulty is that any set of positive instances which confirm a universal generalization H will also confirm some other generalization with which H is incompatible. The example which Goodman takes to illustrate this is that of the generalization that all emeralds are green, and he achieves his result by introducing the unconventional predicate 'grue' which applies to anything

[1] E.g. by W. V. Quine in *Ontological Relativity*, Ch. V. See also my *Probability and Evidence*, pp. 78–82.
[2] In his book *Fact, Fiction and Forecast*.

which is either examined before a given time *t* and found to be green or not so examined and blue. Then any instances of green emeralds which are observed before *t* will also be instances of grue emeralds, though the hypotheses that all emeralds are green and that all emeralds are grue are mutually incompatible. The discovery after *t* that not all emeralds are grue does not remove the problem, since one can then introduce a new predicate which differs from 'grue' only in that the *t* which helps to fix its application is some later time.

There has been some argument about the legitimacy of predicates such as 'grue' into which I shall not enter here, partly because I think that it misses the main point. What we obtain by such devices is the ability to bestow a universal form on hypotheses which we should more naturally express by saying that some A is B and some A is not B. The underlying point, whatever way we put it, is the simple one made by Hume, that however many A's have been found without exception to be B, it remains an open question whether this will also be true of any further A's. The advantage of introducing a special predicate which will be satisfied both by the A's that are B and by those that are not is that the instances which exemplify the hypothesis that All A's are B can then be represented as also exemplifying the rival hypothesis. It is, however, not essential to proceed in this fashion. If we allowed the rival hypothesis simply to be that only such and such a proportion of A's were B, or that all the A's examined before a particular time, or within a particular area, were B and the others not, the same result would be obtained. If there are a hundred marbles in a bag and ninety-nine of them are drawn and found to be green, we have strong confirmation for the hypothesis that all the marbles in the bag are green, but we have equally strong confirmation for the hypothesis that 99 per cent of the marbles are green and 1 per cent some other colour. It is not clear that anything much is gained by so framing the second hypothesis that, whatever colour the remaining marble would ordinarily be taken to be, there will still be some colour-predicate which all the marbles can be said to satisfy.

The moral of such examples, however they are formulated, is that, whatever the evidence, we always have some latitude in the choice of the hypotheses which we are going to project. Our preference for universal hypotheses, at least at the macroscopic level, and for the use of predicates to which we are accustomed, has no better warrant than the success which it has brought us. If anyone maintains that the choice of different hypotheses, or the use of different predicates, will serve us better in the future, we cannot prove that he is wrong; we can only wait upon the event. We can, indeed, say that we are the more likely to be right, but that is only because we measure likelihood in terms of the theories which we accept.

D Cause and Effect

I have so far said very little about the relation of cause and effect with which Hume especially concerned himself. The reason is that not all generalizations of law are causal laws, as this term is ordinarily understood, and Hume's arguments apply to all forms of factual inference. Nevertheless, the concept of cause is of sufficient interest to call for some additional comment.

The two definitions which Hume himself gives of a cause, in his *Treatise of Human Nature*, are first that it is 'an object precedent and contiguous to another, and where all the objects resembling the former are placed in a like relation of priority and contiguity to those objects that resemble the latter' and, secondly, that it is 'an object precedent and contiguous to another, and so united with it in the imagination, that the idea of the one determines the mind to form the idea of the other, and the impression of the one to form a more lively idea of the other'.[1] These definitions are not incompatible, and I suppose that Hume intended them to be combined. They are not, however, entirely satisfactory as they stand. To begin with it should be made clear that the 'objects' to which they refer are particular situations, or events. The requirement that cause and effect be spatio-temporally contiguous needs to be made more precise, in view of the difficulties that attend the notion of contiguity;[2] and it is in any case undesirable to rule out the possibility of action at a distance *a priori*. A more serious criticism is that not all constant conjunctions, even of adjacent events, are taken to be causal: sometimes they are thought to be accidental and sometimes to be the joint effects of an ulterior cause. Finally, it must be a mistake to define causes in such a way that whenever we use causal language, we are not merely exhibiting but actually speaking about our own mental habits.

---

[1] David Hume. *A Treatise of Human Nature*, Book I, Section XIV.
[2] See our discussion of Zeno's paradoxes pp. 17–21.

Nevertheless, in spite of these defects in Hume's definitions, the principles which underly them are correct. The important points are first, as we have seen,[1] that the basis for an ascription of causality cannot be anything more than a *de facto* correlation, secondly, as we have also seen,[2] that the difference between an accidental generalization and a generalization of law consists in a difference in our attitude towards them, and thirdly, that every causal judgement carries an implicit reference to some generalization of a lawlike character.

This last point has been questioned on the ground that we often assign causes without having in mind any causal laws or even being able to meet the demand to formulate them. This is especially so where we are dealing with human affairs, whether on the personal or the social scale. I may think I know why my friend is behaving in such and such a fashion on some particular occasion, without there being any present circumstances with regard to which I am prepared to say that whenever they occur, or only when they occur, does he behave in this way, still less that this is true of all men, or even of all men of a type which he exemplifies. Historians dispute about the causes of wars, or revolutions, or the rise and fall of empires, without their disputes taking the form of an appeal to rival laws; indeed, if the laws were known, they would leave no room for such disputes. It may also be argued that a child does not have to engage in inductive reasoning in order to discover that he can make things happen or that things are made to happen to him. His concept of cause is derived from particular instances in which he knows himself to be an agent or to be acted upon.

The answers to these arguments are first that even if the implicit generalization is not believed by the person who makes a causal judgement, its validity is still required for the judgement to be true, and secondly, that while the generalization must be of a lawlike character, in the sense that it lends itself to projection, it need not be anything more than a generalization of tendency. For the most part, when we speak of the causes of human behaviour, we use the word 'cause' in the sense of 'necessary condition'. We are claiming that the behaviour in question would not have been forthcoming if such and such an event had not occurred. The idea behind this is that there is a finite number of ways in which

[1] See above pp. 147–50.
[2] See above pp. 153–5.

such behaviour comes about. That is to say, the behaviour is linked with different events by different generalizations of tendency. If one of these generalizations is exemplified on a particular occasion, and the others not, we say that the event which enters into the generalization is the cause. So, I may judge that someone is angry because he has been insulted. To arrive at this conclusion, I need not believe that being insulted always makes him angry, or that nothing else does. It is enough that I believe the suffering of an insult to be one of the conditions under which people of his sort frequently become angry, and that I have no present evidence for any rival explanation. In general, this is the way in which motives operate. Philosophers have mistakenly distinguished between motives and causes, because they have overlooked the fact that the generalization on which a causal judgement depends need not be universal. Neither does this apply only to the causes of human behaviour. For instance, when we speak of the causes of changes in the weather, we rely on nothing stronger than generalizations of tendency.

In the cases where there is an appeal to a universal generalization, the state of affairs which is denominated the cause is usually taken to be part of a sufficient condition. The question then arises why it should be singled out from the other factors which are equally necessary to produce the effect. To some extent, this choice is arbitrary, but there are some considerations which tend to govern it. The notion of cause is apt to be associated with that of change, so that when an event is thought to be determined partly by pre-existing and partly by a newly occurrent condition, it is the newly occurrent condition that is picked out as the cause. We are also inclined to pick out factors that result from our own actions or omissions. For instance, if a car which has run out of petrol comes to a stop on the upward slope of a hill, we say that the cause of its stopping is the lack of petrol rather than the gradient. This accords also with the fact that the choice of a condition as a cause is often made to serve the purpose of praise or blame. Thus, omissions tend to be fastened upon some particular person, who is held to have neglected his duty, though so far as the production of the effect is concerned, all that can be relevant is that the action was not done, not that such and such a person failed to do it.

As we have seen in the case of the mind and the brain,[1] it

---

[1] See above p. 130.

sometimes happens that when two concurrent sorts of events are systematically correlated, and therefore might be thought to determine one another, we pick out one of them as the cause of the other because it figures in a wider explanatory system. Thus, we think of the height of an object as determining the length of its shadow, rather than regarding them as mutually determinant, because we can account for the object's height without reference to the shadow, but not for the shadow's length without reference to the object. There is also the fact that when we act in such a way as to alter both the object and the shadow, it is the object and not the shadow that we directly act upon.

The influence of a wider theory also accounts for the cases in which one element in a constant conjunction is treated as a sign of another rather than its cause. That the leaves fall as the days grow shorter is an illustration of the fact that the rhythm of the life of trees matches the rhythm of the seasons. The two processes are not related to one another as cause and effect, because each of them is independently explicable. A change in the barometer is regarded as a sign and not as a cause of a change in the weather, because we accept a theory which explains them both in terms of other factors and also accounts for their concordance.

Since every causal statement can be represented as offering an explanation of the truth of one proposition by reference to the truth of another, it would seem better either to give up thinking of causality as a relation or, if this is asking too much, to conceive of its terms as consisting in facts rather than events. This will also have the advantage of enabling us to accommodate negative causes, since there is no straightforward sense in which the absence of some condition or the failure of someone to do something can be characterized as an event.

Not only that, but the strictly Humean conception of causality as a relation between distinct events does not do justice to the complexity of our usage. The cases in which a causal statement links two states of affairs at the same observational or theoretical level are no doubt the most common, but we also speak of a disposition as the cause of its manifestations, as when we say that a man's actions are caused by his ambition; we speak of the behaviour of an object as being the effect of its composition or structure, as when we say that something stretches because it is made of rubber; we sometimes use causal language to encapsulate a theory, as when we speak of gravitation as a cause. What is common to all these uses is that the state of affairs which we are regarding as an effect is fitted into a wider pattern; but the patterns may be of different sorts.

What then does *propter hoc* add to *post hoc*? At the factual level, nothing at all, so long as the conjunction is constant in either case. At the explanatory level, the difference is that causal statements imply generalizations which we are willing to project. As we have already seen, this is mainly a difference in the realm of fiction.[1] In nature one thing just happens after another. Cause and effect have their place only in our imaginative arrangements and extensions of these primary facts.

[1] See above pp. 151–5.

IX Logic and Existence

A The Laws of Logic

1 The Propositional Calculus

By now I hope that I have said all that needs saying about causal necessity. We have seen that this is not any factual relation, but something that is attributed to facts only in consequence of our bringing them under certain sorts of natural laws; and we have seen that what distinguishes a natural law from a mere generalization of fact is that it is a generalization which we are willing to project over unknown or imaginary instances. What now of logical necessity? Earlier on[1] I said that what was logically possible was what was consistent with the laws of logic. It follows that the negation of a law of logic is logically impossible, and consequently that the laws of logic themselves are logically necessary. We need, therefore, to explain what the laws of logic are and how they come by their truth.

If one looks at a modern text-book of logic, one will usually find that it begins with an account of certain forms of sentences. It is characteristic of these forms that the sentences which enter into them are combined, or in one case supplemented, by members of a class of expressions which are said to represent logical constants. These expressions are usually artificial symbols, belonging to one or other of a number of standard logical notations. When they are rendered into English they appear as the words 'not' 'and' 'either ... or' 'if ... then' and 'if and only if'. This translation is, however, only approximate. The meaning which is assigned to these symbols is not dependent on the niceties of the use of their rough equivalents in any natural language, but is determined explicitly by a set of rules. Since the sentences on which the symbols operate are restricted to those expressing propositions which are either true or

[1] See above p. 149.

false, the rules consist in matching the truth-values of the propositions which result from the various operations with those of the propositions which are operated on. Thus, if '*p*' and '*q*' are any propositions that you please, the negation 'not-*p*' is true just in case '*p*' is false and false just in case '*p*' is true, the conjunction '*p* and *q*' is true just in case '*p*' is true and '*q*' is true, the disjunction '*p* or *q*' is true in every case except that in which both '*p*' and '*q*' are false, the implication 'if *p* then *q*' is true just in case either '*p*' is false or '*q*' is true, and the equivalence '*p* if and only if *q*' is true just in case '*p*' and '*q*' are either both true or both false.

As so interpreted, these logical constants are not mutually independent. They can all be defined either on the basis of negation and conjunction or on the basis of negation and disjunction. For instance, '*p* and *q*' can be transformed into 'not either not-*p* or not-*q*': alternatively '*p* or *q*' can be transformed into 'not both not-*p* and not-*q*'. We can indeed, go further and reduce them all to a single one. This can be achieved either by taking as primitive a symbol which, when applied to any propositions '*p*' and '*q*', yields the proposition 'Not both *p* and *q*', or by taking as primitive one that yields the proposition 'Neither *p* nor *q*'. Thus, if we take '*p*/*q*' as being true just in case '*p*' and '*q*' are not both true, we can define 'not-*p*' as '*p*/*p*' and '*p* and *q*' as '(*p*/*q*)/(*p*/*q*)'. For the purpose of exposition, however, it is convenient to maintain the list that I originally gave.

It is to be noted that all these operators are truth-functional, in the sense that the truth or falsehood of the propositions which they yield is wholly determined by the truth or falsehood of the propositions on which they operate. This follows directly from the way in which they are defined. In many cases the propositions which they yield will have a different truth-value according as different truth-values are assigned to their constituents. For instance, the proposition 'If *p*, then (if *q* then *r*)' comes out true if '*p*' is false or '*q*' is false or '*r*' is true or '*p*' '*q*' and '*r*' are all three true, but comes out false if '*p*' and '*q*' are true and '*r*' is false. There are, however, also cases in which a proposition comes out true whatever the truth-values of its constituents. An example is the proposition 'If (if *p* then *q*) then (if not-*q* then not-*p*)'. Since this is equivalent, by definition, to 'If (not-*p* or *q*) then (*q* or not-*p*)', it is evidently going to be true, whatever the truth-values of '*p*' and '*q*'. If anyone doubts this, all that he has to do is try out all the possibilities. In this instance, there are just four of them. Either 'p' and 'q' are both true, or they are both false, or 'p' is true and 'q' is false, or 'p' is false and 'q' is true. If one follows the rules which govern the operation of the logical constants, one can easily satisfy oneself that our proposition comes out true in every one of these cases. A similar experiment will show that its negation comes out false in every case. Any proposition which can be validated in this way can be said to be logically true, and counted as a law of logic. Correspondingly, propositions which can be so invalidated are inconsistent, or logically false.

The totality of logical truths of this sort makes up what is known as the propositional or sometimes the sentential, calculus. This can be exhibited as a deductive system, with axioms and rules of inference. The propositions which then appear as theorems can, however, be proved independently of the system, by the method which I have just described. When these propositions are very complex, as many of them are, this method can be very laborious, and there are various devices by means of which the labour can be economized. The important point is that we do have a method of deciding, with respect to any proposition, whether or not it belongs to this class of logical truths.

Propositions which satisfy this criterion are often said to be tautologies. The word 'tautology' was given this technical sense by Wittgenstein. Having said, in his *Tractatus*, that 'A proposition is an expression of agreement or disagreement with truth-possibilities of elementary propositions',[1] he characterizes a tautology as a proposition which 'is true for all the truth-possibilities of the elementary propositions'.[2] There is, however, also the implication, which Wittgenstein explicitly acknowledges, that tautologies yield no factual information. As he puts it, 'I know nothing about the weather when I know that it is either raining or not raining'.[3] If one asks what purpose these laws of logic can then serve, the answer is that they can be used as rules of inference. Many propositions which do have factual import can be represented as containing the logical constants which figure in the propositional calculus. If we have good reason to believe that they are true, we can use the calculus to derive other true propositions from them. Since the

---

[1] L. Wittgenstein. *Tractatus Logico-Philosophicus*, 4.4.
[2] *Ibid.* 4.46.
[3] *Ibid.* 4.461.

theorems of the calculus may be very complicated, these derivations are by no means always obvious. Even when they might appear to be obvious, they are not always carried out correctly, as the prevalence of fallacies shows.

The reason why these laws of logic convey no factual information is that their truth is wholly determined by the sense which is given to the logical constants. So long as they have a truth-value, it does not matter what propositions are put in the place of the 'p's and 'q's which figure in logical formulae. Neither does it matter what truth-values they have. They are just elements in a pattern which the logical constants set. The relation to empirical fact arises only in the application of these logical laws. The world has to be such that propositions containing the logical constants can be empirically verified. Once this has been established, we can apply the calculus to them with complete security, knowing that so long as we abide by the rules we cannot be led from truth to falsehood. The reason why this is so is that the contribution made by the logical constants to the propositions with which we start is such that these propositions would not be established unless these consequences held.

2   Predicate-Logic and the Theory of Descriptions

Similar considerations apply to the logic of general terms, which goes back to Aristotle. This brings in further logical constants in the form of quantifiers. The notion of a quantifier was introduced by Frege[1] and is linked in his and in Russell's logic with that of a propositional function. Adapting a definition of Russell's, we may say that a propositional function is what is expressed by a sentence containing one or more undetermined constituents, such that when the gaps that they mark are filled, the sentence comes to express a proposition.[2] Thus, the open sentence 'x is wise' expresses a propositional function and comes to express a proposition when some name or description of a person is substituted for 'x'; the open sentence 'Socrates f', or 'f Socrates', as it is usually written in symbolic notation, expresses a propositional function which yields a proposition when the predicate is made determinate. The letters 'x' and 'f' in these formulae are said to stand for variables, and the objects or properties which are designated by the signs which

[1] Gottlob Frege. *The Foundations of Arithmetic.*
[2] See Bertrand Russell, *Introduction to Mathematical Philosophy*, pp. 155-6.

replace them are said to be their values. Now, instead of giving determinate values to the variables, we can also express propositions by quantifying over them; that is, by using signs which have the effect of asserting that the function is satisfied by at least one value, or that it is satisfied by all the values of the variables in question. Some logicians, like Russell, quantify in this way over both individuals and properties; others, for reasons into which I shall enter later on, are willing to quantify only over individuals, or at most perhaps also over classes. So, if we quantify over the variable 'x' in the function 'x is wise' the use of what is known as the existential quantifier yields the proposition 'For some x, x is wise' or 'There is an x, such that x is wise'; the use of the universal quantifier yields the proposition 'For all x, x is wise'. If we make it explicit that we are referring only to men, we obtain the propositions 'For some x, x is a man and x is wise' and 'For all x, if x is a man x is wise', which would more naturally be expressed in English by the sentences 'Some men are wise' and 'All men are wise' respectively. It is, however, to be noted, that whereas the use of the word 'all' in such an English sentence would be taken to imply that there are several members of the class in question, the use of the universal quantifier does not imply that there are any. For example, the proposition 'All unicorns are wild' is transformed into 'For all x, if x is a unicorn, x is wild', which, according to the rules which govern the use of the conditional, is equivalent to 'For all x, either x is not a unicorn, or x is wild'. Consequently, since nothing is a unicorn, this proposition comes out true, as does its apparent contrary 'All unicorns are tame'. In Aristotelian logic, propositions of the form 'All A is B' and 'No A is B' were treated as genuine contraries; it was assumed that while they could both be false, they could not both be true. Since it was also assumed that at least one of the four propositions 'All A is B' 'No A is B' 'Some A is B' and 'Some A is not B' had to be true, the existence of A's was assured *a priori*, no matter what they might be. To avoid this ridiculous consequence, we have to rule that the Aristotelian assumptions hold only under what may be the false pre-supposition that some A's exist.

An interesting use of the device of quantification has been to eliminate singular terms. This started with Russell's theory of descriptions.[1] Russell took the view that a name was meaningful

---

[1] See his essay 'On Denoting' in *Logic and Knowledge*.

only if there was some object which it denoted, and was, therefore, troubled by the fact that definite descriptions like 'The present King of France', which appeared to function as names, were obviously meaningful even though there was no object which they denoted. His solution of this difficulty was to reparse the sentences in which these expressions occurred in such a way that they ceased to look like names and appeared instead as predicates. Thus, the sentence 'The present King of France is bald' was transmuted into 'There is an x, such that x is now King of France, such that for all y, if y is now King of France, y is identical with x, and such that x is bald'. Since there was no reason to suppose that descriptive phrases which happened to have a denotation functioned any differently, from a semantic point of view, from those which did not, the same procedure was applied to all of them. In all cases, including those of indefinite descriptions like 'some man', the technique is to expand the description into an existential statement that some thing, or, when the description is definite, just one thing, has the property which the description attributes. The subject to which it is attributed is left indefinite, being marked only by the existentially quantified variable.

It is clear that this technique can be applied not only to expressions which have the form 'the so and so' or 'a so and so', but to all nominative signs, including proper names. Thus, Quine has proposed that sentences like 'Socrates is wise' be transformed into 'For some x, x is identical with Socrates and x is wise'.[1] If it be thought that 'being identical with Socrates' is not a respectable predicate it can be construed as doing duty for any predicate or set of predicates, which is uniquely true of Socrates. This will mean that we are paraphrasing rather than translating the original sentence, but there need be no objection to this, so long as the paraphrase only adds and does not omit information. We can even deal in the same way with demonstratives by substituting for them uniquely identifying descriptions of the objects to which they are intended to refer. In the case of spatio-temporal demonstratives like 'here' and 'now', those identifying descriptions may pick out some object or event in the environment of the speaker, or they may simply relate the position of the speaker to some spatial or temporal landmark which itself can be described in general terms. It has been objected that this is to deprive demonstratives, and

[1] See *Word and Object*, pp. 178–9.

indeed all other referential expressions, of the role that they ordinarily play in language, which is to direct attention to the subject of one's discourse; and it is true that the elimination of singular terms leaves all our references indefinite. We can say only that there is something, or just one thing, that has such and such a property, and if we are asked what this thing is, we have to say that it is the thing that has such and such other qualities or bears such and such relations to other things which are described in the same indefinite way. This need not, however, prevent us from being able in practice to pick these objects out; and if the purpose of the exercise is to extend the empire of predicate logic without any sacrifice of information, then, so long as we think of information in terms of what is said and not in terms of what is merely shown, it can be held to have been achieved.

The logic of quantification is not confined to qualities, or one-termed predicates. It extends to relations with any number of terms. In the cases where the values of the quantified variables may be different terms, we need to use different letters for the variables; the custom is to use a few of the final letters of the alphabet, or, if this is not sufficient, to differentiate the variables, by putting a different number of accents after one or other of these letters. The same result can be achieved by using numerical subscripts. Sometimes the nature of the relation will be such that it can hold only between different terms, but this is not always so. There are some relations, like that of loving, that a term bears to other terms and also to itself. In such cases, the use of different letters for the variables will allow for but not guarantee a difference in their values, and it may be necessary to assert that x is not identical with y. However many signs for variables are used, it is essential, in substituting for them, that when the same sign occurs more than once in an open sentence the same substitution be made for each of its occurrences. In view of the fact that some words in natural languages are ambiguous, it is not enough that the signs which are substituted be typographically identical: they must also have the same reference.

The existential and the universal quantifiers are interdefinable, since to say that for all x, fx is equivalent to saying that there is no x such that not-fx, and to say that for some x, fx is equivalent to saying that it is not the case that for all x, not-fx. Nevertheless, it is convenient to employ them both. If they are used together, attention must be paid to the order in which they occur. For example, the sentence 'For all x, if x is an event, there is a y such that y is an event and y precedes x' expresses the proposition that there is no first event. If we reverse the quantifiers so as to obtain the sentence 'There is a y, such that y is an event and for all x, if x is an event y precedes x', we shall be saying just the opposite: for what this sentence expresses is the proposition that one event precedes all the rest.

Turning now to the logical truths of quantification theory, we find that they are all obtained by substitution of predicates for the letters, holding places for them, in various general schemata. For instance, the syllogism 'All cats are vertebrates. All vertebrates have kidneys. Therefore all cats have kidneys' is validated by the proposition 'For all x, if (if x is a cat x is vertebrate, and if x is vertebrate x has kidneys) then if x is a cat x has kidneys' and this proposition is obtained by substitution from the schema 'For all x, if (if Fx then Gx and if Gx then Hx) then if Fx then Hx'. This schema is valid because the resulting sentence expresses a true proposition, whatever predicates are consistently substituted for 'F' 'G' and 'H'. Once again the point of formulating such propositions is to enable us to make secure inferences: and once again the inferences are secure because the propositions in accordance with which they are made are not dependent for their truth upon any actual course of events. They are true in virtue of the rules for the employment of the logical constants which they contain; in this case, the quantifiers, as well as the operators of the propositional calculus. Again, this is not to say that we cannot misapply these rules, or even that it is always obvious what they commit us to. In the case of some schemata, we may even be uncertain whether they are consistent. To prove that a schema is consistent, it is, indeed, enough to find a single interpretation in which it comes out true, and so long as there is a finite number of possibilities, this question can be decided, at least in principle. But when it comes to schemata incorporating serial relations which generate an infinite number of terms, this may not always be so.

3 Set-Theory and The Theory of Types

After dealing with quantification, our logical text-book is likely to proceed to set-theory. It is here that logic and mathematics meet. The claim which was made by Frege, and after him by Russell and

Whitehead, that mathematics was reducible to logic depended on their counting set-theory as part of logic. Not all logicians are willing to follow them in this, preferring to stress the discontinuity rather than the continuity between predicate logic and set-theory. The question of nomenclature is, indeed, of minor interest but the underlying point is important. If one holds, as Quine and others do, that a theory is committed to the existence of the entities over which it quantifies, then the feature of set-theory which principally distinguishes it from predicate logic is that it introduces a new set of entities. It does so because it requires us to quantify over classes. It requires us also to quantify over relations, but this is not an additional commitment since there are methods of representing relations as classes of their terms.

To see how the commitment to classes is incurred, we need only consider the account which Frege, and after him Russell and Whitehead, gave of numbers. The basic idea is that a natural number is a class of classes. So o is the class of classes which have no members, 1 is the class of classes which have a single member each, 2 the class of all classes which are divisible into parts a and b such that both a and b belong to the class which is the number 1, 3 is the class of classes which are divisible into parts b and c such that b belongs to 1 and c belongs to 2, and so on indefinitely, each succeeding number being obtained by adding 1 to its predecessor. As a way of defining numbers, this procedure may look circular, but it is not so in fact, because both o and 1 can be defined in terms of class membership. Thus, any class c belongs to o just in case there is no x such that x is a member of c, and any class c belongs to 1 just in case there is a y such that y is a member of c and such that for all x, x is a member of c if and only if x is identical with y. Not only can we define the natural numbers *seriatim* in this way, but we can give a general definition of number which states in effect that numbers are just those classes of classes that belong to every class to which o belongs and to which the addition of 1 to each member also belongs. This definition applies, however, only to finite numbers. To obtain a definition which covers infinite numbers, we have to quantify over a relation. Following Russell, we may say that two classes are similar just in case there is a relation which coordinates each member of either class with just one member of the other.[1] We can then define any given number as

[1] See *Introduction to Mathematical Philosophy*, pp. 15-19.

a class of similar classes of the appropriate size, and number in general as anything that is the number of some class. Again, this definition will be saved from circularity by the fact that the numbering of classes has already been achieved without reference to number, by means of the quantifiers, the truth-functional operators, and the notions of identity and class-membership.

Not only that but these notions are sufficient to define all the concepts of pure mathematics, including those required for the theory of real numbers into which geometry can be interpreted. The process of quantifying over classes has to be taken to higher levels, but that is all. The meaning of the sign for class-membership is determined by a set of axioms, including such axioms as that classes which have the same members belong in their turn to the same classes, and that the objects which satisfy a one-termed predicate always constitute a class, this being the class belonging to 0, in the case where the predicate is not satisfied. The propositions of set-theory are just those that are deducible from these axioms. It was hoped at one time that the whole of mathematics could be demonstrated on this basis, but this has turned out not to be so. On the contrary, it has been proved by Gödel[1] that in any system which has the resources for the formulation even of elementary arithmetic, there will be true propositions which are not demonstrable within the system. These are propositions which in effect say of themselves that they are not so demonstrable. There is also the problem that unless we take special precautions we shall find that set-theory leads us into contradictions. It might, for example, seem reasonable to assume that every predicate determines a class. But now consider the predicate which is true of just those classes that are not members of themselves. If the classes which satisfy this predicate are themselves allowed to constitute a class, it will evidently be true of this class that if it is a member of itself, it is not, and that if it is not a member of itself, it is.

This contradiction was discovered by Russell and is commonly known as Russell's paradox.[2] His own solution of it was to develop what he called a theory of types, according to which objects are arranged in a hierarchy of such a kind that predicates which are

---

[1] Kurt Gödel 'On Formally Undecidable Propositions of *Principia Mathematica* and Related Systems'. English translation in *Source Book in Mathematical Logic* 1871–1931, ed. J. Van Heijenvort.

[2] See Bertrand Russell, *The Principles of Mathematics*, Ch. X.

true or false of objects of one type cannot significantly be applied to those of a different type. Thus, statements can be made about individuals that cannot significantly be made about classes of individuals; statements can be made about classes that cannot significantly be made about classes of classes, and so forth. In this way the paradox is prevented from arising. It is just nonsensical to say of the class of classes which are not members of themselves that it either is or is not a member of itself. The same treatment is applied to other logical paradoxes, of a similar kind, and also to semantic paradoxes, like that of the liar, in which a proposition is made to say of itself, directly or indirectly, that it is false, with the result that if it is true, it is false and if it is false, it is true. By ruling that if 'p' predicates truth or falsehood of 'q', 'p' must be of a higher order than 'q', the theory makes it impossible that 'p' and 'q' should be identical. It thus becomes meaningless for a proposition to ascribe either truth or falsehood to itself.

The theory of types achieves its object, but at something of a cost. One consequence of it is that terms which one might think capable of being applied in the same way to objects of different types become ambiguous. For instance, numerical expressions have to be credited with a different sense, according as they are used to count individuals, or classes, or classes of classes. Another difficulty is that objects of different types cannot significantly be counted together, so that we have to rely on there being enough individuals to furnish the natural numbers, with the risk that the supply will give out. For these and other reasons, some modern logicians prefer to renounce the theory of types and try to deal with the paradoxes by restricting the conditions under which the objects which satisfy a predicate can be held to constitute a class. This leads them also to give a different account of numbers. Thus, on one theory, which is due to von Neumann,[1] each number is simply identified with the class of its predecessors. This may not be what the ordinary man thinks he means by a number, but then no doubt the same is true of Frege's definition. It does not matter if the propositions of mathematics are presented in an unfamiliar guise, so long as their truth-values are preserved, and so long as they can still be applied in the ways that we want to apply them.

[1] J. von Neumann 'On the Introduction of Transfinite Numbers', English translation in *Source Book in Mathematical Logic* 1879–1931.

4 *Semantic Necessities*

The truths of the propositional calculus, of predicate logic and of set-theory, are not the only propositions that are thought to be logically necessary. The list of logically necessary propositions has commonly been taken to include a number which are true not in virtue of their logical form but because of the meaning of their other constituents. Their truth is supposed to follow from the definition of these other terms. Familiar examples are the proposition that all bachelors are unmarried or that brothers are male siblings. These are not propositions about words, as it is a contingent and not a necessary fact that English speakers employ the sign 'brother' to designate a male sibling, but they are propositions of which the truth can be taken to depend exclusively on the meaning of the words which express them. They are necessarily true because they are not exposed to factual refutation. Nothing would be counted as a contrary instance. This is not to say that the signs in question could not be given a different meaning, or that even as things are they cannot legitimately be used in other ways. This applies even to our examples. Not all bachelors of arts are unmarried. To proclaim that all men are brothers is not to proclaim that all men are male siblings. But then it is equally true of logical constants like 'if ... then' that they have other uses than those which are assigned to them in the propositional calculus, and that if they are construed in those other ways the propositions which they then help to express may not have any claim to logical necessity.

The drawback about propositions like 'Brothers are male siblings' is that the synonymity in the use of different expressions on which their necessity depends is something which we do not have a rule for checking. Our only resource is to ask ourselves whether there are any conceivable circumstances in which we should say that one term was satisfied but not the other. The discovery of such a circumstance will be a proof that the proposition in question is not necessary; the failure to discover one will be at least an indication that it is. There is, however, the further complication that we have to decide whether the suggested counter example is relevant, or whether as in the example of 'All men are brothers' the operative word is being used in a different sense. There is also the problem that the senses of words are liable to change, as we acquire more information about what they are used to designate, so that it may be uncertain how much is included in their meaning at any given time. Has it, for example, by now become a necessary proposition that water has the chemical composition H_2O? Well, probably not if the answer is taken to depend on the considerations which still actually govern most people's use of the word. On the other hand, I should not want to say that someone who did hold it to be necessary was making a mistake. By reading more into the term he would increase the chances of its becoming inapplicable, but he might have sufficient confidence in current chemical theory not to regard this as a serious risk.

There is a more interesting way in which the answers to questions of this kind can depend upon our choice. If we consult a textbook of classical physics we may find that 'force' is defined as the product of mass and acceleration. Accepting this definition, we may then take it to be a necessary proposition that the acceleration of a body is equal to the force which is acting on it divided by its mass. It is, however, also possible to define force in such a way that this same form of words comes to express not a necessary but an empirical proposition, the change being compensated by altering the interpretation of other sentences in the reverse direction. This illustrates the fact, to which I referred earlier,[1] that the propositions of a complex theory are tested not in isolation from each other but as a body. I do not think that this invalidates the distinction between propositions which are true only in virtue of the meaning of the signs which express them and propositions the truth or falsehood of which depends upon the facts, but it does make it a somewhat arbitrary question where this line is drawn.

5 Identity

A proposition which seems clearly to be necessary is that everything is identical with itself. Indeed, the theory of identity is commonly treated as a part of logic. It is developed from axioms of which the first is that for all x, $x = x$. A second axiom which would seem to be equally acceptable is that if x and y are identical they have the same properties. So, if being necessarily identical with x is a property of x, it must also be a property of y, if x and y are identical. Consequently, all true propositions of the form '$x = y$' are necessary.

This reasoning appears sound, but it leads to unacceptable

[1] See above pp. 29-30.

consequences when we proceed to substitute values for the variables. That Dickens is Dickens may pass for a necessary proposition, at least under the pre-supposition that Dickens exists, though if anyone were actually to use these words it would more probably be as a means of saying that Dickens was a law unto himself, or something of that sort, rather than just that he was self-identical. But what of the proposition that Dickens is Boz? Surely it is not logically necessary that the author of *Sketches by Boz* and the author of *David Copperfield* should be one and the same person. What of the proposition that the Morning Star is identical with the Evening Star and that both are identical with Venus? Surely it is a contingent fact that one and the same planet is to be found at the places in question in the morning and at night. It has been claimed that these propositions *are* necessary, even though their truth has to be empirically discovered, but on any natural interpretation of them, it seems to me clear that this is wrong.

The trouble comes, I think, from crediting individuals with necessary properties. We can significantly ask what properties it is necessary for something to possess in order to be a thing of such and such a kind, for that is a way of asking what properties enter into the definition of that kind of thing. We have seen that the answer may to some extent be arbitrary, but at least some answer can be looked for. On the other hand, there is no such definition of an individual. There are, indeed, ways of identifying individuals, by descriptions of their appearances, or their functions, or their behaviour, or merely their spatio-temporal positions; but none of these descriptions picks out a necessary property. This does not mean that if we are referring, say, to a particular person, we can imagine anything whatsoever to be true of him, without prejudice to his identity. There is no single item in his biography that could not be denied him without self-contradiction, but if we deprive him of the whole of it we shall find at some point that his identity has been lost. We have to maintain some anchorage in reality, if our references to him are to be successful. Even so, there appear to be no general rules for deciding what this anchorage may be. For the most part, it would seem that the identity at least of a physical object is not thought to survive complete dislocation in space and time, but this does not apply so much to persons, or even to physical objects which are very distinctive in their qualities. For instance, one could imagine that the Pyramids were built at a different time, or perhaps even in a different country. If one anchors Dickens to other items in his biography one can conceive of his not having been a writer: if one identifies him by his writings one can perhaps conceive of his having lived in a different century. But could we consistently place him in the distant future, or in prehistoric times? Would not the reference then have failed? Unfortunately, as I said, there are no rules for deciding such questions. We just have to ask ourselves whether we should still be willing to say that we were talking about the same man. It is therefore a rather arbitrary question, in this sort of case, at what point a factual falsehood turns into a logical one.

The advantage of eliminating singular terms is that these puzzles about identity no longer arise. If we are content to say just that there is something, or only one thing, x, which satisfies such and such a list of general predicates, then all that is required for the avoidance of logical error is that these predicates be logically compatible. Even this, as we have seen, may not always be easy to decide, but at least we shall have definitions to go by, so long as the predicates do not themselves contain proper names. If we keep proper names and substitute them for the variable signs in the formula '$x = y$', then, as we have seen, the fact that the names have the same reference will be sufficient to make the resulting proposition true, but not sufficient to make it necessarily true. It will not even be enough that the name-tokens be typographically identical, in addition to having the same reference, since the two occurrences of the name might be associated with different descriptions. What is required is that the names should be synonymous, in the sense that they both have the same reference and are associated with the same descriptions. If this can be established, the sentence can be taken as expressing the trivial but necessary proposition that the referent of the name is identical with itself, or what comes to the same thing, that it satisfies a description which it satisfies.

B Analyticity

As we have already remarked,[1] it is customary to use the term 'analytic' to characterize propositions which are true solely in virtue of the meaning of the signs which express them. Sometimes, the term is used more widely so that it also covers propositions which are, in this way, necessarily false. In the wider usage, it is

[1] See above p. 48.

contrasted with the term 'synthetic'. It is tempting to characterize synthetic propositions as those that owe their truth or falsehood not only to the meaning of the signs which express them but also to the empirical facts, but this might be thought to beg the question against philosophers, like Kant, who have maintained that the propositions of mathematics, for example, are both synthetic and immune from the possibility of empirical refutation. It would, however, seem that Kant at any rate employed the term 'analytic' in a rather narrower sense than that which it has since acquired. He characterized a proposition as analytic when it was demonstrable by the law of non-contradiction alone, and took this condition to be satisfied when the predicate was contained in the concept of the subject. Thus his ground for saying that '$7 + 5 = 12$' is a synthetic proposition in that the concept of 12 is not already thought in merely thinking the union of 7 and 5.[1] If this means that a child can understand the question 'What is $7 + 5$?' without being ready with the answer '12', it is surely true, but still does not prevent it from being the case that the equation follows from suitable definitions of the numbers and of the signs of addition and equality: and, according to our present usage, this is sufficient to make it analytic.

Another disputed question is whether the distinction between the analytic and the synthetic coincides with that between the *a priori* and the *a posteriori*. The literal meaning of these Latin terms, which were introduced by mediaeval writers to translate expressions that they found in Aristotle, is 'from what comes before' and 'from what comes after'. In Aristotle's usage of their Greek equivalents, they served roughly to make the distinction between deductive and inductive reasoning. In modern philosophy, since the seventeenth century, a proposition has been said to be *a priori* when it is necessarily true or necessarily false, and can be known to be so independently of experience. It is, indeed, allowed that experience is needed to come to understand the meaning of the words in which the proposition is expressed. The idea is that once we grasp what the proposition is, no further experience is needed to enable us to know that it is true, or that it is false. At this point, however, we have to ask what kind of experience is meant. If working through a proof counts as an experience, the number of necessary propositions that are known to anyone *a priori* will be relatively small. Even the simplest arithmetical truths, such as

[1] See *Critique of Pure Reason*—Introduction.

that $2 + 2 = 4$ are often taught to children through having them assemble objects and count them. Later they may or may not learn to prove such propositions abstractly. It depends on the capacity of the child and the sort of instruction that he receives. Since considerations of this kind are not thought to be relevant to the question whether the propositions of mathematics are *a priori*, it becomes clear that what is at issue is not the way in which such propositions are or could be learned, but rather the way in which they acquire their truth-values. A proposition is said to be capable of being known independently of experience, whenever, its truth or falsehood being established on purely logical or semantic grounds, it is not subject to the jurisdiction of empirical matters of fact. But if this is what is meant, to speak of a proposition as being *a priori* will come to the same as saying that it is true or false by one or other form of logical necessity.

The question remains whether all propositions which are necessary in this sense are also analytic. In other words, can there be propositions of which it is true both that they are not in need of empirical confirmation and that they do not owe their truth-value only to the meaning of the signs by which they are expressed? Those who think that the answer to this question is 'Yes', most commonly defend their view by instancing cases in which an object is denied the possession of incompatible qualities. A typical example, which is due to Russell, is that two different colours cannot coexist in the same place in one visual field. The suggestion is that it is a matter of fact that one colour keeps another out and not just a consequence of the meaning that we attach to colour-words. Thus Russell argues that 'Red and blue are no more *logically* incompatible than red and round'.[1] Again, this is difficult to decide because of the uncertainty as to what is to count as logical, but I think that a case can be made for saying that the incompatibility, whether or not we wish to call it logical, is at any rate semantic. It is a general feature of our use of predicates that they are sorted into categories in such a way that if something is characterized at any given time by one member of a category it is not characterized by another. Thus, being red is incompatible with being blue in the same way as being round is incompatible with being square, or being just 2 inches long is incompatible with being 3 inches long. Red and round are compatible because the predicates in question

[1] Bertrand Russell. *An Inquiry into Meaning and Truth*, p. 82.

belong to different categories. One can conceive of a language in which this distinction was not made. For instance, if we used pictures to represent different possible states of affairs, with the convention that only the picture as a whole was meaningful, then any two different pictures with the same intended reference would be incompatible. In our case, the position is not so simple because we have the power to describe things under different aspects; we abstract different features of the total picture. To resort to another analogy, different moves are permissible in different games. Nevertheless, it remains a logical principle, as I said earlier,[1] that if one has made a particular move in any game, one has made that move and not a different one: and it is on this principle that the incompatibility of terms like 'red' and 'blue' depends. I therefore think that such propositions as that two colours cannot coexist at the same place in one visual field can justifiably be treated as being analytic.

In recent times the whole distinction between analytic and synthetic propositions has been put in question, both on the ground that the notion of meaning is not clear enough to justify the attribution of truth on its score alone, and on the ground, which has been notably occupied by Quine,[2] that the logical and mathematical components of a scientific theory cannot be sufficiently disentangled from its empirical components for them to be regarded as subject to different criteria of truth. On the first count, we have, indeed, discovered that the establishment of necessary truths, outside the domain of formal logic and set-theory, is a rather haphazard affair, so that in practice the border-line between analytic and synthetic propositions is highly indeterminate. Nevertheless, there are many cases in which it is generally agreed that two expressions are synonymous, or that one includes the other in its meaning, and so long as there is a considerable area in which it can be confidently applied, the distinction between propositions which are true on this semantic ground alone and propositions which confront the empirical facts does seem to be worth making. On the second count, we have also conceded that the propositions which constitute a theory do not confront the facts individually, but rather as a body. Even so, it still seems possible to distinguish those elements of the theory that

---

[1] See above pp. 12–13.
[2] See *Word and Object*, Section 56 and *From a Logical Point of View* 'Two Dogmas of Empiricism'.

serve, in the way I have tried to explain, for the arrangement of a special set of facts from the logical and mathematical elements that are common to all theories. Admittedly, as we have seen, it is to some extent an arbitrary question which propositions in the theory are to be taken as true by definition, but from the fact that the lines of demarcation may be drawn in various ways it does not follow that there is nothing which they demarcate.

A point on the other side is that there is also a sense in which the propositions of logic and mathematics confront the empirical facts. As I said earlier,[1] the world has to be such that we can successfully apply them to it. Even if we can rule out the possibility of there being a wholly illogical world, for the reason I quoted Wittgenstein as giving,[2] that we could not say what such a world would look like and therefore could attach no sense to speaking of it, still it is conceivable that the world should not be accommodated, or at least not be so well accommodated, to the system of logic that we have in fact developed. Admittedly, there is a sense in which Wittgenstein was right in maintaining that tautologies say nothing.[3] I do learn nothing about the actual state of the weather when I am told only that it is either raining or not raining. Nevertheless, it is not an entirely trivial fact that these are distinct alternatives. In microscopic physics, the proposition that a particle with an ascertained momentum either is or is not at a particular position at a particular time is not taken to be true; and this has led to some attempts to develop a new system of logic which would be better suited to quantum theory. Neither is it a trivial fact that the combination of physical quantities yields results which are in accordance with the laws of arithmetic. For example, in physics, it is not always safe to apply the commutative law that $a \times b$ is equivalent to $b \times a$. If the quantities are vectors, it makes a difference in which order they are taken. Non-Euclidean geometries had already been developed as a mathematical exercise, before Einstein found a use for one of them in his theory of relativity, but it is imaginable that such a development should take place in response to a scientific need. Only the law of non-contradiction is sacrosanct, not indeed as hallowing the concept of negation which is found in the current propositional calculus, but only in the sense that any system, if it is

[1] See above p. 187.
[2] See above p. 13.
[3] See above pp. 186–7.

to be workable at all, must, as I said earlier,[1] be governed by some principle of consistency.

But if the propositions of logic and mathematics are subject to revision in the light of experience, how do they differ from the empirical propositions with which they have commonly been contrasted ? It is, indeed, true that we are more tenacious of logical and mathematical principles than we are of scientific theories, but then do we not hold with equal tenacity to our judgements of observation ? There is, I think, a little more to it than that. The main difference, as I see it, is that whereas scientific hypotheses can meet with counter-examples, the propositions of logic and mathematics are not invalidated by experience, but at the worst found to be unserviceable. We do not say that Euclidean geometry has been discovered to be false, but only that for certain purposes another geometry serves us better. If we were to give up the law of excluded middle, according to which a proposition must be either true or false, it would not be that the proposition '*p* or not-*p*', as it is now understood, had been found to be invalid, but only that we had found it preferable to operate with different logical constants. We might retain the same signs but we should be giving them a different meaning. Here again, there is an overlap between the analytic and the synthetic, since an explanatory theory may also go out of fashion without being actually refuted. What distinguishes the analytic is that it is accorded truth, without ever being subject to empirical refutation, but only at worst to supersession.

C The Existence of Abstract Entities

This distinction may still seem rather tenuous, but it acquires some importance when one comes to consider the implications of logic and mathematics with respect to what there is, or what there is thought to be. If we conceive of them as having a purely linguistic basis, in the sense that their propositions owe their validity only to the conventions which govern our use of a certain set of signs, the question of their subject matter will be subordinated to that of their application. They will add to our knowledge of the world only by showing us to what we are committed, on pain of inconsistency, by our acceptance of propositions which are empirically testable. If, on the other hand, we think of the propositions of mathematics and logic as themselves embodying general truths about the world,

[1] See above p. 12.

the question of their subject matter becomes a problem. What are the objects of which they are true? This problem becomes serious when we arrive at set-theory. The sentences of the propositional calculus can be treated as presenting schemata which acquire a truth-value when propositions are substituted for the 'p's and 'q's. The entities involved will be those, if any, to which these propositions refer. In predicate logic we can avoid referring to anything but concrete individuals. In set-theory, however, we quantify over classes, and it is currently held that we are committed to a belief in the existence of anything over which we quantify. This is in line with Frege's and Russell's definition of existence, according to which to say that something exists is always a way of saying that some predicate is satisfied. But do we really want to admit classes as entities in addition to their members? Are we prepared to say that when a man makes a pair of shoes he brings three entities into existence, the right shoe, the left shoe and the pair?

The problem of the status of classes is akin to the old philosophical problem of universals. Indeed, the two problems overlap, since logicians have in some cases had recourse to classes in order to avoid quantifying over properties. Not that classes are any the less abstract than properties, but they have been thought to be more respectable because they are provided with a more adequate criterion of identity. If A and B are classes, they can be held to be identical when they have the same members. If A and B are properties, their identity will depend upon our questionable judgement that the predicates which designate them are logically equivalent. The superiority of classes, in this respect, is, however, hardly more than notional. It stands out only in the rare cases where we are able to define a class by enumerating all its members. In the ordinary way, we can define a class only as the extension of such and such a predicate, with the result that we cannot discover that classes A and B are identical unless we can decide that they are the extensions of logically equivalent predicates. This is not, indeed, a necessary condition of their identity, since they might just happen to have the same members, but it is obviously sufficient.

Let us look, then, at the problem of universals. The common ground from which it arises is that we successfully apply general terms to different things. To take a very simple example, there are several sheets of paper on my desk and all of them are white. The question is whether we are entitled, or even obliged to hold that these general terms stand for abstract entities. The so-called Realistic view, which we have seen to be held at one stage by Plato, is that there are such abstract entities, existing outside space and time. On this view, the pieces of paper are what they are in virtue of their bearing some relation – it was never quite clear to Plato what this relation was – to the eternal forms of their various qualities. Another type of Realism is the position, taken by Aristotle, that while universals like whiteness are genuine entities, they exist only in the particulars in which they inhere. The other main views on this question have been that of the Conceptualists, like Abelard, who equated universals with concepts or mental images, and that of the Nominalists, like Hobbes, who maintained that all that things to which the same general term applies have in common is just that the same general term is applied to them.

This controversy aroused strong passions in the Middle Ages, but it is hard to see exactly what is involved in it. How would one set about discovering the existence or non-existence of Platonic forms? How would our experience be different, whether there were such things or not? There seem to be no possible answers to these questions. We can, however, make a little more sense of the problem if we treat it as one of a choice between different explanations of our use of general terms. The Platonic contention then will be that we cannot explain the use of a word like 'white' otherwise than by supposing that we apprehend an abstract entity 'whiteness', thereby inviting the objection that this is itself no explanation, unless one can give a plausible account of the way in which this entity is related to the things which are white. If one says that it inheres in them, or that they are instances of it, one seems to be saying no more than that white things have the property of being white, with rather a loss than a gain in clarity by representing this as a relation between different sorts of entities. If one says that whiteness is a model for particular white things, one is faced with the difficulty, which Aristotle raised,[1] that one will need to bring in another abstract entity to account for what the particulars have in common with the model and so *ad infinitum*. The Aristotelian view that universals exist in particulars could perhaps be construed as a proposal to treat terms like 'white' as bulk terms like 'water' or 'coal'. The white sheets of paper would then be considered as parts of a total expanse of white, rather than as instances of a quality, and

[1] See his *Metaphysics* α.9.

whiteness would become a scattered individual rather than a universal. So far as I can see, there would be nothing to prevent our doing this, but it is also not clear why we should want to. The problem, if there is one, about our use of general terms, would not be eliminated, since the parts of the individual 'whiteness' would still have to be identified by their quality. In fact, what Aristotle probably meant was just that white things, and other things to which a general term applies, do have a common property, which is true but not illuminating. The conceptualist view, on the other hand, is actually mistaken. Not only is it obviously false that whenever one ascribes a property to anything one is talking about one's own state of mind, but the theory that we can identify things only by comparing them with mental images, apart from being factually incorrect, leads, as we have already seen,[1] to a vicious infinite regress. We can, indeed, be said to be making use of concepts when we attribute properties to things, but this comes to no more than our employing signs with the appropriate meanings. As we have also seen,[2] there is no call to assume that a verbal sign must always be reduplicated by an unspoken thought.

The nominalist position is more difficult to evaluate, because it is not so clear what it involves. It could be understood as suggesting that properties are always to be taken in extension, so that to attribute whiteness to this piece of paper would simply be to include it in a catalogue of white things. This sounds harmless until we ask how the catalogue is to be compiled. Clearly we cannot enumerate all the white things that there are, and even if we could, the question would arise on what principle we were associating them. If the answer were that it was in virtue of their all being white there would seem to be little point in the manoeuvre. If, on the other hand, we insisted, most implausibly, that whiteness was attributed to an object because of its figuring in the catalogue, and not the other way around, we should be forced to the conclusion that all true predications of this kind were analytic: for then to say that something was white would be equivalent to saying that it was one of a set of objects which included itself. Not only that but the meaning of the predicate would vary with its denotation, so that every time that anyone whitewashed a blue wall, he would be affecting the meaning of the adjectives 'blue' and 'white'. This is surely not acceptable.

[1] See above pp. 56-7.
[2] See above p. 57.

A version of nominalism, which can perhaps be attributed to Berkeley,[1] is that to say of anything that it has such and such a property is to say that it resembles some other thing, or some other set of things. But the objection to this is that from the fact that this sheet of paper is white, it does not strictly follow that anything else is white, or, indeed, that there are any other things. It is true that I should not be using the word 'white' correctly in this instance unless the thing to which I applied it did resemble everything else to which it was applicable, but this does not mean that in predicating whiteness of it I am asserting that it resembles these other things. We have to distinguish between formulating a rule of usage and actually following it. Furthermore, this talk of resemblance is not only not necessary, but also not sufficient, since any two things resemble one another in some respect. We should need to say that this piece of paper resembles other things in respect of its whiteness, and then it will not be clear what this adds to simply saying that it is white, except the gratuitous information that it is not the only white thing.

Even so, the nominalists had a point. They saw that what makes a term general is its being used to mark recurrent features of the world and not its standing for a special sort of abstract object. Where they went wrong was in supposing that general terms could be translated out. There is nothing simpler by means of which their use can be explained. The notion of 'the same again' is fundamental to any use of language or, indeed, to any ordering of experience.

Well then, are there universals ? If the question is whether these general terms are indispensable, the answer is that they are. If the question is whether we gain anything by taking them to stand for abstract entities, the answer is that we do not. If it is the technical question whether we need to quantify over properties, the answer is again that we do not. We can quantify over classes instead.

But then, are there classes ? The present-day nominalist denies that there are, because he objects to the multiplication of entities. And indeed it does seem absurd to say, as Russell once did,[2] that even if the universe did not exist, there would still be the null-class, two classes of classes, consisting of the class of no classes and the

---

[1] See his *A Treatise Concerning the Principles of Human Knowledge* – Introduction.

[2] See *The Principles of Mathematics*. Introduction to the second edition, p. VIII.

class whose only member is the null-class, four classes of classes of classes, and so on. Rather than accept conclusions of this sort, some philosophers would prefer to disallow quantification over classes, even at the cost of sacrificing some parts of mathematics. It seems to me, however, that a better course would be simply to deny the commitment. If we conceive of logic and mathematics purely formally as being concerned only with the transformation of symbols, then so long as we do not contravene the rules, we need not care what symbols are substituted for the variable-signs. We should be committed only to accepting the existence of the entities which figure in the empirical propositions to which the formulae are applied; and these will presumably always be concrete.

Another disputed question of a very similar kind is whether there are propositions. I have used the term 'proposition' freely, because it is a convenient way of referring to what is true not only of some particular sentence 'S' but of any sentence to which 'S' is equivalent in meaning. I do not, however, pretend that in saying that sentences express propositions one is giving an acceptable account of their meaning, any more than one is giving an acceptable account of the use of predicates if one says that they stand for universals. Neither do I take propositions seriously in another role for which they have been cast, as the objects of mental attitudes. It is harmless to talk of believing propositions, so long as this is taken to imply no more than that there may be various equivalent ways of stating what is believed. This must not, however, be regarded as a step towards the analysis of belief. If we treat propositions as abstract objects, on to which beliefs are directed, we shall find ourselves unable to explain how any belief comes to be true or false. The reason for this is that an abstract object cannot refer beyond itself, so that when propositions are treated in this way, they merely become a barrier between our beliefs and the actual course of events by which they are verified or falsified. It is important, therefore, that our talk of propositions should not be regarded as anything more than a concise way of talking about equivalent sentences.

Some philosophers regard even this usage as objectionable, on the ground that the notion of equivalence is not sufficiently clear to sustain it. They prefer to ascribe truth to sentences. It is, however, doubtful whether this makes much difference, since it obliges us to consider sentences not just as sequences of marks or noises but as signs which are given meanings. Neither do we wish to confine our predications of truth or falsehood to sentences which are actually produced. There is also the difficulty that sentence-forms like 'I slept well last night', which contain demonstratives or tenses, will vary in their truth-values according to the context of their utterance. If we eliminate singular terms by paraphrase, in the way that we have seen to be possible, and use a dating system to do the work which is done by tenses, we can, indeed, arrive at what Quine calls eternal sentences which are timelessly true or false.[1] Thus, it is true or false once for all that a person answering to such and such a unique description slept well on such and such a specified date. Since, however, these eternal sentences are required to preserve not merely a constant form, but also a constant meaning it would seem that the only serious difference made by talking about them, rather than talking about propositions, is that one will not be attributing equivalence to sentences of different languages.

Whether truth is attributed to sentences or to propositions, there is no great difficulty about its definition. As Aristotle put it, 'To say of what is that it is not, or what is not that it is, is false, while to say of what is that it is, or what is not that it is not, is true'.[2] The same account has been given in our own time by Alfred Tarski[3] with his formula ' "p" is true in L if and only if p', where 'L' is a language, the sentence within the quotation marks is a sentence of L, and the sentence which follows the connective 'if and only if', or its equivalent in whatever language one is speaking, is one that is logically equivalent to the one within the quotation marks. An example which Tarski gave is ' "Snow is white" is true in English if and only if snow is white.' For technical reasons Tarski does not treat his formula as a definition of truth but rather as a model of the sentences which any adequate definition of truth for a given language is required to entail. It is also worth remarking that although Tarski treats truth as a predicate of sentences, his theory tacitly admits propositions, since it requires that sentences of different languages be treated as equivalent. The reason for this is that the language in which one defines truth need not be the same as the language for which one defines it. Thus, if one were speaking

---

[1] See *Word and Object*, Ch. VI.
[2] *Metaphysics* 7.27.
[3] See 'The Concept of Truth in Formalized Languages'. *Logic, Semantics, Meta-Mathematics*.

in French his example would read ' "Snow is white" est vrai en anglais si et seulement si la neige est blanche'. But this will achieve what is wanted only if the English sentence 'snow is white' and the French sentence 'la neige est blanche' express the same proposition.

Such difficulties as there are over the definition of truth lie in the need to avoid antinomies, such as the antinomy of the liar,[1] and in the fact that it is not possible to enumerate all the sentences in any natural language which express propositions of which truth or falsehood can be predicated. The important problem, however, is not so much that of defining truth as that of giving some general account of the conditions under which we are justified in attributing it. I have tried to achieve this both by distinguishing between analytic and empirical propositions and by distinguishing between primary and secondary systems. The secondary system of which I gave some account was a scientific one. The question which I now wish to consider is whether an explanatory system of a different sort could also be acceptable. I have so far said hardly anything about theology, of which Russell, in a pessimistic mood, once said that philosophy might be nothing but an unfortunate legacy.[2] I shall now do something to remedy this omission.

[1] See above p. 194.
[2] See his 'Logical Atomism'. *Contemporary British Philosophy*, 1st series, p. 361.

X The Claims of Theology

A The Existence of God

In W. H. Mallock's satire 'The New Republic', which was first published in the eighteen seventies, at a time when the conflict between science and religion was at its height, a character representing Dr Jowett is made to admit that an atheist opponent can disprove the existence of God, as he would define him. 'All atheists can do that'. This does not, however, disturb the doctor's faith. 'For,' he says, 'the world has at present no adequate definition of God; and I think we should be able to define a thing before we can satisfactorily disprove it.'[1]

I said this was a satire, but the words which are put into Jowett's mouth represent a point of view which is still not uncommon. People who try to justify their belief in the existence of God by saying that it rests on faith are sometimes maintaining no more than that the proposition that God exists is one which they have the right to accept, in default of sufficient evidence; but sometimes they look to faith for the assurance that the words 'God exists' express some true proposition, though they do not know what this proposition is; it is one that surpasses human understanding. The first of these positions is discussable, though I think it misguided, but the second is merely disingenuous. Until we have an intelligible proposition before us, there is nothing for faith to get to work on. It can be an article of faith that beings of superhuman intelligence, if there are any, entertain propositions that we cannot grasp. This requires only that we can make sense of the expression 'beings with superhuman intelligence'. But if we really cannot grasp these propositions, if the sentences which purport to express them have no meaning for us, then the fact, if it were a fact, that they did have meaning for some other beings would be of little interest to us; for this meaning might be anything whatsoever. The truth is,

[1] p. 231.

however, that those who take this position do understand, or think they understand, something by the words 'God exists'. It is only when the account they give of what they understand appears unworthy of credence that they take refuge in saying that it falls short of what the words really mean. But words have no meaning beyond the meaning that is given them, and a proposition is not made the more credible by being treated as an approximation to something that we do not find intelligible.

In fact, the world is not without descriptions of Gods, whether or not they severally or collectively count as adequate definitions. Until we are provided with a criterion of adequacy, this is a detail that need not detain us. Thus, those who believe in many Gods tend to ascribe properties to them which fit the human activities over which they are thought to preside. The God of War is martial, the God of Love amorous. In some, though not in all cases, these Gods are at least intermittently corporeal and they operate in space and time. Those who believe that there is just one God are in general agreement that he is an intelligent person, or something like one, that he feels emotions such as love or moral indignation, that he is incorporeal, except in the case of the Christian God, when, for a period of about thirty years, if one assumes the identity of the Son and the Father, he had what are ordinarily supposed to be the incompatible properties of being both corporeal and incorporeal, that, again with this exception, he is not located in space, though capable of acting in space, that he is either eternal or with the same exception not located in time, though capable of acting in time, that he created the world and continues to oversee it, that he is not subject to change, that he is all-powerful and all-knowing, that he is morally perfect and consequently supremely benevolent, and that he necessarily exists.

There may be some doubt whether the predicates that are ascribed to this one God are all of them meaningful or mutually consistent. For instance, we have found reason to think that if the notion of disembodied persons is intelligible at all, they must at least be located in time. Neither is it clear how a being that feels emotions can fail to be subject to change, unless we suppose that he feels the same emotions with the same intensity all the time, in which case there must be some danger of their sometimes lacking their appropriate objects. What is anyhow obvious is that these different predicates are for the most part not logically connected. We shall have to consider later on whether it is possible to make sense of the idea that the world was created. If this is a significant proposition, it may be taken to entail that the creator was intelligent. It may also be taken to entail that he was incorporeal, on the ground that the existence of a physical body could not precede the existence of the universe, though then it is not clear why the same should not apply to the existence of a mind. It surely does not entail that the creator is eternal; he might have come into existence at any time before he created the world or ceased to exist at any time after. Neither does it entail that he is all powerful. He might have wished but been unable to create a different world, and having created the world that he did, he might subsequently have found that it escaped wholly or partly from his control. It might also develop in ways that he was unable to foresee. Clearly also, there is no logical connection between having any degree of power, including the power to create the universe, and being morally good. Indeed, if one thought of the world's history as having been planned by its creator, a strong case could be made for infering that he was malevolent. Finally, even if the creator could consistently possess all these other properties it would not follow that he necessarily existed. If he was thought to be a God, his possession of them might be necessary, in the sense that they were ascribed to any God by definition, but this would not entail that it was not a contingent proposition that the definition was actually satisfied.

The idea that God necessarily exists is worth pursuing, since it is involved in two of the best known attempts to prove that there is a God. The first of these is originally due to St Anselm and has come to be known as the Ontological argument.[1] A version of it, not significantly different from St Anselm's, was also advanced by Descartes.[2] The first premiss of the argument is that God is perfect, in a sense which implies that no greater being is imaginable. This is taken to be true by definition. We are not told exactly what is comprised in perfection or greatness, but this does not matter to the argument, so long as it can proceed to its second premiss, which is that a merely imaginary being is not so great as a real one. This also is taken to be true by definition. It is then argued that if God did not exist, he would not be the greatest being imaginable. But since by definition he is the greatest being imaginable, it follows

[1] See *Proslogion*, Section II.
[2] See *Discourse on Method*, Part IV and Meditations III and V.

that he exists. To say that he exists necessarily is, in this context, just to say that his existence follows from his essence, or, in other words, from the way he has been defined.

Though some philosophers, even in our own day, have been convinced by this argument, it is surely fallacious. The most common way of rebutting it, which was suggested by Kant,[1] is to deny that anything can include existence in its definition. To define an object is to list the predicates which it has to satisfy, and existence, it is said, is not a predicate. For example, one may define a centaur as a creature with the head, trunk and arms of a man joined to the body and legs of a horse. If one then goes on to say that centaurs exist, one is not adding another property to the definition, or predicating anything of the objects to which it applies, as one would be if one said that centaurs were bellicose. One is making a statement of a different order, namely the false statement that the definition is satisfied. In the same way, one may enumerate the properties which constitute a God's perfection, as consisting in omnipotence, omniscience, supreme benevolence, or whatever, but in adding existence one is not listing a further property; one is saying, truly or falsely, that there is something to which they belong.

I think that this answer is along the right lines, but it is not entirely satisfactory because it places too much emphasis on a rule for framing definitions which one might think could be broken. For instance, if one looks up the word 'centaur' in a dictionary one will find that centaurs are credited not only with the properties that I listed but also with being fabulous. If this were taken seriously as part of the definition, then in the improbable event that anything was found to answer to the other specifications of a centaur, it could not properly be called one: some other term would have to be found to designate this creature which differed from a centaur just in not being fabulous. In the same way, I suppose that someone could insist on making it part of the sense of the term 'God', or indeed of any other term, that it carried an assumption of existence. For such a person, to say 'God does not exist' would be a misuse of language, because the attribute of non-existence would deny what the use of the subject-term had presupposed. But now it becomes clear that nothing is gained by this manoeuvre, since it remains an open question whether the subject-term has any use. Let it be written into the definition of a perfect being that he is not imaginary.

[1] See *Critique of Pure Reason*. The Ideal of Pure Reason.

The question whether there is anything that has all the other properties of a perfect being and is also not imaginary can still significantly be answered 'No'. Thus, even if we allow to St Anselm that to conceive of a greatest imaginable being is to conceive of him as existing, it will not follow that there actually is anything to which this concept applies.

Does it make any difference if God is defined as a necessary being? There is some difficulty in understanding what this could mean, but I suppose it might be taken to mean that whatever predicates he satisfied, he satisfied necessarily. In this respect, though presumably not in others, he would be assimilated to a number. This is not, indeed, true of all the predicates which numbers satisfy, but it is true of some of them, and these would furnish the analogy. In fact, I think it very doubtful whether the comparison is tenable, but there is no need to press the point, as this move does nothing to save the argument. For even if it be granted that if the predicates in question are satisfied at all, they are satisfied necessarily, it remains a mere assumption that they are satisfied at all.

Sometimes when it is said that God is a necessary being, what is meant is that he is a being, and indeed the only being, that contains in itself the reason for its own existence. This was the position, or one of the positions taken by St Thomas Aquinas,[1] who did not believe that the Ontological Argument was valid but thought that there had to be a necessary being, in the foregoing sense. This definition of God was accepted by Spinoza and, as we have seen,[2] it led, in his case, to the identification of God with Nature. The difficulty, as we then remarked, is to understand how such a definition could possibly be satisfied. If what is meant by a reason is a logical ground, the implication would be that God's existence follows from his essence, and we are back with the Ontological Argument. If what is meant is a cause, it is hard to see what sense can be attached to the proposition that something causes itself. What is the difference, one may ask, between saying that something causes itself and saying that it has no cause?

In St Thomas's case, the fundamental idea appears to have been that the world cannot just happen to exist in the way that it does. We have theories which account more or less successfully for the observable facts, but the propositions which figure in these theories

[1] See *Summa Theologica* 1a, 2, 3.
[2] See above p. 8.

are themselves contingent, or if the theories take the form of deductive systems, it is a contingent matter that their axioms are satisfied. To bring the facts under laws is not to show that they could not have been otherwise but only to fit them into general patterns. We seek to simplify these patterns by developing more far-reaching theories, but however far we go we always end in the position that this is how things generally are. The question why they are so is answered only by the production of another theory which leaves us with the same question to be asked again. The answer that we need is one that assures us not just that this is how things are but that this is how they must be. But such an answer can be forthcoming only if the final explanation is found in the existence of a deity whose actions proceed from his nature and whose nature could not be different from what it is.

There is an echo of this reasoning in the writings of modern existentialists, who conclude that the world is absurd, just because everything in it might have been otherwise. Those who take this position do not see any reason to believe that there is a God, but they imply that if only there were a God, the world would have a significance which it tragically lacks.

In this, they are mistaken. The search for an ultimate reason is emotionally understandable but it is not intellectually coherent. To begin with, the recourse to a deity will not explain anything, unless it yields hypotheses which we can successfully project, and we shall see presently that it is doubtful whether this is so. Let us suppose, however, that this condition can be satisfied. Let us suppose that we can attribute purposes to God which account for the way in which the world is organized. Would it not be a contingent fact that he has these purposes? No, it is said, because they will be in accordance with his nature. Being what he is, he is bound to have these purposes. But then is it not a contingent fact that he has this nature, that he is, for example, benevolent rather than malevolent? No, it is said again, because his nature is included in his definition. But then we return to the fallacy of the Ontological Argument.

Not only that, but the necessity which is attributed to God's actions and the explanatory role which they are supposed to play are incompatible. From necessary propositions only necessary propositions follow. Their content is wholly abstract. They are consistent with everything that might actually happen. But an explanation derives its power from not being consistent with everything that might actually happen; it favours one actual pattern in contrast to others which are logically possible. So, if one could think of the history of the world as being regulated by a God's decisions, one would have to allow both that its history could conceivably have been different, and that the God's decisions could also have been different, if they were themselves to be explicable. Here too there would have to be a point at which the explanations stopped. No further reason would be given why God's nature was what it was, or, if this were made a matter of necessity, why there was a being with such a nature. If it were rational to settle for an explanation of this sort, the reason would not be that it did away with contingency, but that it made sense of our experiences in a way that scientific theories did not. But then it would have to be shown that this was so. It would not be enough to say that there was some explanation of this kind which we had not fathomed. This would be permissible only if the existence of God had been independently established. If the positing of a deity is to be justified by its explanatory value, the explanation has actually to be given.

B The Argument from Design

Can it be given? Only, it would seem, if we are able to detect a pattern in the course of events which can be held to support the hypothesis that they are planned. We may then be able to develop a theory about the intentions of the planner which can be empirically tested. Again, it will not be enough to say that there is some plan or other. It has to be a system that we can successfully project.

The belief that the world affords sufficient evidence of an ulterior plan is responsible for the argument in favour of the existence of a God which is commonly known as the argument from design. The proponents of this argument do not take it to show that there necessarily is a God, but only that the assumption of his existence is a reasonable hypothesis. Their position is elegantly and fairly stated by one of the participants in Hume's *Dialogues Concerning Natural Religion*. 'Look round the world: Contemplate the whole and every part of it: You will find it to be nothing but one great machine, subdivided into an infinite number of lesser machines, which again admit of subdivisions, to a degree beyond what human senses and faculties can trace and explain. All these various machines and even their most minute parts, are adjusted to each other with an accuracy, which ravishes into admiration all men, who have ever contemplated them. The curious adapting of means to ends, throughout all nature, resembles exactly, though it much exceeds, the productions of human contrivance; of human design, thought, wisdom, and intelligence. Since therefore the effects resemble each other, we are led to infer, by all the rules of analogy, that the causes also resemble: and that the Author of nature is somewhat similar to the mind of man: though possessed of much larger faculties, proportioned to the grandeur of the work, which he has executed.'[1]

Before we try to evaluate this argument, let us take a closer look at the conclusion. What properties is the author of nature supposed to have, and how is he related to the world for which he is made responsible? In the first place, as one of the other participants in Hume's dialogue remarks, there is nothing in the analogy to favour the assumption of a single author, rather than a multiplicity. There is nothing to favour the assumption that the world as we find it is the fruit of his only attempt to make a world, rather than the outcome of previous experiments on his own part or on that of others; if anything the analogy would point the other way. There is nothing either to license the inference that he is eternal or indeed that he is incorporeal; since all the designers that we have actually observed have been mortal and embodied, the analogy, if it were to be pressed, would again point the other way. It would suggest that his faculties are larger than ours, but not that he is omnipotent, nor yet that he is benevolent. The ascription of benevolence to him would require us to find empirical evidence not merely that the world had an author but that it had an author who meant well by the creatures whom he had put into it.

What now of the designer's relation to the world? If one supposes there to have been an act of creation, I do not see how one can avoid the conclusion that it took place at some time. If one supposes this to be the first instant in time, one will find it difficult to say in what sense the author of nature existed antecedently to its creation. The idea that he existed outside time is one to which it is difficult to attach any meaning. It is true that abstract entities can be said to exist outside time, if they can be said to exist at all, but the activities which are attributed to the deity are hardly such as are consistent with his existing after the fashion of an abstract entity. A more intelligible theory would be that events in his history temporally

[1] David Hume. *Dialogues Concerning Natural Religion*, Part II.

preceded the act of creation. This would be, in a way, to include him in the universe, but on the assumption of his existence, he would anyhow have to be included, if the universe was taken to comprehend everything that there is. The creation of the world as we know it would then appear more as a transformation, a radical change in the total course of events, though not necessarily as a transformation of pre-existing matter. It is, however, to be noted that the analogy with the makers of human artefacts is still further weakened if we suppose the material world to have been created out of nothing at all.

In view of these difficulties, the proponents of this argument might be better advised to lay more stress upon the metaphor of the *author* of nature. Instead of comparing the world to a machine, which needed to be designed and built, they could compare it to a play, which needed to be written and directed. Among other things, this accords better with the ordinary concept of creation. The author, who would also be spectator and critic, would exist in time, but the time in which he existed would be incommensurable with that of the incidents in the play, which would have its own spatio-temporal structure. The participants in the play would not be able to verify the existence of its author, except on the dubious assumption that when they had played their parts they were somehow translated into his world, but it might be maintained that they could attach sense to the hypothesis that he existed, as the fundamental principle of a secondary system which they could use to account for the proceedings on their stage.

But now the question arises whether the character of the world as we know it gives any support to these analogies. The fact that regularities are detectable in it is not sufficient, for we have seen that no describable world can fail to exhibit some regularity. Neither is it sufficient that some processes within it are goal-directed, for the fact that ends are pursued and sometimes attained within a system is not a proof that the system as a whole is directed towards any end. What needs to be shown is that the entire universe presents the appearance of a teleological system. If one prefers the dramatic analogy, the play has to have a moral or at least some discernible plot. Can this requirement be met? It does not seem that it can. None of those who have compared the world to a vast machine has ever made any serious attempt to say what the machine could be for. They have spoken of there being an overall purpose, but have not said what it was. Again it will not do to say that there is a plan, but one too intricate for us to fathom. This answer might pass muster if the existence of a deity had been independently established, but if the sole reason given for believing in his existence is that the book of nature must have had an author, then the grounds for taking this metaphor seriously have to be produced.

In so far as theists have held any view at all about the purpose for which the world was created, they have generally assumed that it had something to do with the emergence of man. This is a view which it is perhaps natural for men to take but hardly one that would be supported by a dispassionate consideration of the scientific evidence. Not only did man make a very late appearance upon the scene in a very small corner of the universe, but it is not even probable that, having made his appearance, he is there to stay. As Russell put it, 'The second law of thermodynamics makes it scarcely possible to doubt that the universe is running down, and that ultimately nothing of the slightest interest will be possible anywhere. Of course, it is open to us to say that when that time comes God will wind up the machinery again: but if we do say this, we can base our assertion only upon faith, not upon one shred of scientific evidence. So far as scientific evidence goes, the universe has crawled by slow stages to a somewhat pitiful result on this earth, and is going to crawl by still more pitiful stages to a condition of universal death. If this is to be taken as evidence of purpose, I can only say that the purpose is one that does not appeal to me. I see no reason therefore to believe in any sort of God, however vague and however attenuated.'[1]

C   Religious Hypotheses

At this point it may be objected that it is not fair to assess religious hypotheses in terms of scientific theory. We have seen that our reason for accepting the scientific picture of the world is that it accounts for the primary facts of observation in a way that we find satisfactory. At the same time we allowed that other methods of accounting for these facts might be conceivable. Instead, therefore, of trying to give a religious flavour to a scientific system which it does not suit, ought we not to consider the hypothesis of God's existence as the basis of a rival system which applies directly to the primary facts?

[1] Bertrand Russell. *Why I am not a Christian*, pp. 24–5.

This indeed was the position taken by Berkeley,[1] though he did not put it in quite those terms. Conceiving of percepts as ideas in the mind of their perceiver, for which the perceiver's own volitions were not causally responsible, he argued that they must have some external cause. He rejected the theory that they were caused by material objects, on the ground that the belief in the existence of such objects, beyond the reach of our perception, was not only unverifiable but incoherent, and maintained instead that our ideas were directly supplied to us by God. He did not, indeed, suppose that God was any more perceptible than matter, but he thought that whereas we could have no notion of matter, we did have a notion of spirit, and he argued, invalidly, that because ideas were spiritual, as being in the mind, they had to have a spiritual cause. As I remarked earlier,[2] he also looked to God to keep things in being. Though he sometimes wrote as if he were prepared to conceive of the physical objects of commonsense, in phenomenalist fashion, as permanent possibilities of sensation, his main view was that if they continued to exist at times when they were not otherwise being perceived it was as ideas in the mind of God.

Is such a position tenable? It is certainly not forced upon us in the way that Berkeley claimed. Though I think that he was very largely justified in his attack on the Lockean form of the causal theory of perception,[3] we have seen that it is possible to arrive at physical objects as abstractions out of percepts, and that once a primary physical system has been developed in this way it may be legitimate to admit physical entities, of an unobservable sort, if they figure in theories which have an explanatory value. We have also seen that it is a mistake to start by treating percepts as private entities, and there is nothing in their character to suggest that they must have a spiritual cause. Nevertheless, none of this debars the Berkeleyan system from being an alternative option. If anyone were inclined to take it, he would need to be clearer than Berkeley seems to have been about the nature of the ideas which he attributed to God. For instance, when God keeps things in being, is it through having tactual sensations of all of them simultaneously? If his ideas are visual, from what point of view are they obtained? To avoid such awkward questions, the best course would probably be to

[1] See the second of the *Three Dialogues between Hylas and Philonous.*
[2] See above p. 60.
[3] See above pp. 86-8.

represent God just as thinking continuously of perceptible objects as having such and such properties and standing in such and such relations to one another, and as being constantly disposed to supply us with sensations that match these thoughts.

Such a theory, if it is allowed to be intelligible, cannot be directly tested. No experiments could be devised which would decide between it and a materialistic theory. The only reason there can be for accepting it is that it yields a fruitful arrangement of the facts of our experience. Does it do so? Does it yield any hypotheses that we can successfully project? The answer plainly is that it does not. To obtain a theory which had some explanatory value, one would have to make various assumptions about the tenor of God's thoughts, and derive conclusions from them which our observations would confirm or refute. This is not, however, what Berkeley does. On the contrary, the ideas which he ascribes to God are simply a reflection of the common-sense picture of the world which we elaborate out of our sensations. So far from employing any assumptions about God's thoughts to forecast changes in our experience, he has to wait upon the course of experience in order to discover what God thinks. But this means that the part played by God is theoretically idle. Neither is it easy to see how this could be otherwise. Unless we simply have God thinking in current scientific terms, in which case his introduction is superfluous, it is not easy to see what assumptions could be made about his thoughts that would yield a genuinely explanatory theory.

But is this not to take too narrow a view of our experience? No doubt it can be left to science to order the phenomena which sustain our conception of the material world. But our lives are not wholly spent in the exercise of sense-perception or the reasoning which arises out of it. We also have moral sentiments. Some of us have distinctively religious experiences. There are those who have claimed a direct awareness of God. To account for this range of facts, may not the adoption of a religious hypothesis be not only fruitful but necessary?

So far as religious experience is concerned, we have already answered this question in dealing earlier with mysticism.[1] The problem, as we then saw, is to determine whether and, if so, in what way such experience is cognitive. Again, I do not want to argue that it is impossible for it to be so. If experiences of this kind were

[1] See above pp. 4–7.

widespread, and those who had them agreed in the accounts which they gave of them, I see no decisive reason why they should not be credited with an object. If it is conceivable for there to be mental states which are not associated with a body in the normal way, as we have seen that it may be,[1] this object might even be represented as a person. We should still have the option of accounting for the experiences in question in terms of the physiological and psychological states of those who had them, without allowing them any object, but we might think it unreasonable to follow this course if the accepted criteria of objectivity were very largely satisfied. The consequence, however, of allowing them an object would again be only that we should take a more liberal view of what the world contains. There could be nothing in the character of these experiences to justify any attempt to locate their object outside the world, nor could they sustain any such proposition as that the world had a creator. They might possibly confirm such a proposition if it had been independently established, but this has not been achieved. Accordingly, the answer to the claim that to have an experience of this kind is to be aware of God is that the most that it can come to is that the experience, or its object, if it is thought capable of having one, is endowed with a numinous quality.

D Religion and Morality

Is there any support for religious belief in the fact that men have moral sentiments to which their actions sometimes answer ? The view that there is has been quite widely held. The main arguments which have been advanced in its favour are, first, that only the agency of God can account for the existence of morality, and, secondly, that God's authority is needed to give our moral standards some objective validity.

The first of these arguments seems very weak. The assumption which underlies it is that it is natural for men to behave only in a purely selfish manner. Consequently, if they sometimes forgo their interests, or what they believe to be their interests, in order to serve others, or because they think that the action which promotes their interests is wrong, or that some other course of action is morally binding on them, the ability to behave in this unnatural way must have been given to them by a higher power. Even if the starting-point of this argument were true, the reasoning would not be

[1] See above pp. 124–6.

cogent, since it ignores the possibility that moral behaviour can be adequately explained in terms of social conditioning, but in fact it is not true. Antecedently to any actual observations that are made of human behaviour, there is no reason to expect it either to be selfish or to be unselfish; there is no reason to expect it either to conform or not to conform to any particular moral code. If it seems to us more natural for men to pursue their individual interests, this is only because they most commonly do so, at any rate in our own form of society. I believe that there are, or have been, societies in which it is more common for men to pursue the interest of some group of which they are members, their family or clan or tribe. But even if the prevalent tendency in all societies were for men to behave selfishly, it would not follow that unselfish behaviour was unnatural, in the sense of being contrary to nature. Nothing that actually happens is contrary to nature, though there are some actions that we misleadingly call unnatural as a way of expressing our disapproval of them. In fact, I think that a good case can be made for saying that altruistic impulses are innate, though they may be initially weaker in small children than the self-regarding or aggressive impulses. If they are not innate, at least the evidence shows that we have the capacity to acquire them. But how did we obtain this capacity? This question is on a level with any other question about the causes of human behaviour. It is no more and no less difficult than the question how we obtain our capacity to injure one another. If there were any good reason to believe that men were the outcome of a God's creation, their creator would be equally responsible for all their characteristics, however much or little we esteem them. Conversely, if there is otherwise no good reason to believe that men were so created, the fact that they behave unselfishly as well as selfishly to each other does not provide one.

In dealing with the argument that a God is required to ensure the objectivity of moral standards, we need to distinguish carefully between the motives for morality and its possible grounds. There is no doubt that belief in a God has frequently been the source of moral incentives. Sometimes the motive has been the altruistic one of love for a deity or a saint whose wishes one believes oneself to be carrying out, or love for other human beings on the ground that they are equally the children of God. Perhaps more frequently it has been the prudential motive of fear of future punishment or hope of future reward. It was the belief that men were not generally capable of behaving decently without this prudential motive that led Voltaire to say that if God did not exist it would be necessary to invent him.[1] This is a good epigram, but like many good epigrams, it probably distorts the truth. I do not know that a scientific study has ever been made of this question, but if one were to be made I doubt if it would reveal any strong correlation either of morally admirable behaviour with religious belief or of morally reprehensible behaviour with its absence. Much good has been done in the name of religion but also very much evil. When the long history of religious intolerance and persecution is taken into account, together with the tendency of religious hierarchies to side with the oppressors rather than the oppressed, it is arguable that the evil has outweighed the good. Many bad men have indeed been irreligious, but many agnostics and atheists have led very decent lives. Neither do those who are sincerely religious always live up to their good principles. My own conjecture is that the factors which make for the observance or disregard of morality are mainly psychological and social, and that religious belief has had a smaller influence either way than is commonly supposed. However this may be, it is clear that to show that belief in God had had a predominantly good effect would not be to show that the belief was true, any more than showing that it had had a predominantly bad effect would be to show that it was false.

I suspect that the widespread assumption that religious belief is necessary for the maintenance of moral standards arises not so much from any assessment of the empirical evidence as from a tacit or explicit acceptance of the proposition that if there is no God there is no reason to be moral. What is meant is that there is then no justification for morality, but because of the ambiguity of the word 'reason', the fallacious inference is drawn that there is neither any ground nor any motive. The conclusion sought is that since there is reason to be moral, there is a God. This is the obverse of the Nietzschean idea that since God is dead, everything is permitted.

Whichever way it is taken, this proposition contains two serious errors, apart from the fallacy of thinking that the absence of grounds for morality entails the absence of motives. The first error is to suppose that morality needs an ulterior justification. The second error is to suppose that a God could supply it. The fallacy which is involved in thinking that morals could be founded on divine

[1] Voltaire. *Epistles* XCVI.

authority has been exposed by many philosophers, but perhaps most clearly and succinctly by Russell. 'Theologians have always taught that God's decrees are good, and that this is not a mere tautology: it follows that goodness is logically independent of God's decrees.'[1] The point is that moral standards can never be justified merely by an appeal to authority, whether the authority is taken to be human or divine. There has to be the additional premiss that the person whose dictates we are to follow is good, or that what he commands is right, and this cannot be the mere tautology that he is what he is, or that he commands what he commands. This does not mean that we cannot look for guidance in conduct to those whom we judge to be better or wiser or more experienced than ourselves. To a greater or lesser extent, we can and do take our morals on trust but in so doing we are making a moral decision. We are at least implicitly judging that the rules which we have been brought up to respect, or the verdicts of our mentor, are morally right: and again this is not the mere tautology that these rules and verdicts just are what they are.

But if a moral code cannot be founded on authority, neither can it be founded on metaphysics or on science or on empirical matters of fact. Scientific and factual considerations are indeed relevant to morals, because of the bearing which they have upon the application of our moral principles. We have to know what the situation is in which we are placed and what the consequences of different actions are likely to be. If, for example, we think it right to try to maximize human happiness, a scientific approach to the practical problems may instruct us how best to set about it. The adoption of such a principle is, however, something which is not dictated to us by the facts. It is a decision for which it may be that we are not able to give any further reason, just as we may not be able to give any further reason for the value that we attach to justice or to liberty. In the end, it is a matter of finding principles which one is prepared to stand by and when they conflict, as for most of us they sometimes will, of giving more weight to one or another according to the circumstances of the particular case.

This does not mean that we have to regard every moral standpoint as equally correct. In holding a moral principle, one regards it as valid for others besides oneself, whether they think so or not. In cases where they do not think so, it will depend on their circum-

[1] Bertrand Russell. *Human Society in Ethics and Politics*, p. 48.

stances whether one judges that they are unenlightened or morally at fault. What has to be admitted is that there is no way of proving that they are mistaken. The most that one can do is argue *ad hominem*. One may be able to show that their principles are inconsistent, or that they are based on factual assumptions which are false, or that they are the product of bad reasoning, or that they lead to consequences which their advocates are not prepared to stand by. Even if we are successful in this, we may not persuade them to change their principles, but at least we shall have advanced some reason why they should. It may be, however, that we cannot find any such flaws in their position and still want to regard it as morally untenable. In that case discussion can go no further. This stage is seldom reached because it is nearly always possible to find a sufficient basis of moral agreement for the argument to proceed, but it has to be accepted as a possibility. Neither is this just the outcome of a subjective attitude to morals. The position is no different for one who believes that value-predicates stand for objective, unanalyzable ethical properties. In the case where his intuitions of what is good or right conflict with those of some other moralist he has no means of proving that they are correct. The difference between him and the subjectivist is that whereas the subjectivist is content to say that these are his principles and leave it at that, the believer in absolute values wants to say that his moral judgements are objectively true. Since, however, his only criterion of their truth is his own intuition, the difference is negligible. The merit of this sort of objectivism is that it avoids any suggestion of moral nihilism. Its demerit is its implication that value-judgements are descriptive of something other-worldly, whereas fundamentally they are not descriptive judgements at all. I say 'fundamentally' because they sometimes are descriptive of natural states of affairs; they convey the implication that the objects or actions in question come up to standard, or fail to do so. But then the acceptance of these standards is presupposed.

E The Freedom of the Will

From a logical point of view, the association of religion with morals appears rather arbitrary. Not only can morality not be founded on a God's decrees, but there seems no reason why the belief that the world had an intelligent creator should entail any conclusions about the way in which men ought to behave. If the purposes of the creator were thought to be known, one might derive some conclusions about the ways in which men would in fact behave, but that would be all. In the case of Christianity, however, the association is cemented by the belief that God, in the person of his own son, turned himself temporarily into a man, and underwent torture and a painful death in order to make it possible for sinful men to be redeemed from the punishment which he would otherwise have inflicted. In assessing this belief we have to balance the testimony in favour of such events as the Virgin Birth and the Resurrection not only against their improbability, in the light of the rest of our experience, but also against the strangeness of the motive which is attributed to God. For it is very strange. In the first place, the very notion of vindictive punishment, the idea that if someone does harm to others, or even in certain cases to himself, one is required to do harm to him, is one to which objection may be taken on moral grounds, and it becomes even harder to accept when the suffering is vicarious, where one person is punished on account of what others have done. Neither is the objection removed when the scapegoat himself elects to be sacrificed; for what is objectionable is that there should be need for any scapegoat at all. If God wished to absolve men from their sins, why could he not simply do so, without exacting any price from himself or anyone else ? Why indeed, if he was so deeply concerned with men's behaviour. and had the power to make them as he chose, did he not endow them with a nature and a form of life which would ensure that they always behaved in ways of which he approved ?

The usual answer to this question is that to have contrived that men should live in this fashion would have been inconsistent with giving them free-will, and that it is better that we should have this freedom, however badly we employ it, than that we should simply be a deity's puppets. This answer is sometimes also given in an attempt to reconcile the suffering that men endure with the supreme benevolence which is ascribed to God, but here it wholly fails, if only for the reason that much of this suffering is due to causes which are beyond our control.

Does it fail also in the other case ? It is sometimes argued that the power which is ascribed to God of foreseeing everything that happens is inconsistent with men's freedom, but this is a mistake. There is some difficulty, as we shall see, in understanding what is meant by saying that a man does something of his own free-will, but if a proposition of this sort is ever true, it must be consistent with the tautology that his actions will be what they will be. But if the man's actions will be what they will be, whether they are done freely or not, then equally someone who says what they will be predicts them truly whether they are done freely or not. It makes no difference here whether the predictions are lucky guesses or manifestations of knowledge. From the fact that someone knows what I shall do, it does indeed follow that I *shall* do it, for the purely semantic reason that this is part of what is meant by saying that he knows that I shall. It does not follow that I am compelled to do it, that I shall not be free to act otherwise. The most that can be inferred is that if I do have this freedom I shall in fact not exercise it.

The position becomes different, however, when one thinks of a God as having made men what they are. The suggestion is that he endowed them biologically with certain initial dispositions and capacities but left them free within certain limits to choose whether and to what extent the dispositions are realized or the capacities developed. A man's character, from which his actions largely proceed, is thought to be the joint product of his initial equipment, the physical and social stimuli to which he has been subjected, and his own past choices. The formation of his character may narrow his freedom; he may, through physical or social conditioning, or as the consequence of his own free actions, be deprived of the power to make choices that he once was able to make: but except in abnormal circumstances, such as that of extreme senility, when the man ceases to be a responsible agent, his freedom of choice never vanishes altogether.

But now we may ask how it comes about that he chooses to act in this way rather than that. Through the exercise of his will. But what does this mean? The idea of the will as a piece of psychological mechanism which converts intentions into physical movements appears to be mythical. All that seems actually to happen is that we think about the advantages and disadvantages of different courses of action and having come to some conclusion simply act. More often, where the action is part of some habitual routine, we perform it without any prior deliberation. In neither case do we feel that we are prodded into action by what Ryle has called 'occult inner thrusts'.[1] Perhaps a desire can be represented as such a thrust, but then we do not need another one to enable us to set about fulfilling

[1] See Gilbert Ryle, *The Concept of Mind*, p. 67.

the desire. We may need to concentrate our attention, or to make a physical effort, but that is all. In any case, even if there were a recognizable mechanism with which the will could be identified, we could still ask in any given instance how it came to work as it did. Because that was the way in which its owner chose to operate it. But then we return to the question how he came to make this choice. Was it due to the way God made him, or was it a spontaneous occurrence, a matter of chance? On neither assumption does it seem reasonable for God to hold him responsible for what he did.

But then is it reasonable for us to hold him responsible, whether or not we assign any part to a God? Let us look more closely at this problem. There is no doubt that we think ourselves able to draw a distinction between cases in which someone does something of his own free-will and cases in which this is not so. What then does the distinction consist in? I think that the best way to try to answer this question is to approach it from the negative side. Under what conditions is our freedom of action thought to be non-existent, or else so limited as seriously to attenuate our responsibility?

The most obvious class of cases in which our freedom is thought to be non-existent consists of those in which the prospective action is one which is regarded as being physically impossible for the agent to perform, or physically impossible for him to avoid. These conditions obtain when the circumstances are known to be such that in conjunction with accepted physical laws they exclude the agent's performance of the action or his avoidance of it. This is, however, not always enough to exculpate him, since it may be held that he could and should have prevented the circumstances from arising. It may be physically impossible for me to keep an appointment because there is no means by which I can get there in time, but I was perhaps not obliged to let this happen. I may not be able to avoid falling asleep, at a time when wakefulness is demanded of me, because I have taken a drug, but it can be argued that I did not have to take it. One may also be held responsible for one's general loss of some physical capacity, if this is thought to be due to one's own folly or negligence.

A second class of cases where freedom is taken to be lacking consists of those in which some action is thought incapable of being performed by the agent, or incapable of being avoided, because of the operation of a psychological law. These cases are more contentious, because of our difficulty in finding psychological laws that are agreed to hold universally. It is, however, generally admitted that one has to acquire skills in order to exercise them: one is not expected to speak a language that one has not learned. There are also thought to be neurotic or psychotic states which affect people in such a way that the performance or the avoidance of certain actions is not within their power. Here again they may sometimes be held responsible, to a greater or lesser degree, for falling into this condition.

The circumstances in which our freedom may be thought to be diminished, without being altogether removed, are very various. For instance, one may feel oneself bound by a moral or a legal obligation which would be infringed by some action that one would otherwise wish or think it right to perform. One may be subject to emotional pressures which it is thought excusable to give way to even if they are not thought to be irresistible. One may be acting under the influence of some false belief. One may be under the control of another person, as when one has been hypnotized, or brainwashed. One may be exposed to blackmail or to torture, or to other menaces. Even when one is threatened with death, one is considered free to defy the threat, but in most circumstances this would not be thought reasonable. In all these cases, the idea of what it is reasonable to expect a man to do plays a large part in our assessment of responsibility.

From this it emerges that when one is held responsible for something that one has done, or failed to do, there is always the implication that one could reasonably have been expected to act otherwise. There may, indeed, have been very little likelihood that one would act otherwise, but that may be held to be the result of one's past conduct which could reasonably have been expected to be different at some earlier stage. But now we must ask what is meant by saying of someone, in a given situation, that he could have avoided acting as he did. The answer is, I believe, that the fiction that he did act differently is one that we find acceptable. Whether the fictitious action is thought to be reasonable depends partly on what we consider to be normal behaviour and partly on our moral standards. What makes it acceptable as a possibility is just that it is not excluded by the conjunction of the attendant circumstances, as they are known to us, with the established hypotheses of our explanatory system.

To say that an occurrence is not ruled out by the explanatory system, which we actually have, is not, however, to say that this will always be so. I think it unlikely that there will ever be a working system which enables us to account for every human action in every detail, but equally I do not think that there is any form of action of which one can be sure that it will never come within the reach of established universal laws. Let us, however, assume that we have to be content with statistical laws. In that case it will be a matter of chance whether or not a particular action conforms to the prevailing frequency, and it is not clear why a man should be held responsible for an action which occurs by chance. The same would apply if the action were of a sort that, so far as we could discover, was not governed even by a statistical law, for then we should have to conclude either that there was some explanation which had so far eluded us or that such actions were entirely fortuitous. It has, indeed, been suggested that these are not the only alternatives. Even if a man's actions are not governed by causal laws, he may still have reasons for doing them and therefore be held responsible. But all that this comes to, as we have seen,[1] is that his actions are explained in terms of generalizations of tendency, with the result that, in default of a stronger explanation, the conformity of a particular action to a recognized tendency remains a matter of chance.

Some philosophers have argued that even if we were able to represent all human actions as causally determined, we should still have a use for the concepts of free-will and responsibility. They remark, quite correctly, that we should still be able to distinguish between behaviour which occurs independently of the agent's volition and actions which are done deliberately, in the sense that we do not admit the fiction of their occurrence in the actual circumstances without the agent's having chosen to do them. Free actions can then be characterized, in the way that Locke[2] and others have proposed, as those in which the agent is not prevented from doing what he chooses, no matter how his choices are themselves determined, and the justification of reward and punishment will be that they exert a causal influence upon the agent's future choices as well as on the choices of others who may be expected to learn from the example.

This is a tenable position, but I think that its advocates underrate the extent to which it departs from our ordinary way of thinking.

[1] See above p. 181.
[2] See *An Essay Concerning Human Understanding*, Book II, Ch. XXI.

It is true that considerations of utility are brought to bear upon the character and extent of the rewards and punishments that we think ourselves justified in giving. Even so, our primary reason for rewarding or punishing anyone is that he deserves it; and it is just this notion of desert that our analysis of the concept of free-will has put in question. If our outlook were purely utilitarian, we should take much more kindly than we mostly do to the idea of preventive punishment, and we should be much more ready than we mostly are to allow those who have done wrong to escape any reprisal, when no greater good is likely to result from it.

Not only do we treat freedom of choice as entailing responsibility in a way that seems hardly rational in the light of this analysis, but we also ascribe an intrinsic value to it. We try by various methods of education to impel people along the proper paths, but we dislike the idea of employing means of conditioning, such as the use of drugs, which might effectively ensure this result. We feel that they should be left free to choose what they will do, even if they choose badly: we wish to influence their choice but not wholly to determine it. I admit that I share this feeling, but I do not know how to justify it. So long as we go through the process of choosing, why should it matter to us how our choices are explained? What is the value in their being subject only to statistical laws, let alone in their being totally inexplicable?

F   The Meaning of Life

To say that a God who exacted retribution for men's conduct would not be benevolent or rational is not in itself to say that there is no such God. Even so, the existence of a deity of whatever character would have to have been established on other grounds before we could profitably speculate about his attitude to men, and so far these grounds have not been forthcoming. There are, however, those who would say that in pursuing the question whether there is adequate evidence for a God's existence, we have been approaching the subject of religion in the wrong way. According to them, the question we should have been asking is not whether the proposition that God exists is true as a matter of fact, or acceptable as an explanatory hypothesis, but rather what function the belief in God fulfils in the lives of those who hold it. The justification for the belief may then be said to be that it makes the lives of those who hold it appear meaningful to them in a way that they otherwise would not.

This is substantially the position taken by the pragmatist, William James. Having spoken in one book of 'the craving of our nature for an ultimate peace behind all tempests, a blue zenith above all clouds',[1] he criticizes in another the attempts of what he calls 'systematic theology' to define the attributes of God. 'Wherein,' he asks, 'is such a definition really instructive? It means less than nothing in its pompous robe of adjectives. Pragmatism alone can read a positive meaning into it, and for that she turns her back upon the intellectualist point of view altogether. "God's in his heaven; all's right with the world". *That's* the real heart of your theology, and for that you need no rationalist definitions.'[2] Similarly, in his Gifford lectures on *The Varieties of Religious Experience* he speaks of his wish to vindicate 'the instinctive belief of mankind: God is real since he produces real effects',[3] and what he takes these real effects to be is no more than the feelings of greater energy, security and satisfaction which he thinks are enjoyed by those who hold religious beliefs.

As a psychological hypothesis, this could be questioned. For instance, the thesis of eternal damnation which has been a prominent feature of much Christian teaching is not likely to produce a feeling of greater security. On the other hand, there is no doubt that many people derive solace from the idea of their having a spiritual father who watches over them, especially when it is allied to the hope that he will secure to them in a future life the happiness which they may not have found in this one. To infer from this, however, that there is such a father, one needs to accept James's pragmatic theory that, since it is not to be expected of a religious hypothesis that it will either accord or fail to accord with any observable fact, the criterion for its truth is just that the vague assurance which it gives that 'all's right with the world' is a source of emotional satisfaction. This is in line with the view of some contemporary theists that the doctrine associated with the religious practices in which they engage is acceptable as a useful myth. This view is so modest that it is hard to take issue with it, unless one wants to argue that the myth is harmful, but it does appear open to

---

[1] William James. *The Will to Believe*, p. 180.
[2] William James. *Pragmatism*, pp. 121–2.
[3] p. 517.

the practical objection that the satisfaction which most believers derive from their acceptance of religious doctrine depends upon their not judging it as mythical. A myth which is generally seen to be a myth must be in some danger of losing its utility.

But without the help of such a myth, can life be seen as having any meaning? The simple answer is that it can have just as much meaning as one is able to put into it. There is, indeed, no ground for thinking that human life in general serves any ulterior purpose but this is no bar to a man's finding satisfaction in many of the activities which make up his life, or to his attaching value to the ends which he pursues, including some that he himself will not live to see realized. One may deplore the fact that life is so short, but if it were not independently worth living there would be no good reason to wish it prolonged. Where the discarding of the Christian myth may have a cruel effect is in the denial to those whose lives have not been happy of any serious hope that they will survive to find the balance redressed.

It has sometimes been thought that those who cannot take comfort from religion may find it in philosophy. The idea, which goes back to the Greek and Roman stoics, is that the philosopher, by coming to see things in their proper perspective, is able to detach himself from the vicissitudes of life. Conscious of his own rectitude he remains happy even on the rack. This may be contrasted with the Marxist idea that the business of philosophy is not merely to understand the world but to change it. In fact, not many philosophers have taken either of these positions, nor is there anything in the nature of the subject to make this surprising. A philosopher may become detached from ordinary concerns by being absorbed in his work, but so may an artist or a mathematician. He may think it his duty to engage in public affairs, but the line which he takes need not be connected with his philosophical theories. This is not to say that philosophy is incapable of changing the world. We have seen that the world cannot be prised away from our manner of conceiving it: and our conception of the world is something that philosophy can help to change. Even so this is not the source of its charm for most of those who practise it. For them, its value consists in the interest of the questions which it raises and the success which it achieves in answering them.

Index

FOR THE BEST IN PAPERBACKS, LOOK FOR THE

In every corner of the world, on every subject under the sun, Penguin represents quality and variety – the very best in publishing today.

For complete information about books available from Penguin – including Pelicans, Puffins, Peregrines and Penguin Classics – and how to order them, write to us at the appropriate address below. Please note that for copyright reasons the selection of books varies from country to country.

In the United Kingdom: For a complete list of books available from Penguin in the U.K., please write to *Dept E.P., Penguin Books Ltd, Harmondsworth, Middlesex, UB7 0DA*

In the United States: For a complete list of books available from Penguin in the U.S., please write to *Dept BA, Penguin, 299 Murray Hill Parkway, East Rutherford, New Jersey 07073*

In Canada: For a complete list of books available from Penguin in Canada, please write to *Penguin Books Canada Ltd, 2801 John Street, Markham, Ontario L3R 1B4*

In Australia: For a complete list of books available from Penguin in Australia, please write to the *Marketing Department, Penguin Books Australia Ltd, P.O. Box 257, Ringwood, Victoria 3134*

In New Zealand: For a complete list of books available from Penguin in New Zealand, please write to the *Marketing Department, Penguin Books (NZ) Ltd, Private Bag, Takapuna, Auckland 9*

In India: For a complete list of books available from Penguin, please write to *Penguin Overseas Ltd, 706 Eros Apartments, 56 Nehru Place, New Delhi, 110019*

In Holland: For a complete list of books available from Penguin in Holland, please write to *Penguin Books Nederland B.V., Postbus 195, NL–1380AD Weesp, Netherlands*

In Germany: For a complete list of books available from Penguin, please write to *Penguin Books Ltd, Friedrichstrasse 10 – 12, D–6000 Frankfurt Main 1, Federal Republic of Germany*

In Spain: For a complete list of books available from Penguin in Spain, please write to *Longman Penguin España, Calle San Nicolas 15, E–28013 Madrid, Spain*